UNIVERSITY COLLEGE

BERYL IVEY LIBRARY

D1547854

WEYERHAEUSER ENVIRONMENTAL BOOKS
William Cronon, Editor

Weyerhaeuser Environmental Books explore human relationships with natural environments in all their variety and complexity. They seek to cast new light on the ways that natural systems affect human communities, the ways that people affect the environments of which they are a part, and the ways that different cultural conceptions of nature profoundly shape our sense of the world around us. A complete list of the books in the series appears at the end of this book.

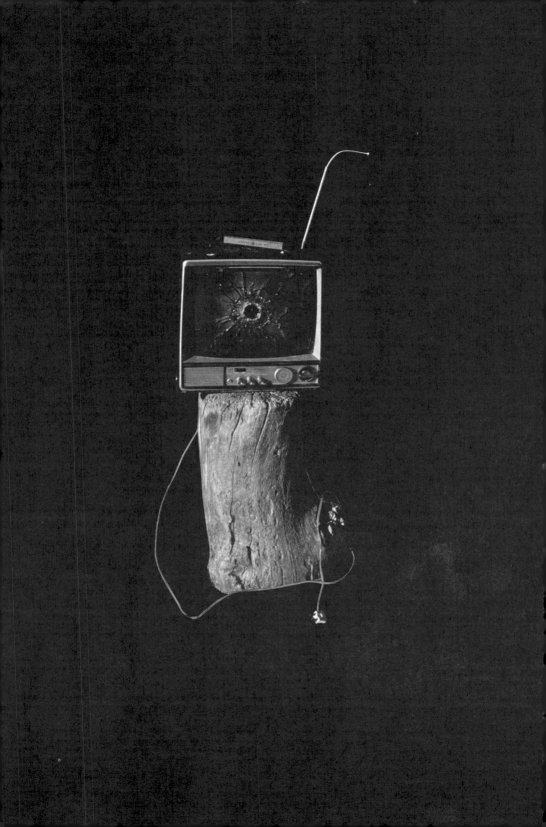

LOVING NATURE, FEARING THE STATE

Environmentalism and

Antigovernment Politics

before Reagan

BRIAN ALLEN DRAKE

Foreword by

William Cronon

UNIVERSITY OF WASHINGTON PRESS

Seattle & London

Loving Nature, Fearing the State: Environmentalism and Antigovernment Politics before Reagan is published with the assistance of a grant from the Weyerhaeuser Environmental Books Endowment, established by the Weyerhaeuser Company Foundation, members of the Weyerhaeuser family, and Janet and Jack Creighton.

18 17 16 15 14 13   5 4 3 2 1

University of Washington Press
PO Box 50096, Seattle, WA 98145, USA

www.washington.edu/uwpress

Library of Congress Cataloging-in-Publication Data
Drake, Brian Allen.
Loving nature, fearing the state : environmentalism and antigovernment politics before Reagan / Brian Allen Drake ; [foreword by] William Cronon.
        pages cm. — (Weyerhaeuser environment books)
ISBN 978-0-295-99299-0 (hardback)
1. Environmentalism—United States—History. 2. Environmentalism—Political aspects—United States. 3. Environmental policy—United States—History. 4. Radicalism—United States. 5. Right and left (Political science) 6. Ideology—United States. 7. United States—Politics and government—20th century. I. Title.
GE195.D78 2013   333.720973—dc23   2013015107

Material from chapters one and three appeared originally in Brian Allen Drake, "The Skeptical Environmentalist: Senator Barry Goldwater and the Environmental Management State," *Environmental History* 15 (October 2010): 587–611, and in "Green Goldwater: Barry Goldwater, Federal Environmentalism, and the Transformation of Modern Conservatism," in Elizabeth Tandy Shermer, ed., *Barry Goldwater and the Remaking of the American Political Landscape* (Tucson: University of Arizona Press, 2013), 214–37.

P. ii: Detail of Edward Abbey and his bagged TV, Tucson, c. 1980. Photo by Terrence Moore
P. xvi: Barry Goldwater at the Grand Canyon, c. 1970. Senator Barry M. Goldwater Papers, Arizona Collection, Arizona State University Libraries

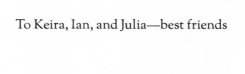

To Keira, Ian, and Julia—best friends

CONTENTS

ACKNOWLEDGMENTS

LIKE MOST ACTIVITIES IN LIFE, WRITING A BOOK IS NEVER A SOLITARY endeavor, even if it feels that way. No one thinks or creates in isolation, and scholarly work is always something of a group project. It gives me immense pleasure to be able to express my gratitude to all the people who assisted me in ways large and small during the time it took to produce *Loving Nature, Fearing the State.*

First, I would like to thank friends and colleagues at, or associated with, the University of Kansas and the city of Lawrence for everything from detailed advice to general support: Jay Antle, Kevin Armitage, Eric Baerren, Bob Blackstone, Lisa Brady, Jeff Bremer, Robb Campbell, Greg Cushman, David and Carol Dewar, Jonathan Earle and Leslie Tuttle, Jeff Filipiak, Jasonne Grabher, Megan Greene and Tony Melchor, Dixie and Gina Haggard, Shen Hou, Maril Hazlett and Brian Trigg, Mark and Laurie Hersey, Crystal Johnson, Marie Kelleher, Brett and Stephanie Knappe, Jim Leiker, Chris O'Brien, the late Phil Paludan, Martha Robinson, Adam Rome, Valerie Schrag, Steve Sodergren, Bill Tsutsui, and Chris White. The staff of the University of Kansas history department, especially Ellen Garber and Sandee Kennedy, was also of much help to me, and I owe particular thanks to graduate director Eve Levin for her support for my scholarship applications. I am also grateful to the department for twice awarding me the Lila Atkinson Creighton scholarship and to the Harry S. Truman Good Neighbor Foundation for its 2005 Eddie Jacobsen Scholarship.

Peter Iverson, Robert Goldberg, Jeffrey Stein, Laird Wilcox, James Calahan, Mark Harvey, John Baden, and Karl Hess Jr. offered me specific advice and for which I am grateful, as did the participants at my various presentations for the Hall Center for the Humanities' Nature and Culture Seminar, the annual meeting of the American Society for Environmental History, and the University of Georgia's Workshop in the History of Agriculture and the Environment.

For archival assistance I am indebted to the staff of the Arizona Historical Foundation, especially head archivist Linda Whitaker, whose enthusiasm and energy were a delight. Thanks also to Robert Spindler at the Arizona

State University Libraries, the staff of the Special Collections library at the University of Arizona, the Cline Library Special Collections at Northern Arizona University, the Special Collections library at Montana State University, the American Dental Association library in Chicago, the Bieneke Rare Book and Manuscript Library at Yale University, and the Kenneth Spencer Research Library at the University of Kansas.

University of Kansas professors Donald Worster, Karl Brooks, Bill Tuttle, Jeff Moran, and Jim Woelfel gave me the benefit of their considerable knowledge when *Loving Nature, Fearing the State* was still in its infancy. My adviser Donald Worster deserves special praise for his unflagging commitment to me and my fellow graduate students and for his trenchant critique of our work. No one who has studied under him comes away from the experience without some profound insights about good historical writing. From Don I learned that it demands both a critical eye and moral passion, it avoids parochialism and overspecialization, and it addresses itself to matters of broad, even timeless, intellectual interest. Good historical writing also requires clear and vigorous prose. I hope that in the course of writing this book I have put his lessons into practice satisfactorily.

At the University of Georgia in the city of Athens, which I now call home, I have had the good fortune to work alongside a number of wonderful colleagues, such as Ari Levine, Adam Sabra, Steve Soper, Steven Mihm, and Montgomery Wolf. Three others deserve special mention. John Inscoe's friendship has been invaluable, and I am convinced that you will not find a more caring and pleasant person in all of academe. Similarly, in my first two years at Georgia, fellow Jayhawk Paul Sutter patiently answered the barrage of questions I launched at him, and his unofficial mentorship did much to ease my transition from graduate student to faculty member. He has since left Georgia for the University of Colorado, but I still count him as one of my important influences as well as my friend. Finally, Stephen Berry is a fabulous historian, and his intellectual interests have enriched my own to no end. He has been a staunch advocate of my professional development, and I cannot thank him enough for that. Nor have I found many people whose outlook on life so closely matches my own. He, his wife, Frances, and his brother Patrick have become some of my dearest friends, and Athens would not be Athens without them.

At the University of Washington Press, senior acquisitions editor Marianne Keddington-Lang, assistant managing editor Mary Ribesky, and Weyerhauser Environmental Series editor William Cronon have been vital to this project. It has been a pleasure to work with people of such professionalism and skill, and I have deeply appreciated their critiques as well as the leeway they have given me to make this book my own. Two anonymous readers for the Press offered many suggestions for improvement as well.

Finally, I am thankful to both the Drake and the Digel families. Most of all, eternal thanks go to my wife, Keira Digel Drake, our son, Ian, and our daughter, Julia. More than anything else, they are the reason I have been able to write this book. Keira supported our family financially for most of my graduate career (as we like to joke, I was the lucky recipient of the prestigious Digel Spousal Fellowship, renewable annually), and her patience with my academic trials and tribulations amazes me to this day. Meanwhile, her emotional support has simply been too important for words. Julia's keen intelligence and affection have been a daily pleasure, and Ian has done his best work by simply being Ian—joyful, friendly, humorous, and energetic. It is impossible to imagine a better trio of fellow travelers on life's journey.

CONSERVATIVE CONSERVATIONISTS

William Cronon

AMERICAN CITIZENS WHO CAME OF AGE AFTER ABOUT 1980 ARE ACCUStomed to elections and policy debates in which the two major parties align themselves pretty predictably on environmental issues. Ask either a Democrat or a Republican what they expect a dyed-in-the-wool environmentalist to do at the ballot box, and both will almost certainly answer that such a person would vote Democratic much more often than not. Democrats, after all, are comfortable with the idea that government in general, and the federal government in particular, has a vital role to play in enforcing environmental regulations to prevent air and water pollution, improve energy efficiency, protect endangered species, reduce exposure to toxic chemicals, respond to the threat of climate change, and other such interventions. Republicans are much more likely to be doubtful about the effectiveness of such regulations and concerned about their impacts on taxes, property rights, economic prosperity, and political liberty. And so most of us just *naturally* assume that being an environmentalist means being a Democrat.

Those with longer historical memories, though, will recognize that there is considerable irony in this seemingly inevitable partisan alignment. It was, after all, the Republican Theodore Roosevelt who first used the bully pulpit of the White House to promote the conservation of natural resources, permanent protection of public lands, and government regulation of corporate misbehavior. The national forests as we know them today are largely the result of Roosevelt's partnership with Gifford Pinchot, who would go on to serve two terms as the Republican governor of Pennsylvania. Despite partisan differences, Pinchot embraced many of the conservation policies of Franklin Roosevelt's New Deal, making Pennsylvania second only to California in the number of camps it hosted for the Civilian Conservation Corps, its expansion of the state park system, and its promotion of other conservation measures. Such activities were not unusual among Republican leaders during the first half of the twentieth century. The conservationist Aldo Leopold, today regarded as a patron saint of American environmentalism, was a registered Republican.

The most striking example of environmental activism by a leading Republican must surely be Richard Nixon, whose efforts to undermine potential Democratic rivals for his second-term presidential election led to an escalating competition between the Republican White House and a Congress in which the Democrats controlled both houses. Most of today's environmental laws at the federal level were passed with large bipartisan majorities during a surprisingly brief period in the 1960s and 1970s. Among them are the Clean Air Act, the Clean Water Act, the Endangered Species Act, and the National Environmental Policy Act. Not only did Richard Nixon sign all of these bills, but his administration also authored some of the most sweeping environmental reforms of the period, including the creation of the National Oceanic and Atmospheric Administration and the Environmental Protection Agency.

In the post-1980 world, this longstanding Republican tradition of environmental concern and commitment to conservation seems about as remote from the modern conservative movement as it is possible to imagine. Certainly Nixon's enthusiasm for large-scale government reorganization and his willingness to create powerful new regulatory agencies to enforce environmental protection have been largely repudiated by many members of his party in the years since 1970. But it would be going too far to say that modern conservatives have severed all ties to these earlier environmental traditions or that the environmental movement did not at least partly originate from values and political convictions that we would today regard as conservative. Liberals, conservatives, and environmentalists alike forget the complexities of their own intellectual traditions when they lose track of these inconvenient political truths.

In *Loving Nature, Fearing the State: Environmentalism and Antigovernment Politics Before Reagan*, Brian Drake sets out to recover this forgotten history by reminding us of the conservative roots of modern environmentalism. He does this in an unusual and intriguing way. Rather than provide a linear narrative of conservative and libertarian environmental thought or an institutional history of the Republican Party's changing relationship to environmental politics, he selects key figures and episodes to explore different strands of what we now recognize as modern conservatism and analyzes how they relate to the simultaneous emergence of environmentalism. By juxtaposing unexpected elements that might today seem quite unrelated, he demonstrates their hidden connections and encourages us to think more carefully about political platitudes that make it too easy to assume that conservatism is intrinsically hostile to environmental protection.

The figure who looms largest in Drake's story is Barry Goldwater, the Arizona senator whose disastrous presidential campaign in 1964 seemed at the time to spell doom for the conservative movement but which is now regarded as the galvanizing episode that ultimately led to Ronald Reagan's election in 1980. Drake demonstrates Goldwater's deep and longstanding passion for the wilderness landscapes of the American West, his skill as an outdoor photographer, and his active involvement in protecting parklands in places he cared about. All of these would seem to mark him as a conservationist in the tradition of Teddy Roosevelt, and there is more truth to that characterization than many modern environmentalists might be inclined to believe. But Goldwater was also deeply suspicious of state power, particularly in the hands of the federal government, and it is his antistatism—the core value of modern conservatism—that we mainly remember today.

The same is hardly true of Edward Abbey, whom environmentalists have long celebrated as one of the most eloquently uncompromising wilderness advocates of the second half of the twentieth century. He is best remembered for a passionate polemic on behalf of the arid Southwest entitled *Desert Solitaire* (1968) and a seriocomic novel called *The Monkey Wrench Gang* (1975), about a group of radical environmentalists who decide to liberate a drowned Glen Canyon from the floodwaters of Lake Powell by blowing up the Glen Canyon Dam. That novel would help inspire a group of environmental activists to form Earth First! in 1979; and when they published a handbook of tactics for direct action in defense of the environment, they entitled that volume *Ecodefense: A Field Guide to Monkeywrenching* in Abbey's honor. His environmentalist bona fides are beyond question.

It is precisely here that Brian Drake's ability to recognize and analyze strange bedfellows shows itself to best advantage. In this book, although the two men probably never met each other and undoubtedly would have had serious reservations about one another if they had, Drake demonstrates that Edward Abbey and Barry Goldwater had more in common than their followers would ever imagine. Both loved the deserts of the Southwest and the wilderness traditions of American culture; both were deeply suspicious of state power. Abbey was no less hostile than Goldwater to the corruptions of power (government and corporate alike), and he opposed bureaucracy, intrusive regulation, and threats to American liberty just as passionately as did Goldwater. Although conservatives today celebrate Goldwater and environmentalists celebrate Abbey, in truth both groups are engaging in selective memory when they overlook what the two men had in common.

The pleasures of Drake's book thus reside in its unexpected juxtapositions and the surprising insights they provoke. *Loving Nature, Fearing the State* sheds new light on an unlikely cast of characters that includes Roosevelt Republicans, free market libertarians, antifluoridationists, Burkean conservatives, and others who feared state power as an enemy of liberty. All today look like forerunners of movement conservatism and the modern Republican Party . . . yet all were quite significantly engaged with environmental politics and saw little contradiction between their hostility to the state and their love of nature. We may be tempted to believe that their conservatism ultimately won out over their environmentalism, but it may equally be true that environmentalism lost something important with their departure from the movement. Certainly the loss of bipartisan environmental politics in the United States means that it would be quite impossible today to pass the 1960s and 1970s legislation on which federal environmental law still depends. Difficult though it may now be for either group to believe it, liberals and conservatives once worked together for environmental protection in the United States. If one wishes to understand how that could possibly have been true—and if one wants to imagine ways that it might someday be true again—Brian Drake's unlikely cast of characters is well worth pondering at length.

Loving Nature,

Fearing the State

INTRODUCTION

NATURE'S STRANGE BEDFELLOWS

> Questions about the proper management of the environment are
> fundamentally intertwined with questions about the proper ends
> and means of governments themselves.
>
> —*Richard N. L. Andrews, 2006*

HENRY DAVID THOREAU SPENT HIS LIFE SPEAKING WORDS FOR NATURE, but his enthusiasm began to wane when it came to people. The Bard of Concord's place in the front rank of American environmental writers comes mainly from his reputation as a lover of the nonhuman world. We think of him as the champion of wildness in the "Walking" essay, the chronicler of natural life around Walden Pond, the man who found the sublime atop Mount Katahdin. We also think of him as something of a curmudgeon, even a misanthrope, grumbling about lives of quiet desperation, marching to a different drummer, longing to take a crowbar to the Billerica dam.[1]

Curmudgeon or not, Thoreau was as much a social critic as a nature lover. His best known piece of writing after *Walden* is his 1849 essay "Civil Disobedience," in which he railed against one social institution that particularly irked him: the central government of the United States. "I heartily accept the motto 'that government is best which governs least,'" he announced in the essay's celebrated opening, adding slyly that he would rewrite it as "that which governs not at all." Thoreau's biggest gripe against the federal government was the recent Mexican War. As it was for many in New England, to him the conflict was nothing but a brazen land grab by a southern slave power using the federal government as its weapon. Furthermore, most of his fellow northerners tacitly supported slavery by supporting the government that waged the war, even as they criticized both. But justice compelled resistance to such complicity. Thoreau did his part by "quietly [declaring] war with the State, after my fashion," refusing to pay his taxes and earning himself a famous night in the Concord jail.[2]

It wasn't just the slavery-enabling American government that bothered Thoreau, though. Government itself made him uneasy, despite his acknowledgment in "Civil Disobedience" that it was sometimes necessary. The problem was that even good government inevitably encroached upon individual freedom. He was no anarchist or one of the "no-government men," he said, backpedaling a bit from his opening line, but he was simply not confident in government's ability to rule well. It was enough to depress him. "I walk toward one of our ponds," he declared in the fiery 1854 abolitionist speech "Slavery in Massachusetts," "but what signifies the beauty of nature when men are base...? The remembrance of my country spoils my walk. My thoughts are murder to the State, and involuntarily go plotting against her." But then the sight and smell of a lily reminded him "that Nature has been partner to no Missouri Compromise..., [bursting] up so pure and fair to the eye, and so sweet to the scent, as if to show us what purity and sweetness reside in, and can be extracted from, the slime and muck of earth."[3]

Thoreau, the antistatist nature lover. Had he lived a century later he might have found a comrade in the postwar environmental writer and social critic Edward Abbey. "Cactus Ed"—fans tagged him with the nickname in honor of his prickly irascibility as well as his love of desert country—was one of the most original voices in twentieth-century American nature writing, a poet, essayist, and fiction author whose major works are classics. At first glance, Abbey bears little resemblance to the quirky, bookish, and sometimes puritanical Henry Thoreau. A hard drinker, a voracious womanizer, and connoisseur of the manly arts of booze and guns, Abbey had a strong and simple literary voice, for he detested the florid style that characterized Thoreau's writing and the ethereal banality of Transcendentalism ("Appearance *and* reality?" he once wrote in his journal: "Appearance *is* reality—the only reality we know, will ever know, will ever need to know"). Yet the two men shared a gift for witty epigrams, the pleasure of playing the gadfly, a wariness of the herd mentality, and a love for the natural world. They also had an affinity for speaking their minds loudly, the response be damned. "A crusty character, Thoreau," Abbey wrote admiringly in a 1981 essay. "An unpeeled man. A man with the bark on him."[4]

Thoreau and Abbey also shared a passionate aversion to government. "All forms of government are pernicious," Abbey declared, in a nod to Thoreau's essay, "including good government." "If you refuse to pay unjust taxes," Abbey once argued, with much the same attitude that landed Thoreau behind bars, "your property will be confiscated. If you attempt to defend your property, you will be arrested. If you resist arrest, you will be clubbed. If you defend yourself against clubbing, you will be shot dead. These procedures are known as the Rule of Law." Modern American conservatives might chuckle in agreement, but Abbey was not a conservative in the conventional sense, for his contempt for industrial capitalism and Christian morality matched his disdain for government. He was not a government-friendly liberal either. His social ideals—fierce individualism paired with strong community ties, local autonomy, agrarian self-sufficiency—ignored partisan divides and drew from a more complex conception of democracy and freedom, the heart of which was a powerful mistrust of centralized power, private or public. For Abbey there was little difference between the two; government, the military, Big Science, and Big Business were all allies in a crusade to enslave people.[5]

It was by dominating nature that they attempted that enslavement. Through agencies like the U.S. Forest Service and the Bureau of Reclamation, staffed and run by willing "experts," the state razed America's wild lands to secure the raw materials of power and create "a world entirely conquered by technology, entirely dominated by industrial processes . . . , the ultimate trap for mankind, threatening us with the evolutionary dead end of the social insects—the formicary of the ants, the termite commune." Freedom meant finding an escape—but to where? For Abbey, wilderness—undeveloped, unmanaged, unpeeled land—was the preservation of the democratic world. Wilderness was the final arena for the exercise of freedom and community in the face of the politicians, industrialists, and technocrats who would make citizens into servants.[6]

While Abbey was not a typical conservative, Barry Goldwater was practically the patron saint of those who were. As Abbey worked on his first books in the late 1950s and early 1960s, Goldwater was establishing himself as the political right's premier national figure. Riding a wave of grassroots Sunbelt conservatism, the Arizona-born Goldwater won election to the U.S. Senate in 1952 and secured the Republican Party's nomination for president twelve years later, going down to legendary defeat at the hands of Lyndon Johnson before recapturing his Senate seat in 1968 and serving for eighteen more years. He was instrumental in creating the Republican Party's postwar conservative wing, which has dominated the GOP since Ronald Reagan's election in 1980, and was perhaps the most important conservative politician in postwar America until Reagan. Goldwater was also the most recognizable champion of conservatism's core ideals: anticommunism, antiunionism, states' rights, free enterprise, property rights, staunch individualism, traditional morality, and, above all, the beauty of a small federal government that, with exceptions like national defense, kept its authority limited and its power restrained.[7]

Like Abbey, Goldwater was wary of centralized government power, but unlike Cactus Ed, the senator's love for nature actually dampened his antistatism. Goldwater was sincerely concerned about the environmental issues of his day, and when the American environmental movement blossomed in the 1960s and early 1970s, he took it seriously. Born and raised amid the Sonoran desert of the early twentieth century, Goldwater was an outdoorsman, a wilderness lover, and a crack nature photographer—avocations that would later lead him to consider federal environmental protection as something more than mere bureaucratic meddling in the affairs of free enterprise. Around the first Earth Day, he proved willing to grant the government substantial powers to manage the nation's environmental affairs. While he was no knee-jerk defender of its environmental policy—there were times when he would regret his previous support—when it came to protecting nature, the federal government was not necessarily Goldwater's perennial enemy. He would advocate ambitious federal research into alternative energy, support air and water pollution legislation, and sponsor a number of bills creating national wilderness areas. In the 1970s, he would startle friend and foe alike by admitting that his support for the construction of the Colorado River's massive Glen Canyon Dam had been his single biggest political mistake—even more so than his failure to vote for the Civil Rights Act—for it had destroyed what was perhaps the river's most beautiful stretch and damaged the ecology of his beloved Grand Canyon.

This last sentiment was one normally reserved for environmental radicals, among them Edward Abbey. Whatever else might have divided them, Abbey and Goldwater could agree on at least two significant points: government as a threat to human liberty, and the concrete colossus athwart Glen Canyon as an insult to nature. In fact, the two men were more alike than perhaps either would have cared to admit, had they known each other personally. Abbey, a Goldwater constituent for much of his adult life, acknowledged a grudging affection for the senator in a draft of a 1972 lecture, dubbing him "too cute [and] loveable to hate." He also hiked many a mile in the Arizona wilderness areas created at least partially through Goldwater's efforts.

Parallel sentiments about nature and the state could, it seems, sometimes make for strange bedfellows.[8]

Postwar American environmentalism's most thorough and influential historian, Samuel Hays, once observed that its adherents' beliefs and philosophies have had a curious tendency "not to fit into traditional political ideologies, but to cut across them." Historians have traced American environmental sympathies back to the early nineteenth century and before, revealing the diversity of the sympathizers and especially their entanglement with class, race, gender, religion, science, and so on. But their relationship to ideas about the individual, government, and the proper relationship between the two—in other words, to classic questions of American political philosophy—is a largely untouched topic, at least explicitly.[9]

Following up on Hays's comment is the aim of this book. It takes as its subject strange bedfellows: "antistatists" with "environmentalist" leanings in the years after World War II. In the conventional wisdom, postwar environmental concerns in the United States are almost always associated with people and organizations with a "liberal" view of state power—that is, a belief in and often a preference for the vigorous application of federal regulatory, statutory, and bureaucratic force to solve social problems, improve quality of life, and protect the public good. Environmental historian Adam Rome has argued persuasively that government-mandated environmental protection was one of postwar liberalism's central components. Reinforcing the idea of environmentalism-as-liberal is the hostility of many post-Reagan conservatives and libertarians, for whom almost any kind of environmental protection is a usurpation of local authority and a violation of individual rights, property rights, and free enterprise. The result is that antistatism and environmental concerns tend, for scholars and laypeople alike, to be paired like matter and antimatter: never the twain shall meet, except in combat. Thus it is that Thoreau, Abbey, and Goldwater form such a striking trio. Their love of nature and fear of government run counter to the belief that green sympathies are the domain of those comfortable with federal power.[10]

Postwar environmental concerns emerged and matured during an era of considerable mistrust of government from both the Left and Right. New Left activists excoriated the supposedly "liberal" federal government for its racism, tolerance of poverty, prostration to corporate power, and, above all, its illegal and immoral war in Vietnam. From the right, conservatives assaulted the federal government for its inefficiency, its do-gooder welfare-state enabling of the lazy and undeserving, its overregulation and assaults on property rights and free enterprise, and its general drift toward an authoritarian-tinged collectivism. Libertarians, meanwhile, occupied a sort of adjacent ideological territory, drawing arguments from both sides in a broader critique of state power per se. But what happened when these two historical trends cut across each other? What happened when the postwar era's antistatism met its environmentalism? Was it simply the meeting of oil and water—or something more complicated? What was the nature of their interaction, and what sorts of amalgams, combinations, fusions, and chimeras might have been created in the process? And why have those amalgams and chimeras been so uncommon since the Reagan era?[11]

Like liberty and justice for all, fear of government is an American leitmotif. It has taken many forms—from sophisticated philosophical critique to visceral disgust—but whatever the particulars, the general sentiment has been there since at least the American Revolution. The Articles of Confederation were nothing if not a blueprint for limited government, as were the tenets of the Antifederalists, whose anxieties about unchecked power inspired the Bill of Rights. A few years later, the musket-wielding farmers of Shays' Rebellion and the Whiskey Rebellion saw themselves in well-justified revolt against governmental tyranny. In the 1830s Andrew Jackson killed the Second Bank of the United States, and during the next three decades the country slid into civil war over the question of slavery and the government's role in its expansion. In the twentieth century the New Deal's critics spoke darkly of collectivism and communism, and after World War II, conservatives would make the federal government their primary target, defining the politics of the century's last two decades in the process. We might cite a hundred other examples.

We might also note an equal and opposite reaction. From Alexander Hamilton to the Great Society, champions of a more powerful state fought hard to expand its reach and power. Anxious about disorder and rebellion, Federalists discarded the Articles and forged a stronger federal government with the Constitution. The National Republicans pushed for financial centralization and federally funded internal improvements in the first decades of the nineteenth century, and the Civil War brought sweeping new economic and legal powers to Washington, D.C., serving as a prelude to the fin de siecle Progressive Era. That in turn foreshadowed the New Deal, which marked the starting point for the massive increases in federal power. Meanwhile, even the staunchest philosophical antistatists could make exceptions in practice. It was easy for Thomas Jefferson to warn against executive power and then invoke it in the Louisiana Purchase and the Embargo Act, or for states' rights advocate Jackson to crack down on South Carolina during the Nullification Crisis, or for late-twentieth-century religious conservatives to legislate morality while decrying "judicial activism." The contemporary massiveness of Washington, D.C., suggests the battle went long ago to friends of government, but the vitality of antistatism remains clear today in the popularity of Tea Party conservatism.

This persistent vacillation about the state also left its mark on the history of environmental concerns. For the most part, American environmentalists—active for decades and even centuries before the term was coined or the modern movement formed—have come down squarely on the side of strong government. Environmental management and state power have been closely linked since before the Revolution, and environmentalists have traditionally relied on government to achieve their aims. But there have been some notable exceptions; at times the federal government has been one of the American environment's worst enemies—and thus one of its defenders' main opponents. Generally speaking, however, environmental protection and government have been long-term partners.

For conservative critics, environmental laws and regulations might be Exhibit A in the case against modern-day government excess, yet environmental regulation is anything but new. In the nation's early years, "environmental policy" focused mainly on putting as much public land as possible into private hands. However, colonial and state governments took a strong interest, and sometimes a strong hand, in regulating the use of water, wildlife, forest, and soil on both private lands and the commons. In the first decades of the 1800s, New Englanders worried about the impact of milldams and manufacturing on rivers and forests. Facing formidable opponents like the textile-magnate Boston Associates, paper mill owners, commercial fishermen, and incorporated timber interests, Yankee proto-conservationists appealed to legislatures and courts as the only effective counterweights. Later, sport hunters and anglers looked to their states to manage fish and wildlife populations, to control predators, and to control poachers and "undesirable" market and pot hunting. By the 1870s the states' role as steward of natural resources was well established in theory, if not always in fact. A similar trajectory marked the urban environment, where problems with industrial wastes, garbage, sewage, and smoke inspired a vigorous public health movement to invoke government regulation.[12]

By the turn of the twentieth century, this stateward trend in environmental stewardship had expanded to include significant federal power, culminating in the Progressive conservation movement. Progressivism writ large was a motley collection of reform impulses: one part moral crusade against social ills and corrupt government, one part patronizing middle-class "uplift" of immigrants and the poor. But its unifying mission was to rationalize a messy, inefficient, and inequitable American society with scientific expertise, technical skill, and large doses of government regulation. Poverty, urban blight, disease, labor unrest, and other ills, created and magnified by massive disparities of wealth and power, were at heart problems of technique and implementation, said the Progressives. Traditional politics had failed to solve them, but a modern scientific approach offered new hope. Muster enough data, feed that data into the latest analytical frameworks, empower government to act on the results, and these problems were solvable. Thus the future belonged not to crass partisanship but to the highly trained, objective, amoral government expert working for the greater good.[13]

Conservation was Progressivism's environmental wing. For those interested in natural resources and with a penchant for rationalization—scientific foresters, hydrologists, range and wildlife managers—the traditional American approach to resource use was hopelessly flawed. Conservationists had no problem with economic exploitation of land per se—on the contrary, they were profoundly utilitarian in their attitudes—but they argued that the unregulated free market was uncoordinated, shortsighted, and badly executed, dominated by an every-man-for-himself mentality that led to inequitable and wasteful resource use. Lack of regulation actually hindered economic growth by permanently damaging watersheds and forests and threatening the nation with resource scarcity while enriching the few. With experts like themselves in charge, however, they believed resources could be managed with both scientific skill and moral impartiality—"the greatest good for the greatest number for the longest time," as Progressive forester Gifford Pinchot said. A strong central government would be the conservationists' enforcer, supplying the legal and political muscle for their stewardship of the nation's public lands. As the Progressive Era unfolded, conservation came to dominate the federal approach to resource management. The U.S. Division of Forestry, founded in the 1880s and led by Chief Forester Bernhard Fernow, exemplified the philosophy until Pinchot and the U.S. Forest Service superseded them in 1905. Most of the West's public lands not otherwise managed by the Forest Service fell under the wing of the Grazing Service, later renamed the Bureau of Land Management. Meanwhile, federal hydrologists worked to harness the rivers of the West with the creation of the Bureau of Reclamation in 1902; the older U.S. Army Corps of Engineers pursued similar goals in the East.[14]

Complementing conservationists—and sometimes squaring off against them—were preservationists, who argued that the wisest use of nature was often little or no use at all, at least of the utilitarian kind, and who emphasized the recreational, aesthetic, and spiritual value of public lands over the economic one. Historians have spilled copious amounts of ink analyzing (and overanalyzing) the differences between the two, but both conservationists and preservationists shared the belief that government, not private interest, was often the most appropriate tool for managing the natural world. Preservationists secured national park status for Yosemite, Yellowstone, Rainier, Glacier, and other areas in the late 1800s and early 1900s before finding an official federal guardian in the National Park Service in 1916. They also worked to protect birds, game, and other wildlife with landmark federal legislation like the Lacey Act of 1900 and bureaucracies like the Bureau of Fisheries and the Biological Survey, later combined and renamed the U.S. Fish and Wildlife Service. Among the preservationists' staunchest allies was Republican president Teddy Roosevelt. While certainly a use-oriented conservationist, his love of wildlife and wild land inspired him to vigorous efforts to establish the nation's first federal wildlife preserves and to invoke his executive authority under the Antiquities Act of 1906 to set aside the Devil's Tower area in Wyoming, Chaco Canyon in New Mexico, Arizona's Petrified Forest, parts of Washington, California, and South Dakota, and vast tracts of the Grand Canyon.[15]

Yet differences between conservationists and preservationists were not insignificant. Because conservation dominated the federal government's approach to environmental management, preservationists could find themselves at odds with the very federal government that they appealed to for help. The Hetch Hetchy debate foreshadowed what would become, in the postwar years, a contentious relationship between preservationists and "wise use" bureaucracies like the Bureau of Reclamation. In the wake of the famous 1906 earthquake and the fire that followed, the city of San Francisco unveiled plans to build a reservoir in Hetch Hetchy Valley, then a part of Yosemite National Park, to serve the city's water needs. Preservationists and their allies (with a variety of motives) put up determined resistance but collapsed in 1913 under the weight of arguments from dam boosters, many of them working for the federal government. Meanwhile, federal game-management and predator-control programs devastated hawk, wolf, coyote, bobcat, and cougar populations, triggering an explosion in the numbers of deer and mice, and fire suppression and intense timber management wrought ecological havoc in some national forests.[16]

The 1930s were a high point in the federal government's interest in conservation, with the Civilian Conservation Corps' trail-cutting and tree-planting programs, the Soil Conservation Service's erosion-control efforts, and massive reclamation projects on the Columbia and Colorado Rivers and in the Tennessee Valley. Preservationists got new national parks and monuments in Big Bend, Death Valley, the Everglades, Black Canyon of the Gunnison, Organ Pipe, Joshua Tree, the Channel Islands, and elsewhere. But federal environmental management came into its own after World War II, particularly during the 1960s and 1970s, when "the environmental-management state [joined] the national-security state and the welfare state as a central concern."[17]

Much of this concern came about because the public demanded it. Economic growth and increasing affluence were hallmarks of the first two decades after the war, and although that growth and affluence were neither shared equally nor without significant costs, fostering them was an article of faith in the era's post–New Deal political climate. A significant side effect, as Samuel Hays showed in *Beauty, Heath, and Permanence*, was increased environmental concern among the burgeoning middle classes. Postwar middle-class life was a consumer's life: a suburban house loaded with appliances, a new television, a V-8 parked in the driveway, and a front lawn like shag carpet. Even as the consumer lifestyle devoured resources and fouled the air and water, it also fostered a parallel desire for "ecological amenities," for an environment free from toxic chemicals, full of abundant wildlife, and with increased outdoor recreational opportunities and wilderness experiences. With anxieties about nuclear technologies adding a tense undercurrent to their consumer desires, these new middle-class environmentalists looked, as their predecessors had, to the federal government to battle developers and polluters. Given the liberal-consensus politics of the period, with its faith in government as a tool for change and examples like the civil rights movement, which aimed to bring federal power to bear on segregation, this embrace of government was a logical response to the tenor of the times as well as the continuation of a historical trend.[18]

The 1960s and 1970s were high-water days for federal action on environmental issues. Wilderness advocates, for example, secured passage of the Wilderness Act in 1964, which provided, through an official federal "Wilderness" designation, permanent protection for public lands that retained their "primeval character and influence" and where "the imprint of man's work [is] substantially unnoticeable." But the new environmental management state spread well beyond conservation and preservation to take on issues like air and water pollution, solid waste, and the control of toxic substances, which were traditionally the realm of local and state government. In 1962, marine biologist Rachel Carson's *Silent Spring* struck Americans' environmental nerve and inspired federal bans on a number of pesticides. In 1970 alone, President Richard Nixon authorized the National Environmental Policy Act, the Environmental Protection Agency, and the Clean Air Act. Congress took a particular interest in water pollution, passing the Federal Water Pollution Control Act of 1972 (the Clean Water Act), the Endangered Species Act (1973), the Resource Conservation and Recovery Act (1976), the Federal Land Policy and Management Act (1976), the Toxic Substances Control Act (1977), and the Superfund Act (1980).[19]

Yet government was not always the nature lover's friend. The biggest battles came over federal reclamation projects. Since 1902, hydrological engineers with the Bureau of Reclamation had been drawing up plans to tame the free-flowing rivers of the West, and by the 1950s they were well on their way to success. As a classic conservation bureaucracy, the bureau had never been the kind of organization to let misty-eyed sentimentality stand in the way of a good project, and two of its biggest after 1945 included a proposed dam inside Dinosaur National Monument and two more in the legendary Grand Canyon. Preservationists launched desperate campaigns to stop them. To the bureau's horror, they were successful—an indication of the power of the era's burgeoning environmental sentiments. Meanwhile, environmentalists were at odds with the Forest Service's industrial-friendly, timber-mining mentality and with the National Park Service for its obsession with park development and "ease of access," evident in programs like the road-building Mission 66 project. They also found themselves, in the 1970s, cracking the whip on the EPA, irritated by what they saw as the bureaucracy's failure to do its job.[20]

And so it has remained. The Reagan administration's assault on federal environmental regulation in the early 1980s temporarily slowed environmentalists' momentum but failed to eliminate it and in fact produced a considerable public backlash. Similarly, the George W. Bush administration's virtual war against everything from federal logging moratoriums to regulation of greenhouse-gas emissions spoke volumes about just how important the federal government's power has been to the cause of environmental protection.

Just as the environmental-management state was hitting its stride, critics of government were gathering at the margins of American political life. The New Left, weaned on C. Wright Mills and Herbert Marcuse and disillusioned by the listless conformity of postwar America, had notable anti-statist tendencies. Participatory democracy, equality, community, and local control were its watchwords, and it unleashed much of its criticisms on what it perceived as the ever-widening gulf that separated power from the people. The "democratic" U.S. government, according to New Left adherents, was actually a bureaucracy-encrusted authoritarian partner of corporations and universities—all of them linked in a self-replicating Establishment determined to keep and hold power at any cost. The Vietnam War, the draft, and the repression of social protest were all evidence of its dictatorial drive and fundamental corruption. The later counterculture movement also viewed the American government with a jaundiced eye and generally preferred dropping out of mainstream politics rather than attempt to reform the seemingly unreformable.[21]

But another, and eventually much larger, assault on government came from the Right. "Conservative" is a slippery adjective, and "postwar conservatism" was actually a hodgepodge of individuals and groups of greater or lesser intellectual and philosophical sophistication, whose particular agendas could vary widely and who argued with one another as often as they agreed. A movement that housed Robert Welch, Phyllis Schlafly, William F. Buckley, Russell Kirk, Barry Goldwater, and Milton Friedman under the same terminological roof defies easy categorization. Historians typically divide the postwar Right into two groups: traditionalists and libertarians. Traditionalists included devout Christian moralists and Burkean defenders of tradition, social hierarchy, and law and order, staunch anticommunists and champions of free enterprise, and a smattering of anti-Semites and white supremacists. For them, the fundamental goals were containing the godless Soviets, maintaining social stability, individual morality and "family values," supporting states' rights and defending capitalism, private property, and deregulation.

Libertarians placed far more emphasis on individual rights. They were cheerleaders for private property and free enterprise, but they put just as much emphasis on personal freedom of expression and action, taking their cue from John Stuart Mill in opposing the regulation and criminalization of individual behaviors such as drug use or sexual activity. Libertarians were also intensely antistatist, opposed to state power beyond the limits necessary for maintaining social order and protecting individual rights. This often put them at odds with traditionalists who supported a large military and aggressive foreign policy, defended the war in Vietnam, and itched to use police power against protestors, drug users, and the morally deviant. Many libertarians felt an ironic kinship with the New Left, especially those in organizations like Young Americans for Freedom, from whose ranks traditionalists purged them in 1969.[22]

Whatever the differences between them, one thing traditionalists and libertarians shared was a profound mistrust of central government and "the growing tendency of the state," in historian Lisa McGirr's words, "to organize social and economic life in the name of the public welfare and the social good." They might have disagreed about the state's specific role in personal and moral life, or military defense and law and order, but neither sung praises to federal power. They agreed that government was inefficient, profligate, and blundering when it wasn't trying to relieve individual Americans of their rights, and like modern-day Antifederalists, they saw endless plots against their liberties in the machinations of the federal contraption in Washington, D.C. Thus it was that Ronald Reagan could declare in his first inaugural address that government was the problem, not the solution, to the nation's problems, a statement that neatly encapsulated four decades of resentment toward the New Deal's ideological legacy.[23]

In fact, postwar conservatism/libertarianism had little to hold it together except its contempt for Big Government, but that was enough to fuse it into an alliance that would change the face of American politics in the last thirty years of the twentieth century. In 1964 conservative Republicans would try, with the Goldwater campaign, to take their place on the national political stage, and they would fail badly. But the war in Vietnam and the protests against it, the increasing militancy of the civil rights movement and the New Left, the rise of the counterculture movement, the failures of the War on Poverty, the Oil Crisis of 1973, and the end of two decades of postwar prosperity would badly damage the federal government's credibility, eventually bringing the "unraveling of America," as historian Allen Matusow described it, and with it liberalism's political dominance. In 1980, Ronald

Reagan would win the presidency and put the conservatives in the seat of national power they had long coveted. Matusow may have exaggerated liberalism's death in the 1970s, but it would be hard to deny that conservatives have deeply influenced, even dominated, American politics ever since.[24]

By looking at Barry Goldwater, Edward Abbey, supporters of the antifluoridation movement of the 1950s to the 1970s, and "free market" environmentalists of the 1970s and 1980s, we can unravel the complicated ways in which antistatism and environmental sentiments influenced, interacted with, and hybridized with each other to create fascinating amalgamations of ideas about nonhuman nature, human health, economics, individual rights, and state power. The four share a pronounced mistrust of government and an equally pronounced appreciation for the environment and a concern about threats to it, and thus are ideal for teasing out the relationships between "loving nature" and "fearing government." In other respects, they couldn't have been farther apart, and readers might argue that any discussion of similarities would seem forced. But this book constructs bridges between historical actors, ideas, and movements that are rarely linked in historical analyses, and an open, fluid approach is necessary to appreciate the complexities and ambiguities involved. Here, as with historical reality more generally, vagueness and contradiction are the norm.[25]

The term "environmentalism" and phrases like "environmental concerns" are similarly capacious, and I use them in the book to identify broadly defined environmental concerns—not just the political movement that emerged around Earth Day 1970, but also the conservation and preservation movements that preceded it, as well as apprehensions about pollution and bodily health and a wider sense of the sublime and the pastoral. "Environmentalism" is an unwieldy bundle of ideas, values, and impulses, and broader definitions are vital to the sort of the intellectual bridge building that I engage in here.

What, then, does such bridge building reveal? We see Goldwater and the free-market environmentalists struggling to reconcile their environmental concerns with their ideological ones. Goldwater, moving against his deepest political instincts, tried to carve out a place for federal environmental protection in the midst of his suspicion of regulation and his faith in unfettered capitalism. Not given to rigorous philosophical thinking, he was unable to fully reconcile the tensions between the two. As academically trained economists and political scientists, however, the libertarian free-market environmentalists worked meticulously to develop a philosophically consistent template for government-free environmental protection based on clear property rights, market incentives, and tort law. Like Goldwater, they too had difficulty harmonizing the elements of their critique.

Meanwhile, antifluoridationists developed a unique antistatist-oriented defense of bodily health. For them, sodium fluoride, added to public drinking water in an effort to eliminate cavities in children, was the greatest single threat to Americans' physical well-being. Their sentiments had close parallels with concerns about DDT coming from organic farmers and critics like Rachel Carson, who in most other respects were as different from the conservative-leaning "antis" as could be imagined. Because it had the blessing of the U.S. Public Health Service, "fluoridation" suggested to many antis that a major consequence of federal social welfare programs was an environmental one: the literal pollution of an individual's flesh, the violation of his or her right to a chemical-free environment, and the usurpation of the right to manage his or her own body. Reducing the size and power of the federal government, then, was also to protect human health and place responsibility for its management back into the people's hands.

For Edward Abbey, the preservation of wilderness was the key to parrying state power. As an anarchist raised in rural Appalachia by a Marxist father, Abbey's politics were a jumble of agrarian/labor/Left and libertarian Right, but they were firmly anchored in an aversion to centralized power, high-technology, and consumer capitalism. The State and its corporate allies wanted power and control, he believed, and it was by dominating the natural world that they hoped to dominate individuals, for the exploitation of people and nature were inextricably linked. It followed that environmentalism was a form of resistance to the State. To champion the preservation of wilderness—to resist the nation's ever-expanding suburbanization, its hyper-consumerist lifestyle, its superhighways, corporate farms, and shopping malls—was not simply some feel-good effort to save the planet. It was to undercut the very source of power that the State depended on and thus to save its human victims.

At about the time of Ronald Reagan's election, antistatists had largely abandoned environmentalism, especially of the federal variety. Reagan himself was as good example of this. His aversion to government rivaled Goldwater's, but he lacked the Arizona senator's deep personal connection to nature, and as president Reagan abandoned Richard Nixon's environmental legacy in the name of regulatory relief and a true believer's faith in economic growth. Meanwhile, the larger ideological shifts that brought Reagan to power also pushed the Republican Party in the same direction, to the point that environmentally friendly Republicans were as rare as spotted owls by the 1990s—an ending that did not necessarily have to be that way.

With all the variables involved, exploring the postwar quest to square a love for nature with a fear of government can be an exercise in frustration. To *not* do it, however, is to miss a persistent ideological complexity in Americans' environmental thinking. The relationship between environmentalism and antistatism has been decidedly ecological, as it were—pick the two up and you find them hitched.

—1—

ARIZONA PORTRAITS

The Natural World of Barry Goldwater, Part I

> I like to think that all human effort takes place within the context
> of something permanent, like that river and its canyons.
> —*Barry Goldwater on the Colorado River, 1970*

THEY CALLED HIM "MR. CONSERVATIVE." TO HIS SUPPORTERS, BARRY
Goldwater was the personification of everything they held dear: a crusader
against big government, an unblinking foe of the global Communist peril,
a defender of states' rights, free enterprise, right-to-work laws, and old-fashioned individual initiative. He was a man's man to boot, with rugged good
looks, a sense of humor, and a no-nonsense disposition that complemented
his success as a Phoenix businessman, military pilot, and eventual five-term
U.S. senator from Arizona. He was also their white knight.

The 1950s through the early 1970s, the years of Goldwater's prominence,
were not the best ones for the American Right. It was an age of liberal
centrism and consensus, at least on the surface, with both Republicans
and Democrats working in the long shadow of the New Deal and an ever-expanding federal government. Rock-ribbed conservatives had few champions to whom they could turn, but when Goldwater, seemingly against
the odds and certainly against conventional wisdom, captured the 1964
Republican nomination for president, it was as if a prophet had emerged
from the desert Southwest to lead them home. "In your heart," went their
hagiographic campaign motto, "you know he's right."[1]

To his opponents, he was a menace. Goldwater's rejection of social welfare legislation, they said, revealed a hatred of the poor and the working classes, and his support for states' rights and his vote against the Civil Rights Act of 1964 suggested common cause with white Southern racists. His trigger-finger approach to the Cold War, they charged, was just plain dangerous in a nuclear-tipped world. After all, hadn't he been an enduring supporter of Joseph McCarthy when others had long since come to their senses? Didn't he enjoy the support of the crackpot John Birch Society? Had he not urged an invasion of Cuba during the tense days of October 1962 and pushed for the military liberation of rebellious Soviet Bloc nations like Hungary? To his critics, a vote for Goldwater in 1964 would be a vote for World War III, an idea captured famously in opponent Lyndon Johnson's TV ads that same year. "In your guts," ran a Democratic parody of the Goldwaterite motto, "you know he's nuts." Johnson's drubbing of Goldwater in November confirmed to liberal critics that the Right was going the way of the dodo, an obituary that proved to be rather premature.

Goldwater's ascent rested on one of the most important political transformations of the postwar years—the rise of the Republican Party's conservative wing. The GOP was deeply fractured in the 1950s and early 1960s. Conservatives bemoaned what they saw as its wishy-washy quasi-liberalism and eastern elitism. "Establishment" Republicans like Dwight Eisenhower and Nelson Rockefeller, they said, had turned the party from its core conservatism into an imitation of the Democrats, complete with eastern-style patrician attitudes, New Dealish welfare plans, social and racial liberalism, and a dangerous tendency to coddle the Reds. The GOP was sorely in need of ideological purification, a return to its proper role as champion of small government, states' rights, laissez-faire capitalism, and private property. It needed to reassert its anticommunism and be willing to back up those sentiments with military action, to leave issues like civil rights to local and state authorities who "understood" such things, and to abandon its tacit acceptance of regulation and the welfare state. The modern party offered only an echo of Democratic ideals, conservatives complained, and, to make things even worse, the Establishment prevented them from fixing it. Their champion, Robert A. Taft, had been denied the Republican candidacy for president in 1952 by the Eisenhower mainstream, and twelve years later they still flinched at the memory.

To "establishment" Republicans, the conservatives were hopeless extremists. The political future ran toward the political center, said Eisenhower and others. Like it or not, social welfare, civil rights, and activist government were here to stay, and right-wing dogma would only drive ordinary

Republicans into Democrats' hands. The conservatives would have none of it. They itched for a showdown, and in Barry Goldwater they found not only a man sympathetic to their ideals but also a charismatic leader who could rally the troops. Combining their ideological passion with superb grass-roots organizing and skillful use of party rules, they secured Goldwater's nomination in 1964 and took control of the party by the late 1960s. By 1980 the second generation of GOP conservatives would finally place another of their heroes, Ronald Reagan, in the White House.[2]

Barry Goldwater's own political beliefs were like a hundred-proof shot of conservative antistatism. For him, the federal government was a barely necessary evil, limited by the Constitution to a handful of activities, and its growth in the twentieth century suggested a national slide toward social-ism. As a businessman, he loathed the New Deal's legacy and preached the gospel of individual initiative while damning unions, government regula-tions, and welfare programs. His mistrust of communism was total; when it came to national defense, he urged Americans to resist, by force if neces-sary, the totalitarian designs of the Soviet Union and its (supposedly) obe-dient client states. No compromise was possible, and victory the only road to peace; talk of peaceful coexistence was treason born of "a craven fear of death." Not surprisingly, such attitudes made many people nervous and sometimes angry.[3]

This side of Goldwater has often hidden the rest of the man, for he was never the cardboard figure constructed by worshippers and detractors alike. His sanity was never in question, of course, notwithstanding the Democrats' "nuts" comments. He was not an ideological saint or a political visionary sui generis. Nor was he a segregationist, a hater of the poor, a Bircher, or a war-monger, even if his ideas heartened those who were. It is certainly true that he leaned well to the right, and he ranks as one of the most significant politi-cal figures in postwar American conservatism. Despite that, however, it was not always easy to pigeonhole Goldwater on a particular issue, for he had a fierce libertarian independence that could push him offscript and frus-trate even his most loyal followers. He disappointed gay-rights opponents in the 1990s, for example, by supporting homosexuals' right to enlist in the armed services and arguing for their legal protection from discrimination. He was a lifelong advocate of Planned Parenthood and once declared that the conservative Christian activist and staunch Republican Reverend Jerry Falwell needed "a swift kick in the ass" for meddling in Americans' personal lives. To the horror of his conservative fans, in 1992 he even supported a

Democrat's bid for Congress. No one could tell Barry Goldwater what to think and expect full compliance.[4]

That independence extended to environmentalism and the natural world. In the wake of Reagan's war on the Greens, one might expect that the uberconservative Goldwater, godfather of the postwar Right and icon of the libertarian West, would have had no use for environmentalism. It would be easy to assume that he saw the natural world as nothing more than a collection of resources in the raw and environmentalists as just another group on a long list of regulation-happy eastern liberals bent on using the federal government to hamstring capitalism and create a socialistic welfare state. But such a view would be an oversimplification. A closer look at his life, both the political and the personal, unveils a man with a complicated relationship to the postwar environmental movement in general and the role of government in environmental protection in particular. It reveals one of America's consummate conservative antistatists thinking about nature, and humans' place in it, in ways more sophisticated than mere "antienvironmentalism." Goldwater came of age in a region of tremendous natural beauty, which inspired in him a lifelong passion for it. Later, after World War II, like so many middle-class, urban- and suburban-dwelling Americans, he longed for beauty, health, and permanence and had serious concerns about the central environmental issues of the time: wilderness preservation, pollution, sustainable energy, overpopulation, and the general ecological quality of life. In short, nature mattered to Barry Goldwater.

But his passion for the natural world often clashed with his ideology, waxing and waning with particular issues and the broader environmental and political context in which they arose. There was constant tension between Goldwater's environmental values on the one hand and his antistatism on the other, especially his support for unfettered capitalism and his fears of federal power. He believed wholeheartedly in laissez-faire economic growth, yet he embraced federally sponsored conservation and reclamation projects to achieve it and later came to regret the environmental damages wrought by some of the very projects he had so enthusiastically supported. He celebrated Arizona's phenomenal postwar economic expansion and the associated population and construction booms, yet fretted over the rampant suburban sprawl and the air and water pollution that came with them, all the while grumbling about the excesses of doom-and-gloom environmental "radicals." Influenced by the climate of the first Earth Day, he claimed in 1970 that agencies like the Environmental Protection Agency were necessary exercises of federal power and then went on to complain about their excessive regulations. He loved national parks and wilderness, even as he voted against the Wilderness Act of 1964 and later expressed his sympathy with the Wise Use and Sagebrush Rebellion movements.

In the end, Barry Goldwater as environmentalist emerges as a man trying to serve two masters, pulled by loyalties and sentiments that did not always complement each other. Contradictions abounded in his thinking, and it was seldom clear if he was aware of them or fully cognizant of their significance. He recognized that economic growth could have its downside and that the resulting environmental problems might require more than a simple reiteration of the joys of small government, but there was always the other side, the antistatist, market-worshipping, growth-loving, boosterish Barry Goldwater, for whom federal regulation was Hell's tenth level. Even when he was aware of his competing values and views, he could not get fully past them.

Goldwater's bifurcated response to postwar environmentalism might be seen as a kind of symbolic transition between an older eastern-oriented Republican tradition of federally centered environmental and resource management and a newer, less government-friendly, more western one represented by Reagan's antienvironmental crusade. Until 1980, support for federally enforced environmental protection was largely a bipartisan issue, as Republicans wrestled with Democrats to seize the mantle of leadership. In fact, before that year, as the historian William Cronon has noted, Republicans "could claim with considerable justification that their party's environmental record was no less distinguished that that of the Democrats," despite their ideological discomfort with excessive government power. This was especially true of northeastern Republicans, who could trace their concerns about the environment and their support for government action to the federal activism of Teddy Roosevelt, Gifford Pinchot, and beyond to the reformist traditions of antebellum New England. Despite Goldwater's western roots, his reputation as the New Right's godfather, and his mistrust of the GOP's eastern-elite old guard, his environmental sympathies reflected this older Republican tradition. But he was also in the vanguard of a changing party, one moving away from its already limited embrace of government regulation as well as shifting in its geographical orientation. In his environmental thinking, one can see the GOP's antienvironmental future as well as its Progressive Era past.[5]

It would have suited the Goldwater mystique if he had been born in a log cabin, but Barry Morris Goldwater was a city boy and a child of privilege, at least by territorial Arizona standards. He came into the world on January 1, 1909, in the small but growing capitol city of Phoenix. His father, Baron, was the highly successful proprietor of Goldwater's, one of the few department stores in Arizona that specialized in high-end fashion goods. Its motto was "The Best, Always," and it was in that spirit that Barry, along with brother, Bob, and sister, Carolyn, came of age in a two-story Victorian house at 710 North Central Avenue, complete with a maid, a nurse, and a chauffeur.[6]

Baron Goldwater had little use for the outdoors. His father, Michel "Big Mike" Goldwasser, had emigrated from Poland in the 1850s, anglicized his name, and bounced around California before settling in Arizona. Like others who sought wealth in the West, Big Mike struck gold in the form of merchandising and established the store in the 1870s. Mike's wife, Sarah, longed for a life less rustic than that of a frontier merchant family, however, and spent much of her time in San Francisco with their children. Baron was thus no hardscrabble son of a pioneer, and it showed. His wife, Josephine, recalled him as a "Beau Brummel" who tipped well, dressed with flair, and parted his hair stylishly down the middle. He enjoyed a good drink, a good card game, and good conversation, and the idea of physical hardship and outdoor work didn't appeal to him in the slightest. "My father couldn't drive a car or a nail and never shot a gun," Barry Goldwater remembered later. "He had a motto: never do anything you can pay someone else to do." An emotionally distant father, not one to enjoy the exuberance of his children, Baron spent much of his time absorbed in his own affairs. It fell to Barry's mother to raise the couple's children, foster their values, and introduce them to Arizona.[7]

Josephine Williams Goldwater was a far more important influence on Barry than his father, and Barry was deeply attached to her. She was fiercely independent and adventurous, and he credited her strength of character for his life's successes. In the early 1900s Josephine Williams left her native Nebraska and came alone to Arizona for the desert air, seeking a cure for a case of tuberculosis. Missing a connecting train to Prescott, she stalked down the tracks on heels, suitcase in hand, until a passing locomotive picked her up. Josephine had feared that her health made death imminent, but she survived and went on to marry Baron Goldwater in 1907. She would live another six decades.[8]

Barry Goldwater's conservatism had its roots in his mother's beliefs. "She was always a very patriotic woman," he wrote in 1985, and one of his first memories was of her sewing two stars onto the family flag when

Arizona and New Mexico joined the Union. Jo Goldwater regularly dragged Barry and his siblings to the nearby Indian school, where they watched the nightly lowering of the flag while she instructed them to stand and salute. She was a strict disciplinarian, who never punished her children physically but instead forced them to stare at the family's grandfather clock for hours (sixty years later Barry still remembered how much he had dreaded it). Though the proper moral instruction and conduct of her children was her supreme goal as a mother, Jo tempered her corrections with kindness and affection. "I loved her smile," Barry once wrote, in a revealing metaphor. "It was big, like sunrise over the Grand Canyon." Above all, she demanded honesty, integrity, patriotism, and self-reliance from her children, lessons that would not go unlearned by her eldest son.[9]

Goldwater's mother had an irrepressible love of the outdoors, and it was she who first acquainted him with the desert. "A convert to the beauty of Arizona," writes historian Peter Iverson, Jo "made sure that her children . . . appreciated its unique grandeur." This involved more than mere aesthetics, for to her the natural world was also an important source of spiritual inspiration. A member of Trinity Episcopal Church in Phoenix, she was sincerely if not deeply religious, and she instilled in her children a strong faith in God and a sense of Christian morality. She was firm in the conviction, however, that religious faith need not be cultivated only within the walls of a church, for God also dwelt in His Creation. "She always said," Barry Goldwater once observed, "that you can find God [by] walking through the desert, or walking through the forest, or climbing the mountains just as easily as you can find God in a church." As an adult, Goldwater would never be much of a churchgoer, his religion more of a vague "ethical commitment," as historian Robert Goldberg has written, than anything else, but the idea of nature as sacred space, especially the wild nature of his home state, would stay with him.[10]

Following her convictions, Jo Goldwater made certain that her children spent time in the bosom of God's nature. She was good with a rifle, and she took Barry, Bob, and Carolyn on hunting trips throughout the state (even into her eighties she was still hunting dove and bagging the limit). More often, she would throw the children into her automobile and set off to camp under the stars. Usually their final destination was the California coast, where they would rent a house and spend a few weeks enjoying the beach. Sometimes they rolled across the desert to Prescott, Flagstaff, Sedona, Oak Creek Canyon, the Grand Canyon, Roosevelt Dam, or to Blue Point on the

Salt River for some fishing. When they stopped for the night, the children gathered firewood and washed the dishes. Jo "did the driving and the bossing," Goldwater remembered, and also lectured the children on local history, taught them to identify the desert vegetation, and read to them about Arizona's geology.[11]

The trips made a big impression on young Barry, for car camping could be a serious undertaking in early twentieth-century Arizona. Dressed for adventure in rolled leggings and a World War I–style campaign hat, Jo would pack the car with gear—spare tires hanging from the rear, bedrolls, canteens, pots and pans stashed inside and in boxes slung on the running boards—and they would rattle off, windshield open to relieve the heat. The roads were terrible and very hard on the tires (Barry later recalled changing thirteen flats during one trip to Prescott), and it would be many hours before they would stop, camping out among the yipping coyotes and the craggy, saguaro-studded mountains. One can imagine how it all must have felt to an impressionable young man eager for fun and physical challenge.[12]

These trips exemplified a rapidly growing national trend. The 1920s saw an explosion in car-camping, an outgrowth of that decade's emerging consumerism. Nature travel had once been the domain of upper-class tourists, pricey rail excursions, and grand hotels, but those were giving way to middle-class automobiles, "improved" roads, and campgrounds. Americans seized on the chance to escape their crowded cities and seek temporary solace in nature. "Roughing it" became a national pastime, and in this way large numbers of Americans came to appreciate nature as more than a place to be conquered by an ever-advancing civilization. Ironically, "escaping civilization" by "roughing it" in the "wild" relied heavily on technology, economic growth, and consumerist urges, and Goldwater would later struggle to reconcile wilderness preservation with his support for the economic growth that both threatened the wild and provided the financial and technological means for its enjoyment.[13]

Whatever the contradictions, in the course of these youthful ramblings with his mother and siblings, Barry Goldwater came to love nature's Arizona. Six years before his birth, nature writer Mary Austin said of the California desert in her classic Land of Little Rain that "none other than this long brown land lays such a hold on the affections." Goldwater no doubt would have made the same claim about his home state. Its desert wildernesses would keep calling him back as he grew older and would take a prominent place in both his personal life and his career.[14]

There was more to Barry Goldwater's youth than camping trips, of course, and he spent much of his time in the classic activities of young boys: games, sports, and goofing off. He was street-smart but not intellectually inclined, more interested in having fun and pursuing his own interests than in studying, and consequently he was an abysmal student. His high spirits and lax academic attitude inspired his exasperated father to ship him to military school in Virginia during his teens, where (no doubt to Baron's pleasant surprise) Barry blossomed under the discipline, the pomp, and the honor code to become a model cadet. Even as a wild-eyed kid, though, Goldwater's more serious interests were becoming apparent. As an adult, he would be a great lover of technology and gadgetry, for example, with a knack for tinkering. He was particularly fascinated by radio communication, and his first job was as a sweeper and "gopher" in Arizona's first radio station. He later built his own car radio for his Ford Model A and was a devoted ham radio operator.[15]

Aircraft proved a powerful attraction. Goldwater saw his first airplane at a state fair during World War I and fell hard for it. Around 1930, having graduated from military school and studied for a short time at the University of Arizona (where his stint was cut short by his father's death), Goldwater returned to Phoenix to live with his mother and run the family store. In the mornings before work, he took flying lessons at what would become Sky Harbor airport. Aircraft would become one of the great passions of his life. Goldwater would go on to train pilots and fly across the Atlantic and The Hump as a courier pilot during World War II. As senator, the U.S. Air Force would be his area of expertise (and pet branch of the service) as a member of the Armed Services Committee.[16]

But it was landscape photography, another legacy of his mother's camping excursions, that would bring Goldwater's first brush with fame and eventually ease his entry into politics. Jo Goldwater had owned a box camera, and Barry was soon using it to document their trips. When he got his pilot's license, Goldwater took the camera along with him, taking photographs of Phoenix and the Salt River valley from the air. In 1934 his new wife, Peggy, gave him an Eastman camera for Christmas, and soon he was picking up tips from local photographers, roaming the Arizona backcountry with camera in hand, and studying photographic masters like Ansel Adams and painters like Gunnar Widforss for inspiration. After meeting on the trail to Rainbow Bridge in the 1930s, Adams and Goldwater became correspondents, and the legendary photographer and Sierra Club activist would later pen a laudatory foreword to Goldwater's 1976 book of photographs, *Barry Goldwater and the Southwest*.[17]

Goldwater was never a world-class talent—"Ansel Adam's crown is still safe," the renowned *Washington Post* editor Ben Bradlee teased in a 1984 letter—but he was nevertheless an excellent and dedicated photographer, trekking into remote canyons and mountains to practice his art. He also photographed Arizona's native peoples, especially Navajo and Hopi, and some of these images became his most famous. By 1940 he was confident enough in his abilities to put together the first of several coffee-table photography books, a self-published collection of twenty-five black-and-white plates entitled *Arizona Portraits,* which revealed an artist with a keen eye for land, light, and shadow. A number of the photographs had a rather conventional Old West feel to them—horses, cattle on the range, old wagon wheels, and the like—suggesting an Arizonan's pride in a harsh land tamed by humans. But there were also ten "pristine wilderness" shots, some of them quite striking, like that of Oak Creek Canyon or another of a mule train entering a slickrock-sided canyon. *Arizona Portraits*'s simultaneous glorification of both the wild and the developed landscape foreshadowed Goldwater's later ambivalence about environmental protection and economic growth. There was nothing particularly unusual about such ambivalence, especially when it came to the desert. Many desertophiles in the first half of the twentieth century, writes historian Patricia Nelson Limerick, "combined a sentimental fondness for nature with a practical interest in commercial development and reclamation . . . , equally disinclined to perceive contradiction or strain in loyalty extended both to nature and the growth of the American economy."[18]

The subtler tensions in its environmental philosophies aside, *Arizona Portraits* was a success in its namesake state. Harvey Mott of the *Arizona Republic* praised Goldwater as "a photographer of the first rank," and admiring letters poured in, which Barry mounted proudly in a large scrapbook. Meanwhile, his talents garnered notice in the world of professional photography. The Royal Photographic Society of London elected him to membership, and one of his photographs graced a cover of *Arizona Highways,* the famous travel magazine that, like Goldwater, trafficked in picturesque desertophilic ambivalence.[19]

By the early 1940s, Barry Goldwater was becoming a locally known figure, not for his conservative politics or political ambitions (he had few if any at the time) or for his association with the Goldwater store but for his artistic interpretations of the Arizona landscape. Later, as a senator and presidential nominee, his photography would remain important to him, and photography books continued to come. One of these was a collection of images that appeared in 1964, *The Face of Arizona*. What made this particular volume special was its role as a fundraiser for the Goldwater presidential run. *The Face of Arizona* was impeccably executed, with forty photographs captioned by the senator, separated by translucent leaves, and bound in a bright white cover. For fifteen hundred dollars, gift contributors received a free autographed copy; two thousand to twenty-five hundred dollars got the donor one of the first twenty copies. It is another of the small ironies of Goldwater's life that as one of the most conservative presidential candidates of the twentieth century, he funded his campaign with photographs that a modern, liberal environmentalist might hang on a living room wall.[20]

In July 1940, just three months before *Arizona Portraits* was published, Goldwater's twin passions for photography and wilderness came together in dramatic fashion. Thirty-one years old and the father of two young children (with another on the way), he fulfilled a lifelong ambition to run the Colorado River through the Grand Canyon. He was a busy man now, with the demands of family and part-ownership of the Goldwater store, but for someone fascinated by Arizona's history and in love with its beauty, the prospect of such a trip would be too tempting to ignore. When the chance came, Goldwater jumped at it. He joined the eminent river guide Norman Nevills and seven others at Green River, Utah, on July 10, still and motion-picture cameras packed among his gear.[21]

The Nevills party was to be only the fourteenth group to complete the journey since the Powell expedition of 1869, and Goldwater the seventy-third person. But if he was aware of the historical significance of his trip, Goldwater made no mention of it, the prospect of adventure apparently foremost in his mind. Having begun the journey three weeks earlier, the party pulled ashore on July 9 to pick up its new passenger. They pushed off again the next morning, floating gently down the Green for four days until reaching its confluence with the Colorado. The shallow stretches of the lower Green seemed to disappoint Goldwater a bit, as he grumbled in his journal about seemingly endless sandbars and the necessity of the expedition's outboard motors. But soon, he noted excitedly in his journal, "the fun starts." The rhapsody started as well, as Goldwater sat at the confluence and "gazed long and wonderingly at the Colorado . . . and the indescribably beautiful country through which it flows."[22]

With that beauty came a dose of peril, for in 1940 the Colorado ran unhindered from its headwaters in Rocky Mountain National Park until finally backing up against Hoover Dam, just outside Las Vegas. It was a wildcat of a river, sometimes swollen to raging heights by spring runoff, other times withered by summer drought. Driftwood and boulders clogged side canyons or rumbled menacingly as they slid downstream beneath the current. The river's sediment load was fearsome, so thick it gave the water a brownish-red color that inspired the river's name (the silt was so bad, Goldwater wrote in his journal, that it discouraged swimming, clinging afterward to the swimmer's body like a wiener skin as it dried in the sun). Meanwhile, the rapids made navigation a constant challenge.[23]

For a month the Nevills party slowly made its way downstream. The accoutrements of modern life—canned food, air mattresses, outboard motors—and proximity to civilization made the trip rather less adventurous than previous ones, but there were still hazards. Many rapids had to be lined rather than run directly, the boats tethered and floated through empty and the gear portaged to still water. The rapids of Cataract Canyon pounded the group as they had the Powell expedition seventy years earlier, at one point stranding one of three wooden boats on a rock and tearing holes in the hull and port bow. Farther downstream, another mishap stranded the boat containing Goldwater's film, flipping it on its side and filling it with rushing water (the film survived). And then there were the standard hazards of desert living: heat, sun, wind, nighttime cold and rain, insects, and the endless quest for silt-free drinking water.

Despite the hardships, Goldwater was clearly enchanted, at times unable to refrain from a foray into John Muiresque Romanticism. "Today we have been passing," he wrote on the night of August 7, 1940, "between sheer, red sandstone cliffs . . . indescribably beautiful. . . . The tall spires near the rim . . . look as though God had reached out and swiped a brush of golden paint across them, gilding those rocks in the bright glow of a setting sun. Below the heights the canyon is filled with a blue haze that is not unlike smoke. The river winds lazy and brown through all this beauty. Above this grandeur float soft cumulus clouds, tinted with pastel shades of evening." He concluded, "No, I fear the lenses of my camera will never record what my eyes see and my hand tries so feebly to capture in words."[24]

Goldwater peppered the journal with similar sentiments that, next to other passages, suggested a man with complicated and contradictory views about wilderness. The river's power, the immensity of its canyon, and the intimacy of its side canyons left him in poetic awe. But he also dreamed of a Colorado River harnessed for human use, penned up behind dams with purring dynamos, and diverted into swollen irrigation canals bound for fields blooming in the desert. The tension would not escape him entirely, although it would be some time before he would ask serious questions about taming the Colorado. His photographs of the trip reinforced these contradictory feelings. Along with photos of high canyon walls and water-falls were shots of the Crossing of the Fathers, old settler cabins at Hite's Crossing and Lee's Ferry, and steps cut into the canyon walls by Mormon immigrants at Hole-In-The-Rock. One photo showed Goldwater himself, bearded and shirtless, painting the phrase "Arizona Welcomes You" on a canyon wall near the state's border with Utah, his boosterism having apparently survived the trip intact.[25]

By the end of his journey down the Colorado River, forty-three days after he had begun, Goldwater was ready to go home. "Tomorrow we return to three squares, soft beds, dry and clean clothes," he wrote on the day before the journey's end. "But I will think often of the experiences we've had out here. Maybe I'll even miss them." The next morning the Nevills party motored across Lake Mead to Boulder Dam, where his wife and daughter arrived to greet a stubble-faced, tired but grateful Barry.[26]

Had it not occurred during the summer of 1940, as the Battle of Britain raged, Goldwater's river adventure might have garnered more national attention (although it caught the eye of Kentucky governor Keen Johnson, who appointed Goldwater an honorary "Kentucky Colonel"). Still, it did make him a minor celebrity within Arizona. Goldwater emerged from the canyon with some three thousand feet of motion-picture film, and by November he had begun showing it to audiences around the state, from the Heard Museum in Phoenix to the Rotary Clubs of Kingman and Prescott, Arizona State Teachers' College in Tempe, and Scottsdale High School. He traveled to some of these venues in his own airplane, which only increased the mystique surrounding his new reputation as an adventurer. The response to the film itself was enthusiastic, and Goldwater posted news clippings and letters from admirers in his scrapbook. The film was "exciting and filled with many thrills," the newspaper in Kingman effused, and the Phoenix YMCA urged members to "make reservations early" because of the film's "extreme popularity." By the winter of 1941, Goldwater estimated that some eight thousand people had seen the film; by spring the tally included another ten thousand. At one point he was showing it five times a day.[27]

Goldwater's film may have thrilled audiences, but its real importance lay in the speaking experience, the public exposure, and the network of acquaintances he collected in showing it. "In communities throughout Arizona," Robert Goldberg writes, "Barry sowed political seeds . . . , making personal contacts with men and women who would not forget him." Lecturing, fielding questions, shaking hands, forging connections—all would prove vital in his later political career. As Goldwater later observed, his film gave him "access to so damn many Arizonans that it was just a natural step for me to go into politics." He also published some of the trip's best photographs and parts of his journal, adding to his growing image as a sturdy outdoorsman in classic western style. Without the wild Colorado River as his backdrop, it is conceivable that Goldwater might not have had the initial political success he did. On the national stage his appeal may have come from his uncompromising conservatism, but when he first entered politics with a run for Phoenix city council in 1949, victory came in part from his fame among Arizonans as the man who ran The Canyon.[28]

Goldwater entered politics largely on a whim. While he was concerned about corruption in Phoenix's government, he was also curious if he had a talent for serving in government. He did, and political office soon became his permanent line of business. His rise followed swiftly. By November 1952 he was Arizona's Republican junior senator, defeating longtime Democratic incumbent Ernest McFarland in a tight election. Goldwater's victory was something of a bellwether for the state's political future, once the seemingly inevitable inheritance of the Democratic Party. World War II and the Cold War brought tremendous economic development in the American West, much of it a product of federal effort: military bases, technological research facilities, highways, and reclamation projects. Arizona's economic fortunes had always depended on federal aid, even before statehood (Goldwater's grandfather had established his retail business in part on contracts to supply local U.S. Army outposts), and the trend continued during the 1950s. Following the federal government's trail, private corporations streamed into the region, bringing thousands of residents who settled in places like Phoenix and Tucson. Many of the new arrivals brought conservative political values with them, and they despised central government even though their new home was supported by massive federal largess. In Goldwater they found a native politician who shared their feelings.[29]

From 1952 to 1964, Goldwater's political activities centered on the classic issues of postwar American conservatism. As he discharged practical

duties as chair of the Senate Republican Reelection Committee, he fulminated against the Soviets, championed a strong, high-tech military, and
bemoaned America's lack of resolve in countering communist aggression in
Europe and elsewhere. At home, he supported Senator Joseph McCarthy's
campaign to root out communist infiltrators in the federal government and
warned of governmental meddling in the free market. Labor unions received
an extra helping of his ire, as he locked horns with United Auto Workers
leader Walter Reuther during Senate committee hearings on union corruption. Democrats and liberals received most of Goldwater's castigation, but
he could be critical of his fellow Republicans as well, especially President
Eisenhower, whom he saw as too accommodating to liberals and insufficiently firm with the communists. On the strength of such convictions,
Goldwater soon became a darling of the Right, from William F. Buckley and
the *National Review* to Robert Welch's John Birch Society.[30]

It was during this time that the postwar environmental movement also
began to coalesce. Concern about pesticides, pollution, and overpopulation
would not come into full flower until the next decade, but the 1950s were
hardly without environmental concerns. In the West those concerns centered on federal reclamation and public power projects, national parks, and
wilderness preservation; despite his preoccupation with Moscow and Big
Labor, Goldwater would take a keen interest in such things. One would be
hard-pressed to call him an "environmentalist" during this era, because he
often found himself at odds with national sympathies for wilderness protection. He was a disciple of old-school conservation, and his environmental
views involved virtually everything that label implied: a dedication to ever-
increasing economic growth; a pragmatic and functional view of nature as
the raw material of that growth; a faith in science, engineering, and high-
technology as the means to growth; and human happiness as the ultimate
end. As the environmental movement matured in the late 1960s and early
1970s, Goldwater would move closer to its camp, but for now his faith in old-
fashioned economic progress was strong.

Brought to life by the Reclamation Act of 1902, which officially launched the
U.S. government into the dam-building and irrigation business, the Bureau
of Reclamation may have been the most important federal bureaucracy in
the twentieth-century West. In terms of its impact on the region's economy
and physical infrastructure and certainly its ecological health, it rivaled the
Bureau of Land Management, the U.S. Forest Service, and even the military.

From its inception, BuRec, as it was called, was a conservation organization in the classic Progressive Era mold. "Conservation" here meant the full economic utilization of natural resources via government-oriented science and technology and the concurrent avoidance of "waste"—that is, nonutilization—an attitude that, despite its technical emphasis, was heavy with moral overtones. Consequently, few bird watchers or wilderness lovers worked for BuRec. For its staff of zealous hydrological engineers, any western river not fully dammed, diverted into canals, and lined with irrigated fields was a situation that demanded immediate redress.

Beginning after World War I with Roosevelt Dam and the Salt River Project, located just east of Phoenix, BuRec went to work taming the great rivers of the West with equal parts engineering wizardry, anthropocentric conceit, and near-religious fervor. It was intent on fulfilling of its unambiguous official motto: "Total Use for Greater Wealth." Just who got that wealth, though, was a thorny issue. As Donald Worster has argued, BuRec's mission to harness the waters of the West, originally undertaken in the Jeffersonian spirit of fostering agrarianism and 160-acre family farms, eventually mutated into a massive subsidy for corporate agriculture and private power interests, which in turn promoted the vigorous growth of their political muscle. Meanwhile, the larger ecological consequences of total use, never a matter of much interest for most BuRec projects, wreaked havoc on the West's riparian and agricultural ecology.[31]

But civilizing missions can be hard to resist, and after an early period of financial and technical struggle, BuRec was building apace across the region. For New Dealers and other 1930s political liberals, BuRec's great western reclamation projects, along with the similarly motivated Tennessee Valley Authority, were the preeminent symbol of government toiling for the public good. The great Hoover and Grand Coulee Dams, for example, not only tamed the Colorado and Columbia Rivers but also produced awesome amounts of cheap electricity, employed thousands of workers and, perhaps most important, provided concrete emblems of national faith and purpose for a populace wracked by self-doubt and fear of the future. Other projects accomplished the same thing on a smaller scale, opening up vast sweeps of undeveloped land to farming. Such were federal reclamation's myriad attractions that even many conservatives embraced it, especially if they came from regions that hosted projects. In the West, as elsewhere, ideological opposition revealed its perennial tendency to fold under the weight of pork.

BuRec reached the peak of its power after World War II, and it had big dreams for the upper Colorado River. In the late 1940s the agency concocted the Colorado River Storage Project (CRSP), a mammoth reclamation plan for the upper Colorado basin that outstripped anything BuRec had attempted before. CRSP was, in BuRec terminology, a "multiple use" project. Utilizing more than a dozen dams on both the Colorado and its tributaries, its creators claimed, the project would tame the rivers' spring floods, trap silt and prolong the life of Lake Mead downstream, and provide irrigation water for upper-basin farmers, all while generating enough salable electricity to finance itself. The details could be found in *The Colorado River: A Natural Menace Becomes a National Resource,* a 1946 publication chock full of the gospel of conservation, resource use, and the domination of nature. "Tomorrow," BuRec predicted, "the . . . river will be utilized to the very last drop. Its waters will convert thousands of additional acres of sagebrush desert to flourishing farms and beautiful homes. . . . Its terrifying energy will be harnessed. . . . More water—water from the Colorado River—is the hope of the future."[32]

Not surprisingly, upper-basin politicians supported the CRSP with gusto. As regional boosters, they were keen to anything that promised economic growth, but taming the Colorado for that purpose had always been a task too great for local government. Now they saw a golden chance to expand local private enterprise on the national dime; the federal money to be spent and the contacts to be landed during the construction phase were no small enticement, either. The project offered other benefits as well. First, it would allow the upper-basin states, in accordance with the Colorado River Compact of 1922 (of which they were all a party), to deliver an annual 7.5 million-feet of river water to the lower basin. Second, it would help secure the upper basin's share of the Colorado against the designs of its perennial rival California, which most politicians in the intermountain West were convinced would eventually find a way to appropriate the entire Colorado if not prevented from doing so. Finally, BuRec had helped reclaim enough agricultural land in California to make the state, and at least some of its residents, fabulously wealthy. Now it was the upper basin's turn.[33]

The CRSP's keystone dam was to be the Echo Park Dam on the Green River in western Colorado, a concrete beast of a size and cost to rival Hoover Dam downstream. For BuRec's engineers, it was as if Fate itself had designed Echo Park for damming: a "gunsight" canyon with high walls of good rock, with relatively little surface area in the resulting reservoir, an important consideration for reducing losses to evaporation. Unfortunately for the champions of the CRSP, Echo Park also sat snugly within the borders of Dinosaur National Monument, a small unit of the national park system that preserved not only the fossils that inspired its name but also some stunning stretches of high desert. The result was the biggest environmental battle of the 1950s.

The Sierra Club, the National Parks Conservation Association, and the Wilderness Society plunged into a desperate crusade to stop the dam, and activists like the Sierra Club's David Brower would come of political age in the campaign. For wilderness lovers the dam was triply pernicious. First, Echo Park was beautiful and worth saving in itself. More important, however, was saving the idea of national parks. If BuRec could build inside the borders of a national monument, then was any national park safe from development? Preservationists cringed at the precedent that might be set by a dam in Echo Park, tortured by visions of future reservoirs in Yosemite Canyon and the Grand Canyon. Similar things had happened before. In the early twentieth century, John Muir and the fledgling Sierra Club had fought to prevent the city of San Francisco from damming Hetch Hetchy valley inside Yosemite National Park, a loss that still haunted wilderness lovers a half-century later and that, according to Sierra Club lore, literally broke Muir's heart. This time, the preservationists vowed, they would not only save Echo Park and the national park idea, but they would exorcise Hetch Hetchy's ghost in the process.[34]

To the horror of reclamation boosters across the West, the preservationists succeeded, although not without cost. A massive publicity campaign, complete with newspaper advertisements, coffee-table books, and a traveling road show and film helped turn public opinion and a majority of congressmen against BuRec's plans. Questionable engineering data, revealed dramatically by David Brower in CRSP hearings, put the final nail in the coffin. When Congress finally approved the CRSP on April 11, 1956, the Echo Park dam had been stripped out of it. The role of "keystone dam" now fell to Glen Canyon Dam, to be built on the Colorado River just south of the Utah-Arizona state line, a stretch of the river that many believed was actually far superior in beauty to Echo Park. But Glen Canyon was not a part of a national park or monument, and despite the blossoming sense of regret among activists like Brower—who was soon campaigning against Glen Canyon Dam as vociferously as he had against Echo Park—it began to fill in 1963, eventually creating the 186-mile-long reservoir that BuRec would name Lake Powell.[35]

Despite Goldwater's love affair with the Colorado and his appreciation for wilderness, his support for reclamation trumped any desire he might have had to preserve Echo Park. Whatever aesthetic splendor the place might have, he would not sit idly by as the river's economic potential flowed, unused, to the sea. One of his first actions as a freshman senator in April 1953 was to cosponsor S. 1555, a bill to authorize the CRSP. Like other critics of wilderness preservationists, he rejected the idea that the dam threatened the area's beauty. In fact, Goldwater claimed that the opposite was true. Before Hoover Dam, he observed, Black and Boulder Canyons had been almost inaccessible. "I would say that fewer than 25 persons a year visited there," he averred, but now "approximately 2 ½ million persons were able to visit" and see the two canyons' spectacular geography—or at least the parts that had not been submerged by Lake Mead—by boats and on new roads. The Green River and Echo Park were similarly "impossible to reach by boat or automobile," and the great attraction of the Echo Park dam was not only its reclamation potential but also that "millions of Americans will be able to visit this beautiful section of the country each year." There was an alluring populism to such arguments, and other CRSP supporters employed them relentlessly. Enough of Echo Park would remain to attract lovers of wilderness and natural aesthetics, they said; instead of fighting, the dam preservationists ought to be embracing it for bringing a beautiful area within reach of the common people.[36]

When it came to reclamation generally, there were few projects that Goldwater did not support, especially if they were located in Arizona. One of the great tensions in his political life was between his pro-reclamation sentiments, his conservatism, and his love for wild rivers. Beginning in the 1950s, environmentalist critics would hammer reclamation as both ecologically and aesthetically damaging as well as financially indefensible, and in time Goldwater would come to recognize the ecological problems of at least some projects. Still, he clung tenaciously to the idea that federal reclamation, a big-government welfare program as blatant as any in American history, was somehow exempt from his conservative critique.

This is not to say that Goldwater was uncritical or slavishly supportive of all federal water management. A good example was his dislike of federal hydropower generation. Between 1952 and 1964 he filled more pages of the *Congressional Record* with criticism of the proposed Hells Canyon federal "high dam" and the Tennessee Valley Authority than any other environmentally oriented topics on which he spoke. Taken alone, such criticism was standard-issue postwar conservative antibureaucratic rhetoric; but placed next to his views on irrigation and reclamation, they highlighted his attempt to have his ideological cake and eat it too.

The Hells Canyon controversy was an acrimonious dispute between advocates of private and public electricity production on Idaho's Snake River. In the late 1940s the Idaho Power Company applied for and received permission from the Federal Power Commission to build a number of small dams on the Snake. Public-power proponents vigorously protested the company's plans, however, and argued instead for a single federally funded "high dam" with accompanying power-generation facilities. The resulting conflict raged for years before being settled by the courts in favor of a three-dam Idaho Power Company plan. Debate on the plan filled many pages of the *Congressional Record*, with Goldwater prominently railing against the government's proposal with an ideological passion reinforced by rafts of facts, figures, and testimonials. He approved enthusiastically of damming the Snake; the only question was who should do the damming, and for what reasons.[37]

Goldwater's problems with the federal plan were numerous. Most of all, it offended his laissez-faire sensibilities. Why, he asked in 1955, "if private funds can construct adequate dams" on the Snake, "should the United States be deprived of the use of a half billion dollars [the estimated cost of the federal plan], when private resources are ready to spend the money?" Meanwhile, the Idaho Power plan, Goldwater claimed, would save Americans some $465 million. A federal dam would also cheat local and state governments out of the tax dollars that private dams would provide, he argued, because federal payments in lieu of taxes would never equal lost tax revenue. It was simply not fair for the people of Arizona and elsewhere to be forced to subsidize rural Idahoans' electrical bills. The worst thing about the federal proposal was that it was a gross violation of free enterprise; the government simply had no right to compete with private electricity producers. Why propose federal electrification of an area like Hells Canyon, Goldwater asked, when private interests stood ready to serve? It was a situation that he simply could not abide. It was not only inefficient and unfair, but it also set an ominous precedent. If the government could produce and sell power, then what would stop it from moving into other areas of the market? "The next step," he warned, "will be toward coal, oil, gas, land," and other resources. "Our distinguished majority leader [Democratic senator Lyndon Johnson of Texas] has termed it legislation from the heart," Goldwater concluded. "I agree with the heart part of it. It would put a knife right through the heart of our free enterprise system."[38]

Goldwater leveled similar charges, only with more vigor and regularity, at the great dam-building colossus of the New Deal, the Tennessee Valley Authority, which in his eyes was perhaps the ultimate example of economic absurdity and bureaucratic authoritarianism. It was true, he admitted, that the TVA might have a worthy flood-control and irrigation component, and it might once have provided much needed employment during the Depression, but its forays into public power production were dangerous. It wasted taxpayers' money with its inefficiency and mismanagement, usurped the market from private power producers, deprived local government of tax income, and unfairly relieved local citizens of their duty to take care of their own needs. "It is no more appropriate," Goldwater observed in his first lengthy congressional attack on the TVA in 1954, "for the Federal Government to assume responsibilities for supplying the power needs of an area than it is for it to assume the responsibility for supplying drinking water, sewage service, police protection, or even transportation." Furthermore, like the Hells Canyon project, the TVA subsidized the electric bills of one region at the expense of the others. The people of Arizona, Goldwater assured TVA supporters in 1957, "are not interested one whit in supplying the hundreds of millions of dollars necessary . . . [for] cheap electricity" in the rural upper South, "electricity made cheap by the absence of costs which are absorbed by established private enterprise."[39]

The real threat, however, was ideological. If projects like the Hells Canyon Dam were models of creeping collectivism, then the TVA was collectivism on the dead run. "Galloping socialism," Goldwater termed it derisively in 1961, a mercenary bureaucracy "conceived in the minds of socialistic planners, born in a period of economic distress and nurtured and expanded in deceit," dedicated only to its own ruthless expansion, whatever the costs to the treasury or to democracy. At the same time, the TVA lauded itself cynically as a populists' dream. "Its greatest achievement to date," sneered the senator, "has been in spreading propaganda—with Federal tax funds, of course—eulogizing its accomplishments." Not content with monopolizing power production in the Tennessee Valley, the TVA had designs on the entire South and, in fact, the whole nation. 'If the Government [controls] power" across the country, Goldwater warned, "it [will] have an iron grip on industry and even our domestic life."[40]

Seduced by its celebratory cant, TVA supporters saw nothing wrong in the expansion of the project, but Goldwater sensed ominous developments everywhere. He objected vigorously to suggestions in the late 1950s that the TVA fund itself through the sale of bonds, because it was only the purse strings of Congress that kept it from running roughshod across the country. Bonds would give it "a freedom of action never before granted to any Federal agency." Meanwhile, he charged, the TVA's subsidized electricity steadily drained the capitalist spirit from its customers even as it seemed to enrich them. "I want to tell my friends in these [TVA] states," Goldwater warned in September 1961, "when you become beholden unto government for your economic progress you seem to lose a part of that initiative and independence which under our free enterprise system has brought such great prosperity to our country." The TVA could sometimes bring out the hardshell conservative Jeremiah in Goldwater, as he argued on at least one occasion that federal power projects were so odious that even God Himself objected.[41]

The only sure way to cage the burgeoning TVA monster was to privatize it, or perhaps to turn it over to the states, a proposal that elicited a vigorous response from critics who accused Goldwater of wanting to dismantle the entire operation. But he usually stood firm. "I am quite serious in my opinion that TVA should be sold," Goldwater wrote to a concerned Tennessee citizen in 1963, for "it would be better operated and would be of more benefit to more people if it were a part of private industry." The political implications of such a stance were clear in the run-up to the 1964 presidential election, when fond memories of the New Deal ran high in the rural South. Tennessee congressmen Joe Evins, Clifford Davis, and Richard Fulton denounced Goldwater, as did Arkansas senator William Fulbright. Fulton even challenged Goldwater to come to the region for a debate on the TVA's merits.[42]

On the surface Goldwater's attitude toward the Hells Canyon project and the TVA seemed of a piece with his larger conservative faith in private enterprise, local government, and minimal bureaucracy. The problem was that, when it came to reclamation in his own backyard, Goldwater proved unable to follow his beliefs to their logical conclusion. For him, subsidized power generation was unfair competition, a welfare handout, and a destroyer of initiative; subsidized irrigation and flood control were simply a helping hand for upright citizens who would handle such things themselves if only they could. Public power violated the Constitution; reclamation was a legitimate governmental responsibility. Public power was creeping socialism; reclamation enriched and glorified the region and the Republic. That his criticisms of the one might apply equally to the other was an ideological quandary that Goldwater chose to rationalize away or simply to ignore.

If ever there was an enterprise that confirmed conservatives' warnings about the perils of federal bureaucracy, reclamation was it: a welfare program of vast scale and a money-waster of almost breathtaking proportions. A typical BuRec or U.S. Army Corps of Engineers project in the years after World War II—and there were literally hundreds of them—might cost tens of millions of dollars, and by the 1960s the budgets of some proposed projects, such as the Corps' Rampart Dam in Alaska, topped three billion dollars. In theory, such expenses would be repaid in relatively timely fashion, typically a few decades, by water-usage fees and power generation. In reality, most projects would take hundreds of years to pay themselves off, if they ever did, even though BuRec shifted many of the costs to taxpayer-funded categories like flood control and "wildlife enhancement" and gave water users a generous financial head start with below-market rates and, later, relaxed acreage limits. Often the acres irrigated by federal reclamation produced only low-value crops for a market already awash in cheap food and fiber, and there was not always a reliable market for electricity from the "cash register" dams intended to pick up the projects' financial slack. As with most government operations, a large majority of reclamation projects ran well over budget, and BuRec became remarkably adept at convoluted accounting procedures designed to conceal what was essentially a fiduciary black hole. The result was a spectacle of taxpayer-funded economic irrationality: massive volumes of water sucked from reservoirs across the West by electricity-hungry pumps, lifted by giant pipes over mountains, sent hundreds of miles though tunnels and canals to fields that often grew only alfalfa or feed corn in direct and subsidized competition with farmers in the East who could produce larger crops without irrigation.[43]

But the pork was delicious; for its recipients, reclamation's benefits were too valuable to pass up. Agricultural interests enjoyed water at rates well below market value while letting Uncle Sam absorb the costs of construction and maintenance. Regional municipalities got water for population growth and the attendant increases in economic development and the tax base. Consumers got electricity at some of the lowest rates in the nation. BuRec and the Corps of Engineers got every bureaucracy's manna from heaven: increased funding, more and bigger projects, more authority, and more opportunity to elbow each other out of the way in pursuit of all three. And politicians got kudos from everyone for bringing Progress, freed from the whims of capricious Nature, to their cities, states, and region. It would have taken considerable honesty, self-reflection, and a full comprehension of the reclamation system to have rejected it. Goldwater would prove no more resistant to the charms of federal reclamation than most other western politicians, although it must be stated that, if he had been, he would have been promptly tossed out of office. Reclamation's value was a bipartisan article of faith in the West, and voters expected their candidates to bring water projects home, whatever their affiliations. But Goldwater needed little prodding from his constituency. He was a true believer, and although he was never as politically active in pursuing reclamation projects as Arizona's senior Democratic senator Carl Hayden, he remained an adamant champion of them for his entire life.

Goldwater was not unaware that his attitudes toward public power versus reclamation could be perceived as contradictory, even hypocritical, and consequently he took pains to explain the logic behind them. First, he argued, the federal government had a Constitutional duty—"by inference," if not one "specifically stated" in the Constitution itself—to provide flood control. Second, reclamation projects differed from federal power projects in that they were loan programs, not welfare. The TVA lost money it would never recoup, but reclamation projects were designed to pay themselves back quickly through usage fees; if that didn't work, "secondary" power sales from the dams could fill in the financial gaps. Here, Goldwater liked to point proudly to Arizona's Salt River Project as proof. It provided flood control, irrigation, and electric power, he noted with satisfaction, all while paying itself off by the 1940s. The problem was that one solvent reclamation project was not evidence of the financial health of them all, and it is worth noting that the Salt River Project was hardly a model of democratic irrigation, as large agribusinesses monopolized the water, ignored BuRec acreage limits, and grew even larger.[44]

Most important, though, Goldwater simply asserted that his home region "needed" reclamation, a defense that he shared with most westerners. The West was an honest place, their argument went, a proud and self-reliant region with economic greatness shimmering on its horizon. It was the kind of place where free-market capitalism might flourish as nowhere else on earth, if only it could get enough water. Independent westerners, on principle, would pay for their own water if they could, but environmental obstacles loomed so high over the region that it lacked the monetary resources to harness its rivers on its own. And without sufficient water, the

West would not only fail to develop economically, it would also lose what it already had. Reclamation helped the region help itself. It provided a crucial beachhead in the West's battle to overcome its environmental constraints, pull itself up by its bootstraps, and build a society worthy of both its pioneer ancestors and the nation. Thus reclamation was emphatically not welfare. It was seed money that would be repaid in full and then some as the West rose to its economic destiny, a temporary loss leader for the long-term growth of both the region and the nation—a "real advantage to the people" of the country, as Goldwater observed in 1961. He seemed not to notice that this argument bore more than a passing resemblance to those made by public-power advocates, who regularly invoked "national greatness" in defense of their own pet dam projects.[45]

If the federal government wanted to bring reclamation to Arizona, then Goldwater would stand at the front of the receiving line, and during the 1950s he tried several times to prod it into doing so. He sponsored bills to authorize the construction of a number of projects: Buttes Dam, the Colorado River Indian Irrigation Project, the Navajo Irrigation Project, the San Juan–Chama Project, and various "improvements" on the Gila and Salt Rivers. In 1956 he introduced a joint resolution urging BuRec to study the feasibility of piping seawater to Arizona from the Gulf of California and sponsored a bill in 1961 for federally funded investigations into the possibilities of irrigating with desalinized water. Meanwhile, with the CRSP's passage in 1956, Goldwater worked hard to make sure his home state reaped its benefits, urging BuRec commissioner Wilbur Dexheimer to make northern Arizona the center of operations for the construction of Glen Canyon Dam, lobbying interior secretary Fred Seaton to employ Arizona's Native Americans on the project, and complaining about federal ownership of the dam's powerlines. Most of all, Goldwater championed BuRec's mammoth Central Arizona Project (CAP), destined to be one of the most ambitious in its history.[46]

The CAP was designed to save Arizona agriculture from itself. Local boosters had been dreaming since before statehood of capturing water from the Colorado River and sending it to fields around Phoenix. By the 1940s that dream had taken on some urgency as agriculture in the area, combined with an exploding urban populace, drained the local groundwater supply to perilously low levels and began to collapse the land above it—a phenomenon known as subsidence. In the late 1940s BuRec offered the CAP as a simple but immense solution. Giant pumps would suck over a million acre-feet of

Colorado River water (approximately 8 percent of its entire average annual flow) out of Lake Havasu, the reservoir behind Parker Dam on the Arizona-California state line, pump it via a tunnel through the Buckskin Mountains, and pour it into Granite Reef aqueduct for a three-hundred-mile trip southeastward to the Phoenix-Tucson area. There it would be used to take the pressure off the groundwater supply and aid in its recharge. Thus augmented, agriculture would again flourish and Arizona would climb to new and triumphant heights of economic prosperity. Local businessmen and politicians loved the idea—they had been clamoring for just such a project for years—and Carl Hayden considered the CAP's final congressional approval in 1968 to be one of his crowing achievements. BuRec loved it too; great projects like this one were a hydrological engineer's dream.[47]

Although Hayden was the main political advocate, for the CAP, Goldwater was equally enthusiastic. Arizona, he warned, "desperately [needs] water for continuing development." Meanwhile, California loomed over the lower Colorado, hungering to devour it whole—"with the covetous eyes of buzzards waiting for death," as he put it, in only half-jest, in July 1957—and the CAP would ensure that Arizona could use its rightful share. To make things worse, while Arizona went thirsty, socialistic public-power schemes elsewhere soaked up federal funds that could be turned to the CAP. "It is going to be expensive to bring additional water into Arizona," Goldwater complained in 1963. "But where is the money coming from for that development if the Interior Department and Bureau [of Reclamation] are going to continue seeking huge appropriations from the Federal Treasury to construct power projects?" Goldwater's disdain for public power came not only from ideology, it seemed, but also from the fact that it took pork out of Arizona's mouth.[48]

Even more revealing was the fact that Goldwater was willing to offer up the Grand Canyon in pursuit of the CAP. Granite Reef aqueduct would start high and run downhill, but moving more than a million acre-feet of water out of the Colorado and over the mountains in western Arizona to get it there would require astonishing amounts of electricity, so much that another dam would be needed to generate it. Long discussed and finally proposed officially in 1963—as part of BuRec's massive Pacific Southwest Water Plan, of which the CAP was in turn a part—Bridge Canyon Dam was to be located at the western end of the Grand Canyon, just outside the border of Grand Canyon National Monument. Its generators would power the massive CAP pumping station on Lake Havasu's shore, and remaining power would be sold, "cash register" style, to finance the project. The Bridge Canyon reservoir would back up far enough to flood a thirteen-mile stretch of the Colorado inside the national monument.[49]

Preservationists howled. Not to worry, said the CAP's many champions (among them Arizonan Stewart Udall, John F. Kennedy's secretary of the interior). The reservoir would hardly be noticeable amid the staggering vastness of the landscape. In fact, it would enable more visitors to experience the Grand Canyon's beauty, an argument that closely followed those favoring the Echo Park dam a decade before. Once again preservationists rejected such arguments and dug in their heels. The national park idea was at stake once more, but this time it was no obscure canyon that would be inundated. It was the Grand Canyon. David Brower and the Sierra Club led the battle again, sponsoring a publicity campaign with books, films, editorial essays, and newspaper advertisements so effective that angry letters from around the nation inundated both Congress and BuRec. Even *Reader's Digest,* never friendly to anything that smacked of political radicalism, editorialized against the dam in the spring of 1966. Shortly after, the government revoked the Sierra Club's nonprofit status, a move that many interpreted as punishment for its opposition.[50]

Goldwater may have loved the Grand Canyon and the Colorado River, but that love could not compete with the attractions of the CAP. He had not blinked in 1956 when the CRSP doomed Glen Canyon upstream, and he would not do so now. His reputation as a canyon lover led some to hope that he might be amenable to changing his mind, but they would find themselves disappointed. In fact, he used his outdoor reputation to add credibility to his support for the dam. "I realize," he wrote to a correspondent who demanded an explanation,

that the dam at Bridge would raise the water level of the river along the boundary of the Grand Canyon National Monument[;] however, I believe that such circumstances must be balanced against the needs of the entire state and its economic future. As one of the few who have visited the Monument from both the rim and inside the Canyon, I believe the lake behind Bridge would create even more beauty and make the canyon more available to hikers and outdoor lovers than it is now. . . . I have traveled every foot of the river through the Canyon, and I believe that no one exceeds my own zeal for the Grand Canyon, and I honestly feel that in this case, the dam at Bridge would prove advantageous.

If a true and knowledgeable canyon lover could favor the CAP, then only the inexperienced and the naively romantic could oppose it.[51]

In the end the preservationists emerged victorious, as much from the intricate compromises of interstate water politics as from their own efforts. When the CAP was finally authorized in 1968, Bridge Canyon Dam had been shorn from it, and the electricity for the pumping stations on Lake Havasu would come instead from the coal-fired Navajo Generating Station. The CAP was destined to become one of the premier financial boondoggles in BuRec history, which had no shortage of them. Its total cost ran to over four billion dollars by the 1980s, making it the most expensive aqueduct project in American history, and its water became so expensive that most irrigators in central Arizona could not afford it if usage fees were not kept artificially low. Today its biggest consumers are not farmers but the thirsty urban residents of Phoenix and Tucson. The CAP now subsidizes the region's drinking water, a state of affairs that, had it occurred anywhere else, Goldwater surely would have denounced.[52]

Other issues confirmed Goldwater's differences with the era's environmentalists. In the mid-1950s, for example, he was vocal in his support for President Eisenhower's interior secretary, former Oregon governor Douglas McKay, whom wilderness preservationists had tagged with the nickname "Giveaway McKay" in response to his relationship with forestry and mining interests. The senator also stood behind Eisenhower's veto of a bill to amend the Federal Water Pollution Control Act of 1948, declaring water pollution to be a strictly local issue. A few years later he blasted the Kennedy administration's Youth Conservation Corps, an outdoor-oriented job-training program for disadvantaged urban youth. While Goldwater appreciated the idea that some exposure to nature might be good for them, he said, "supplying them with suntans and an appreciation of outdoor living will simply not find them jobs."[53]

The biggest environmental issue of the early 1960s, however, was the debate over the Wilderness Act of 1964. Signed into law by President Lyndon Johnson on September 3 of that year, the act marked the culmination of efforts to establish a legal basis for protecting undeveloped public lands. It authorized Congress, on the recommendation of the president, to set aside "primitive" lands in the U.S. Forest Service, the Bureau of Land Management, the Fish and Wildlife Service, and the National Parks as designated "wilderness" areas in the National Wilderness Preservation System.

Additional wilderness areas could then be proposed by members of Congress, pending approval by that body and the signature of the president. Once a part of the system, official "wilderness" areas would be managed by their respective bureaucratic administrators as places where, in the act's famously poetic phrase, "the earth and its community of life are untrammeled by man, where man himself is a visitor who does not remain." In practical terms, this meant that federal wilderness, with some minor exceptions, was immune from development: no logging, mining, or road-building. It was a stellar victory for preservationists, who had herded the act through years of contentious congressional debate, a multitude of amendments and revisions, and the heated opposition of the resource industry.[54]

Goldwater might have been expected to have been a grudging proponent of the Wilderness Act. After all, it was a measure of the general attraction of the wilderness idea that the act had widespread bipartisan support—the final version got only one dissenting vote in the House of Representatives and twelve in the Senate—and one of its original sponsors was Republican congressman John Saylor. And Goldwater's love of wild land was both sincere and long-lived; surely he, more than most senators, would have cause to support the act. Instead, he was one of the dissenters. Some of his reasons for voting against the act were ideological. Goldwater fretted about tax revenue being denied to the states as a result of "locking up" land with a wilderness designation. Only 12 percent of Arizona was taxable private land, Goldwater argued in April 1963, and "what the Federal Government is doing [with the act] . . . is to hasten the day when the Western States will not be able to tax themselves adequately to run their own governments. Of course, when that happens, the only place to turn will be the Federal Government."

He also found procedural problems with the act. It "does not provide for [enough] positive control of Congress," he told a Tucson constituent who demanded an explanation for his "nay" vote, because it allowed the president and his bureaucrats too much leeway in the designation process. The act also violated Goldwater's perennial sense of states' rights and regional autonomy. "I do not think the time has yet come," he declared in 1961, in a statement that foreshadowed the Sagebrush Rebellion twenty years later, "when a handful of people in this country can dictate what we must do with many millions of acres of land in the Far West." Besides, Goldwater argued, there were enough national parks and more than enough wild land in the West to satisfy demands for wilderness experience, "enough to satisfy everybody who wishes to take advantage of the natural beauty of those areas. I see no need for expanding the areas . . . [by] putting the Federal Government more and more into the business."[55]

The most provocative argument Goldwater offered against the Wilderness Act was that it would destroy the very wild land that it aimed to save. A wilderness designation for a given area would be akin to giving it a four-star travel guide rating, he predicted. Suddenly everyone would want to go there, whether they really appreciated wilderness or not. No matter what prohibitions the act made against development, increased tourist pressure would ensure that, sooner or later, roads and associated improvements would be built in wilderness areas. The protected landscapes would die of their own popularity. "The moment we set aside the wilderness areas," warned Goldwater during Senate debate on the act in 1961, "roads will be cut into them. . . . The next thing to happen will be that other individuals will come—those we call dudes—who will not drive on any highway unless it is paved. Then what was once a beautiful section of the United States will be overrun by people who have no desire at all to go into a wilderness."[56]

Goldwater elaborated on this argument during debate on the bill in 1963. He had seen, he said, his favorite fishing spot on the remote middle fork of the Salmon River in Idaho "opened up" as "some kind of wildlife area." It had been promptly invaded by "people who have no appreciation for this kind of scenery," leaving empty beer cans and whiskey bottles and dead fish scattered everywhere. The experience had convinced him of the perils of official wilderness designations. "Instead of preserving these areas as wilderness areas," he cautioned, with the Wilderness Act "the tendency is to have them more and more opened up. The public will demand that they be opened up. As a result they will lose their scenic value. I am in hearty accord with the preservation of areas for people who really like to get into the wilderness. . . . However, I am not in favor of opening it up to the abuse of people who want to say they have been there and in the process leave their trade mark." Goldwater was especially fearful for the wild areas of northern Arizona. "What is going to happen when [a tourist] cannot get in there?" he asked. "What if . . . he does not like to ride a horse and he does not like to walk . . . but, instead, likes to drive his car on a paved road and find good accommodations when he gets there? Can the Interior Department and . . . Congress withstand pressures to provide the funds to open these places?" He dreaded the day "when the Federal Government will start putting sewer lines, gaslines, waterlines, and paved roads into . . . the canyon lands." He would have to vote against the act.[57]

It was an argument that on one level came off as inconsistent, disingenuous, and even hypocritical. After all, this was the same Barry Goldwater who had sung the praises of the Echo Park dam precisely because it would increase access to Echo Park and who was currently making similar arguments in support of the dam at Bridge Canyon. Such contradictory logic could only be employed, cynics might charge, by nominally laissez-faire western conservatives who wanted to exploit the wealth of public lands without regulation and have taxpayers pick up the costs. Critics of wilderness preservationists called them "elitists" who wanted to make the Wild West into their personal fiefdom. Goldwater was among those who made such charges during the Echo Park controversy, but now, with his obvious contempt for "dudes," he bore more than a slight resemblance to the stereotypical elitist wilderness lover.

A more sympathetic interpretation suggests something rather different. First, his predictions about wilderness areas being loved to death were not without merit, for recreational use of wilderness exploded in the 1960s and 1970s, threatening it with damage from overuse, a condition historian Roderick Nash has termed "the irony of victory." More important, Goldwater's contradictory reaction to the act was an honest clash between two of his most dearly held convictions. On the one hand, he was a capitalist, with a deeply utilitarian conception of the natural world and an unapologetically anthropocentric view of humanity's place in it. That side of him wanted to tame the wilderness with all due speed for the glory of private enterprise, commerce, and progress. He was also a sincere political conservative whose mistrust of the federal government ran to the core of his being. But on the other hand, Goldwater's photography, his trip through the Grand Canyon, and his enduring love for the Arizona desert revealed that he also saw much of noneconomic value in wild land. Indeed, that value made him particularly protective of Arizona's wild places, which he had come to see as his own. Goldwater wanted to have his wilderness and develop it too.[58]

By November 1964, Goldwater was out of the Senate courtesy of Lyndon Johnson. Four years later he would recapture his seat, but what is remarkable about the interim is what Goldwater chose to do with his time. Today, flying into Phoenix's Sky Harbor Airport in Phoenix, passengers looking to the north see a massive, convoluted stone ridge rising dramatically amid the city's suburban sprawl. There is no development on most of Camelback Mountain, the city's most famous natural landmark, and many of Sky Harbor's arriving travelers will never know that Barry Goldwater was one of the major reasons for its preservation. Phoenix had grown dramatically since World War II, and by November 1964 it was home to several hundred thousand people. Development had necessarily exploded into the desert surrounding the city, and it was now lapping against the edges of Camelback Mountain, to the growing concern of local conservation and civic-beauty organizations. The Preservation of Camelback Mountain Foundation formed in the mid-1960s with the mission of rescuing the mountain from the schemes of house-builders and land speculators. In Goldwater they found an enthusiastic ally. He may have had reservations about preserving wilderness by federal decree, but he welcomed the chance to save local open space through private initiative.[59]

"Saving that mountain has become the most important goal of my life," Goldwater declared in the spring of 1965. "If it's the last thing we do, we're going to preserve Camelback." He was as good as his word. He threw himself into the campaign, donating twenty-five-thousand dollars to the foundation and serving as its chairman, using his influence to raise money, and encouraging Camelback landowners to sell or donate their holdings. He pitched in at fundraisers, even dressing up as one of the Beatles and playing trombone in order to win a thousand-dollar donation from his brother. "A Camelback cluttered with roads and utility poles and bulldozed scars and houses would be the shame of the state," Goldwater warned, with all the passion of a stereotypical wilderness lover. "If we ruin Camelback, ever afterward people will think of Phoenix as the city that made something ugly of the most beautiful thing it had." The undeveloped mountain was "worth the fight."[60]

Goldwater and the foundation's efforts, however, were not enough to save the mountain. They had raised $250,000 by 1966, but without matching funds they would be unable to purchase all of the remaining private lands. So it was that Goldwater, hat in hand, went to the federal government to ask for help. The Preservation of Camelback Mountain Foundation wanted to protect the mountain, he told the assistant secretary of the Department of Housing and Urban Development, "by any means." Private initiative had hit "the bottom of the barrel," and federal largess was the only hope. In May 1968, Interior Secretary Stewart Udall rode to the rescue with a $211,250 check from land and water conservation funds, and in July 1969 the foundation turned its hard-won Camelback holdings over to the city of Phoenix.[61]

Goldwater's Camelback campaign was a harbinger of things to come. When he returned to the Senate in January 1969, he would find that much had changed in the four years he had been absent. Environmental issues were becoming more and more important, not just in Arizona but also in the nation as a whole. They would take up an increasing amount of his time in the years to come, and they would also present him with a conundrum: how necessary was federal involvement in the quest for a clean, safe, and beautiful environment? His response would be a mixture of conservative anxiety and a grudging embrace of federal regulation. Government help might be hard medicine for the nation's environmental ills, but it was perhaps the only medicine that would work.

While Goldwater fretted the environmental consequences of wilderness tourism and suburban growth, Americans were growing increasingly alarmed by other threats. If sprawl menaced the natural landscape, then pesticides, herbicides, nuclear fallout, and a host of other new and unnatural substances endangered the health of the people who inhabited it—a danger often ignored or dismissed, some charged, by the very government that was supposed to protect them. According to the government-averse and conspiracy-minded—whose antigovernment sentiments were sometimes so intense that they made Goldwater look like a socialist—authorities and experts in Washington, D.C., were actually guilty of deliberately contaminating the American populace. Beginning in the late 1950s, this extreme antistatism would merge with rising anxieties about pollution and chemical contamination to create the antifluoridation movement.

— 2 —

PRECIOUS BODILY FLUIDS

Fluoridation, Environmentalism, and Antistatism

Each is the proper guardian of his own health, whether bodily or
mental and spiritual.

—*John Stuart Mill, On Liberty, 1859*

AS BARRY GOLDWATER STUMPED FOR RECLAMATION, LOCKED HORNS WITH
wilderness preservationists, and was anointed the Great Conservative Hope,
Rachel Carson was crafting a book that would change the world. *Under the
Sea-Wind, The Sea around Us,* and *The Edge of the Sea* had established Carson
as a first-rate naturalist and popular writer in the 1940s and 1950s, but *Silent
Spring* would make her a legend. Published in 1962, just two years before her
death from breast cancer, Carson's last major literary work was a blistering
indictment of the postwar breed of pesticides: aldrin, dieldrin, endrin, heptachlor, parathion, 2, 4-D (dichlorophenoxyacetic acid) and, above all, DDT.
Silent Spring was also a lyrical defense of nonhuman nature and the intricate ecological bonds that held it together. Both the book's popularity and
its power came from this rare blend of scientific and artistic skill, as Carson
wove wildlife biology, ecology, chemistry, and toxicology together with the
prose of a literary master. As a result, *Silent Spring* quickly became one of the
most important writings in the environmentalist canon.[1]

In the wake of the book's debut, Carson, a former doctoral student in
biology at Johns Hopkins University and chief scientific publications editor
for the U.S. Fish and Wildlife Service, found herself awash in praise for taking on powerful vested interests in industry and government. Some correspondents aimed at more than mere congratulation, however, and followed

up their accolades with pointed requests for Carson's assistance. Would she be willing, they inquired, now that *Silent Spring* was behind her, to strip the veil from yet another insidious substance—"the most deadly of all," as one writer put it—and the sinister parties who promoted it?[2]

Large numbers of people were exposed to this substance every day, they said, but most were unaware of its dangers. Like DDT, the substance could be used as a pesticide—it was particularly well known as a rat and cockroach killer—and had a tendency to accumulate in human flesh and bone, touching off an avalanche of health problems. Yet, as they did with DDT, "experts" declared the substance perfectly safe. Indeed, they actually called it healthy, and the U.S. Public Health Service even promoted the idea of adding the substance to the nation's tap water so that the American people could reap its "benefits," whether they wanted them or not. The end result was nothing less than a federal program of compulsory poisoning in the name of the "public good," and a gross violation of the individual's right to manage her own health. The nation needed to know the truth, the letter-writers concluded, and Carson's reputation as DDT's slayer would "carry a great deal of weight," as one told her, in the growing crusade against the substance. Rumors about Carson's thoughts on the subject were already circulating, another correspondent informed her, and a third saw a Carson-penned exposé about the substance as a "natural sequence [*sic*] to your excellent book," later requesting her editorial guidance when he decided to write the exposé himself under the title *A Struggle with Titans* (Carson politely declined). Well aware of the controversial nature of their claims, Carson responded cautiously to her beseechers and refused to take a stand either way until she had studied the substance in depth, an answer that probably disappointed them but underlined her commitment to scientific objectivity.[3]

The substance that got Carson's correspondents so agitated was sodium fluoride. Fluoridation—the controlled addition of very small amounts of sodium fluoride to municipal drinking-water systems—was one of the signature advances in twentieth-century American dental care. Beginning in the late 1940s and early 1950s, medical specialists and public-health advocates around the nation promoted the procedure as a cheap and safe method for preventing cavities in children, and by 1953 several hundred American communities fluoridated their tap water. But despite the blessings of numerous scientific and government organizations, some Americans eyed fluoridation suspiciously. To these so-called "antis," sodium fluoride was one of the most hazardous substances known to humankind, a major culprit—perhaps *the* major culprit—in a hundred different health problems ranging from mottled teeth to cancer. By the late 1950s and early 1960s they had coalesced into a loose but powerful constellation of opposition groups who scoured medical journals, consulted sympathetic doctors and dentists, published newsletters, pamphlets, and books, attended public hearings, confronted local fluoridation supporters, lobbied elected officials, swapped literature, and drew inspiration from fellowship in a righteous cause. In the process they were able to throw pro-fluoridation scientists, doctors, dentists, bureaucrats and civic leaders back on their political heels and stymie numerous fluoridation proposals across the nation.[4]

Anxieties about dangerous substances in food, air, and water, at home and at work—smoke, offal, excrement, dyes, lead, arsenic, pesticides, radioactive fallout, and on and on—are nothing new in American history, and sodium fluoride might easily be categorized as just another on a very long list. It might even be argued that sodium fluoride doesn't belong on the list at all because its dangers are debatable. Organizations from the American Dental Association to the Environmental Protection Agency to the World Health Organization have defended fluoridation's safety for decades, and critics have attacked it with equal vigor, each without appreciable effect on the other. Perhaps this is why historians have seemed content to view the antifluoridation movement as a status anxiety–oriented "revolt of the powerless," who "latched onto fluoridation as a symbol" of the scientists, bureaucrats, and business leaders they perceived as threatening. This is unfortunate because whatever the truth about sodium fluoride's safety, the "anti" movement offers a spectacular example of what could happen when the environmental concerns of the postwar period crossed paths with the era's growing mistrust of the federal government, particularly of the conservative/libertarian variety.[5]

The antifluoridation movement should be understood not merely as a manifestation of status anxiety but also as a sincere expression of postwar environmental concerns. Accepting the judgment of mainstream science, I assume that fluoridation poses little danger to human health, and I will not argue that profluoridationists have suppressed information about sodium fluoride's dangers or that antis have been victims of conspiracies to silence them. I intend, however, to take the antis seriously as people deeply influenced by postwar environmental concern. In the 1950s and 1960s Americans lived in a world where compounds like DDT, aminotriazole, and thalidomide turned out to be more curse than blessing, and part of the postwar environmental campaign for "beauty, health, and permanence" involved restricting or eliminating their use. When antis railed against the dangers of fluoridation, they were echoing those concerns. That so many of them wrote to Rachel Carson and linked her crusade against pesticides to their own suggests they saw sodium fluoride as an environmental issue, even if many of them would not have considered themselves "environmentalists" per se. Strong parallels between *Silent Spring* and the antis' condemnations of sodium fluoride reinforce this idea.[6]

But the thing that made antifluoridationists' fears different from other postwar concerns about pollution, contamination, and health was the intense antistatism that informed their environmental critique. For many antis the problem was not simply that sodium fluoride was dangerous to human health. It was that the federal government, via the U.S. Public Health Service and in league with scientific experts and corporate villains, insisted on forcing Americans to drink poison in the name of the public good. Federal power was running amok. Consequently, the movement—which drew much of its membership from "alternative" health practitioners and devotees, nutritionists, organic farmers, and others skeptical of mainstream medicine, science, and technology—also attracted large numbers of libertarians and conservatives, many of them acutely suspicious of federal power.[7]

The end result was a fascinating mash-up of postwar anxieties about pollution, contamination, bodily health, and the power of the State. For antifluoridationists, government was not the solution to an environmental threat like sodium fluoride. It was the problem. Thus the antifluoridation movement emerged as a distinctly libertarian-tinged antistatist version of the more familiar government-friendly "liberal" postwar environmentalism. In the process it revealed one of environmentalism's most interesting characteristics: its ability to serve as a vehicle for ideological critiques. On the left, environmentalism has often been the partner of progressive social justice movements, race, class, gender, and labor issues, and criticisms of capitalism. The postwar antifluoridation movement suggests that a similar kind of ideological hybridization could occur on the postwar right as well. The war against sodium fluoride reflected the general influence of environmental concerns, but it also did double-duty as a condemnation of the bureaucratically intensive, social engineering–oriented, "authoritarian" postwar liberal welfare state that so many conservative and libertarian antis so deeply despised.

Recognition of sodium fluoride's power to prevent cavities came in the early twentieth century, and like so many other scientific discoveries, it grew from a combination of observation and curiosity. It had long been known among dentists that certain populations suffered from the "mottling" of their teeth: specks, blemishes, and black patches on otherwise healthy—unusually healthy, as it turned out—incisors, canines, and molars. The precise cause was unknown, although it appeared to be related to the geographical location of the teeth-owners. In 1901 a dentist named Frederick McKay, concerned about mottling among his patients in Colorado Springs, joined forces with dental specialist Green Vardiman Black to isolate the cause. For the next two decades McKay and Black surveyed the United States, compiling data from regions where mottling was known to occur. That data suggested mottling was closely related to drinking water; something in the water was causing it, but McKay and Black lacked adequate testing facilities.[8]

With the help of the Aluminum Corporation of America and its research head H. V. Churchill, McKay went on in the early 1930s (Black died in 1915) to identify naturally occurring fluorides as the culprit. Of far more import, however, was the ancillary observation that people with fluoride-induced mottling had far fewer cavities than those not exposed to the substance, especially if that exposure began in childhood. In the 1930s researchers confirmed sodium fluoride's cavity-preventing properties in experiments with rats, and near decade's end biochemist Gerald J. Cox suggested that fluorides might be intentionally introduced into drinking water to inhibit tooth decay. Other specialists concluded that one part per million sodium fluoride would be the optimum amount for artificial fluoridation, enough to prevent cavities while also avoiding mottling.[9]

In the mid-1940s the U.S. Public Health Service (USPHS) decided to test the idea in the field with a fifteen-year experimental fluoridation program in Grand Rapids, Michigan, under the direction of H. Trendley Dean, future director of the National Institute of Dental Health. Meanwhile, the state of New York initiated its own experiment at Newburgh, and shortly after World War II a number of other communities also began to fluoridate their water experimentally. The USPHS and Dean were inclined to take a go-slow approach to approving fluoridation for extensive use, as was the American Dental Association (ADA) and the Wisconsin state board of health, then monitoring experimental fluoridation in Sheboygan. But such prudence frustrated a number of activist dentists, especially in Wisconsin. They argued that people had been drinking naturally fluoridated water for centuries with no ill effects, and they lobbied city governments and civic groups to push for artificial fluoridation's widespread adoption. When preliminary results from Grand Rapids, Newburgh, and Sheboygan showed a dramatic plunge in cavity rates, pressure from the Wisconsin dentists moved the USPHS to endorse fluoridation in May 1950, followed closely by the ADA in November. The American Medical Association (AMA) and the Wisconsin Medical Society did likewise in 1951.[10]

The rapid approval of such powerhouse groups (far too rapid for antifluoridationists, who saw clear evidence of a conspiracy in the speed with which the AMA and its ilk caved in) inspired a flood of profluoridation arguments from public health advocates and dentists. By 1953 several hundred communities around the United States had fluoridated their water, and halcyon days of widespread oral health seemed to be on their way. But within months, public opposition began to mount, beginning in Stevens Point, Wisconsin, where a referendum defeated a fluoridation proposal decisively. By 1954 fluoridation proposals around the nation were becoming increasingly subject to referenda, where a considerable majority of them met a similar fate. At decade's end, antis were a force to be reckoned with, as sodium fluoride's proponents were now keenly aware. A growing body of research indicated that sodium fluoride posed no threat to human health at the one ppm level, and profluoridationists, most of them politically inexperienced and accustomed to deference from the public on health issues, had assumed that opposition would fade accordingly. But now they found themselves under an unfamiliar and withering assault from opponents who took issue with nearly everything they said, forced to defend fluoridation in city halls, public meetings, state legislatures, and even Congress. Hand-wringing over the antis became a regular feature in dental and public health journals, accompanied by no little amount of frustration, combative rhetoric, and spirited ad hominem attacks. So it would remain throughout the 1960s and into the 1970s (and beyond—battles over fluoridation rage on today, as a perusal of local newspapers or a visit to the Internet will attest).[11]

Who were these new postwar antis, and what was their problem with fluoridation? Less charitable opponents were usually content to lump them together as charlatans, quacks, megalomaniacs, or gullible followers. Sociologists, who found them especially fascinating, took a more dispassionate look beginning in the late 1950s, analyzing the relationships between antifluoridation sentiments and age, education and income levels, number of children, degree of social "alienation" and powerlessness, level of scientific literacy, and so on. Results varied, with early studies suggesting that antis were generally older, less affluent, less educated, and more alienated than profluoridationists, while later studies qualified or even refuted such correlations. Thus, describing a "typical" postwar anti is tricky.[12]

If we categorize postwar antis in terms of their objections to fluoridation, however, we can divide them roughly into two groups. The first included practitioners and supporters of "alternative medicine": nutritionists and other "food faddists" (as opponents termed them), Christian Scientists and other religious objectors, rogue dentists and doctors who rejected conventional medical practices in favor of nontraditional treatments, and so on. It also included members of a closely related (and often overlapping) group with more explicitly "environmental" interests: organic farmers, among the most active being Jerome I. Rodale and his Rodale Press, famous for its magazines *Prevention* and *Organic Gardening and Farming*. "Natural" was the organic watchword, and Rodale and his followers saw human health as inseparable from "natural" agriculture. What people needed to thrive, they said, was "pure" food and water, which were products of the judicious tilling, planting, and harvesting, untainted by chemicals or other technological manifestations of a cash-crop mentality. Thus the "organic creed" rejected artificial fertilizers, herbicides, pesticides, and industrial philosophies of mass food production in favor of compost, rock-dust fertilizers, biological/cultural pest control, and small-scale planting. Not surprisingly, organic farmers were among Rachel Carson's most ardent defenders in 1962, having been severely critical of DDT and similar pesticides well before that time. They were also among the earliest and staunchest antis. *Organic Farming and Gardening* and *Prevention* editorialized regularly against fluoridation as early as 1954, and the Rodale Press also published a short-lived magazine sometime in the early 1960s called *The Anti-Fluoridationist*. Rodale was even inspired to produce an antifluoridationist play entitled *Enemies of the People* (modeled on Henrik Ibsen's similarly named play), excerpts of which *Organic Farming and Gardening* published in early 1961.[13]

Taken together, the alternative-medicine and organic-farming components of the anti movement suggest a close connection to postwar environmental anxieties, and we will explore that connection later in the chapter. Meanwhile, the second rough category of postwar antis encompassed those who objected to fluoridation on ideological grounds. To them, the procedure was a violation of the individual's right to manage one's own dental health, since it subjected entire populations to sodium fluoride without their consent in order to treat a particular subgroup. In the process it placed too much power in the hands of the federal government, which pushed fluorida- tion on the public via the USPHS when neither the Constitution nor natu- ral law gave it the right to do so. With their antistatist bent, such criticisms were especially popular among antis who tilted to the right politically, some far enough that they traced the blame for fluoridation to Soviet or Com- munist Chinese subversion. The label "fluoridation opponent" has usually been synonymous with "paranoid right-winger," conjuring up images of wild-eyed John Birchers and McCarthyites pounding the table about Red infiltration. We might call this the Ripper Effect, after the cigar-chomping U.S. Air Force general in the 1964 film *Dr. Strangelove,* whose deadpan rants about the contamination of his "precious bodily fluids" by "Communist subversion" have done more than anything else to define the stereotype of the antifluoridationist as raving reactionary lunatic. Most ideologically ori- ented antis, however, found the U.S. government a sufficient target in itself. They worried far more about bureaucrats and authoritarians in Washing- ton, D.C., than those in Moscow or Beijing.[14]

Rarely did postwar antis fit neatly into one category. Individuals might lean clearly in one direction; some antis tended to be more concerned about the environmental ramifications of fluoridation than the ideological ones, and vice versa. Far more often, though, environmental and ideological cri- tiques came so bound together that it could be extremely difficult to disen- tangle them. Organic farmers and "food faddists" condemned federal abuses of power as readily as they did the environmental effects of sodium fluoride, while libertarian and conservative antis did the same thing in reverse. Put simply, when it came to fighting fluoridation, easy distinctions among envi- ronmentalism, conservatism, and libertarianism were anything but.[15]

Other characteristics of the antis further blurred the categories. One was the importance of women in the movement. From Ellen Swallow to Rachel Carson to Lois Gibbs, much American environmental activism has been the work of women, especially concerning industrial and urban pollution, bodily health, and threats to children. Women also played a vital role in the rise of postwar conservatism, with "kitchen-table activists," as Lisa McGirr has termed them, doing vital grassroots organizing for Barry Goldwater's 1964 presidential campaign and national leaders like Phyllis Schlafly taking the lead in battling second-wave feminism. As with male antis, many of these women had very conservative political leanings, and for them, fighting fluoridation and the corrupt government that pushed it was a legitimate activity within the feminine political sphere, a postwar conservative version of Progressive Era "municipal housekeeping." Meanwhile, a favorite publisher of both political conservatives and antis was Devin-Adair, whose catalog featured a quirky combination of anticommunist screeds and treatises on organic farming and the dangers of pesticides. Joseph McCarthy's *The Fight for America* and *America's Retreat from Victory,* for example, could be found alongside Leonard Wickenden's 1956 book *Our Daily Poison,* which decried "the Effects of DDT, Fluorides, Hormones, and Other Chemicals on Modern Man."[16]

People were ready for *Silent Spring* in 1962. Fears about nuclear fallout, thalidomide, aminotriazole, and "cranberry scares" combined with more long-standing concerns about lead and arsenic to make Carson's book seem especially relevant. If *Silent Spring*'s popularity was a keen expression of postwar environmental anxieties about unsafe substances and their effects on human and ecological health, then antifluoridation sentiments were no less so. Carson and the antis were both the inheritors of over a half-century's worth of worry about exposure to harmful substances. Industrial phosphorous and lead poisoning had been a chief concern of Progressive activist and Hull House resident Alice Hamilton, for example, and her reform campaign foreshadowed environmental justice and consumer-protection crusades of later years.

One of the first synthetic pesticides was a compound called "Paris green," made from an arsenic-containing pigment of the same name. It was in use as early as 1867, though by the turn of the century lead arsenate (and, later, calcium arsenate) had supplanted it. Given arsenic's fame as a poison, it is no surprise that arsenical pesticides produced considerable hand-wringing among those concerned about public health. The debate over lead arsenate, in fact, presaged the later controversy over organic phosphates and chlorinated hydrocarbons. As DDT did after it, lead arsenate seemed at first to be a miracle cure for insect problems. It was fast-acting, persistent, and effective, and agricultural scientists and farmers sang its praises and resisted most attempts to regulate it. Dissension came mainly from medical and chemical professionals amid arcane technical debates far from public scrutiny. Pesticide defenders could thus claim that most concerns about arsenic poisoning were emotional, irrational, and unscientific, and at any rate a steady rain and a thorough scrubbing would be sure to wash any residues off.[17]

But an expanding list of scientific concerns about both lead and arsenic in agricultural produce, growing medical recognition of the distinction between acute and chronic poisoning, and an emergent "consumer muck-raker" business in the 1920s brought lead arsenate under increasingly heavy fire. Mounting evidence prompted the Food and Drug Administration (FDA) to set tolerance levels in the 1930s and 1940s, in the face of fierce resistance from agribusiness. The threat was great enough that by the 1920s the public was "already becoming curious," writes historian James Whorton, "and would soon be positively inquisitorial" about arsenical pesticides. A number of popular books appeared in the 1930s with chemical poisoning as their focus. The first and perhaps most famous came in 1933 with Arthur Kallett and F. J. Schlink's *100,000,000 Guinea Pigs*, an exposé of contamination in consumer goods, which dedicated an entire chapter to the dangers of lead arsenate. Brimming with populist contempt for agribusiness and its allies in government, it took both to task for allowing the mass poisoning of American consumers in the name of profit. Three years later, FDA information officer Ruth deForest Lamb published *American Chamber of Horrors*, whose ninth chapter told a similar (and more thoroughly documented) story of excessive lead arsenate use, inadequate regulation, and terrible human health risks born of chronic exposure, even at low levels. The book also questioned the safety of one of lead arsenate's few rivals, fluoride-based pesticides, which Lamb warned could cause severely mottled teeth. *American Chamber of Horrors* became a bestseller, and there was even talk of a movie deal. "By the time Miss Lamb completed her catalogue," Whorton concludes, "none but the most hardened could even look at a piece of fruit without apprehension."[18]

But it was DDT that sealed lead arsenate's fate by replacing it. Its insecticidal properties were discovered by a Swiss chemist in the 1930s but developed in the mid-1940s by U.S. government scientists as a quick, easy, and seemingly safe method for controlling malaria and typhus, insect-borne diseases that had produced tremendous casualties among Allied troops. It worked like a charm, at least in the beginning. The new pesticide made its grand entrance in Italy, where it was used to great effect against the Naples typhus epidemic of 1943–1944. Agricultural interests soon clamored for access to the new miracle killer, and shortly after the war DDT flooded onto the civilian market at the rate of millions of pounds per month.[19]

It was a classic case of better life through chemistry—or so it seemed. Although preliminary government tests suggested DDT was safe for human exposure, long-term dangers became more and more apparent as research progressed. Even before its release for civilian use, scientific work by the FDA and the National Institutes of Health revealed the pesticide's tendency to accumulate in body fat and breast milk and its toxic effects on everything from nerve cells and muscles to the kidneys, the liver, and the brain (one researcher spoke of its "startling toxicity"). Meanwhile, entomologists and wildlife biologists added to the cautionary chorus with studies that showed DDT was toxic not only to pests but to bird and bees as well, killing them and other animals in droves and often in a hideously painful manner. As a result, the U.S. Army banned DDT for domestic use in April 1945. It was only because of the military's need for an effective method of insect control that DDT saw use overseas during the war, and even then only in hard-to-ingest powder, mist, and aerosol forms.[20]

Concern about DDT, however, was not limited to scientists or the military. Residents of Long Island, New York, for example, opposed DDT spraying in the late 1950s, and mainstream newspapers such as the *New York Times* had carried cautionary articles about the pesticide since 1945. Gardeners, sportsmen, and conservationists were also alarmed by government-sponsored aerial spraying campaigns in the 1950s against the fire ant and gypsy moth, which involved not only DDT but a host of other pesticides. Meanwhile, there were more general anxieties about spraying. Despite the best publicity efforts of its champions, DDT could not escape its roots. It was a product of war, as historian Edmund Russell has shown, and particularly of research into poison gases and nerve agents. For many Americans, after World War II the sight of a spray plane trailing mist was less a sign of progress than an ominous parallel with aerial warfare, and they had a difficult time separating DDT from chemical weapons like sarin gas, then being studied for its potential to incapacitate troops. But economics and technological optimism won out over both scientific and lay concerns, and DDT became the pesticide of choice in postwar American agriculture. Doubts about its safety faded into the background as it was quickly "civilianized" (in Russell's phrase) in the years after the war, to resurface with a vengeance in the next decade.[21]

The 1950s and early 1960s manifested an intense preoccupation with other contamination issues as well. The shadow of Alamogordo hung over those Cold War years, as the United States and the Soviet Union tested dozens of atomic weapons in preparation for a seemingly inevitable World War III. Despite their pride in and fascination with high-tech weapons, many Americans were uneasy about the potential for health and environmental damage from the resulting radiation. Complaints from western stockmen and ranchers about strange increases in mortality among their livestock, as well as their own nausea and skin and hair loss, received national media coverage. In March 1954 a Japanese fishing crew working in the Pacific suffered terrible illness and one death after being coated in fallout from a U.S. bomb test. Then, in the early 1960s, the Saint Louis "baby tooth survey" revealed that Strontium-90, a radioactive isotope produced by nuclear testing, could be found in the teeth and bones of the nation's children. Shocked by the ubiquity of such nuclear contaminants, which were potentially carcinogenic and mutagenic, the public's anxiety found expression in science fiction, movies such as *Them!* and *On the Beach*, the bomb shelter craze, and the pure-milk ideology of the Consumers Union. It also manifested itself in *Silent Spring*. It was no coincidence, as scholar Ralph Lutts has argued, that Carson's book opened with a parable of a town destroyed by a powdery white pesticide that closely resembled fallout, or that it included several references to Strontium-90. It was a mark of Carson's skill, Lutts concludes, that "she was able to recognize and take advantage of [this] deep-seated cluster of social concerns [about fallout] . . . and tap into this anxiety and direct it towards pesticides . . . , [using] the public's understanding about the hazards of fallout to teach of the similar hazards of chemical poisons."[22]

The horrific side effects of thalidomide added to the mix. Thalidomide was the active ingredient in Contergan, a West German–made sedative aimed at pregnant women with insomnia and morning sickness. In 1960, Merrell, an American pharmaceutical company, applied to the FDA for permission to market the drug in the United States. It was supposed to be harmless, but a rash of "phocomelia" birth defects—malformed limbs that resembled seal flippers—across West Germany and elsewhere revealed that thalidomide could be toxic to fetuses, and the manufacturer withdrew it from the European market. Meanwhile, in the United States an FDA employee named Frances Kelsey, concerned about phocomelia in Europe, used her bureaucratic authority to resist pressure from Merrell to rubber-stamp its application to sell thalidomide in America. As a result of her efforts, the nation was spared an epidemic of its own (only seventeen thalidomide babies were born in America), and President John F. Kennedy awarded her the Presidential Gold Medal in 1962. Still, the American public was spooked.[23]

Then came the "cranberry scare" of 1959, which involved the pesticide aminotriazole. Recent research had suggested that aminotriazole was a carcinogen, inducing thyroid tumors in rats. Unfortunately, the pesticide had already been in use on cranberry crops since 1956, where it was intended for application after harvest but in practice had often been applied before, thus contaminating berries with trace amounts. To complicate matters, even after testing indicated aminotriazole's carcinogenic potential, contaminated berries still made their way onto store shelves in 1959, despite industry promises to prevent just such an occurrence. In response, Arthur Fleming, secretary of Health, Education and Welfare, recommended that the cranberry crops of 1957–59 be pulled from the market until the cranberry industry delivered workable plans for detecting aminotriazole contamination. This had the side effect of depriving Americans of their traditional Thanksgiving cranberry dish. Predictably, the industry complained loudly, but the public seemed more shocked by the fact that a potential cancer-causing agent had been used so widely and incautiously.[24]

It was in the midst of these issues and on the crest of years of disquiet about chemical contaminants and bodily poisoning that the antifluoridation movement emerged. While the antis' critics dismissed them as ignorant and crazy, the historical context of antifluoridation sentiments makes them seem far less so. In a world full of "safe" poisons and contaminants, suspicion about fluoride could make sense.

Silent Spring's main argument was that the new chlorinated hydrocarbon and organic phosphate pesticides were not modern miracles but "elixirs of death" whose capacity for environmental damage was enormous. Radically different in molecular structure than naturally occurring substances, they were applied to fields, forests, cities, and homes with startling ubiquity, and worked their way along ecological connections to bring illness and death to fish, mammals, and birds. Nor were humans out of harm's way, Carson warned. The death of wildlife was a devastating spiritual and aesthetic loss for the human world, but in that loss we could also see the fate that might await us.[25]

The danger began with the new pesticides' cumulative properties. Acute, short-term contact was certainly a problem, Carson allowed, but long-term exposure to minute amounts could be just as devastating. This was because many new pesticides had an affinity for the body, embedding in fatty tissues in the testicles, ovaries, intestines, or breasts, or in the bones and teeth. They passed through the placenta and into embryonic flesh, and they contaminated breast milk. After years of low-level exposure, bioaccumulation could render a person a walking bank of pesticides. "This piling up of chemicals from many different sources," Carson wrote, "creates a total exposure that cannot be measured. It is meaningless, therefore, to talk about the 'safety' of any specific amount of residue."[26]

The health effects could be terrible, potentially "[destroying] the very enzymes whose function is to protect the body from harm . . . , [blocking] the oxidation process from which the body receives its energy . . . , [preventing] the normal functioning of various organs, and [initiating] in certain cells the slow and irreversible change that leads to malignancy." For instance, many of the new pesticides inhibited production of adenosine triphosphate, a key component of cellular oxidation and energy production. They could also affect a cell's genetic material in ways reminiscent of radioactive fallout, triggering cancer. The liver and kidneys were susceptible to damage, as was the nervous system, where certain residues could prevent the breakdown of the impulse-carrying enzyme acetylcholine, with potentially deadly results. Other symptoms included "sensations as of prickling, burning, or itching," aches, pains, extreme fatigue, tremors and convulsions, nightmares, cognition problems, "confusion, delusions, loss of memory, mania," paralysis, and death. Meanwhile, synergistic interactions between different pesticide residues could increase the toxicity of one or more. Similarly, human bodies damaged by pesticides were often more vulnerable to other normally benign chemicals. It was "a heavy price to pay," Carson concluded, "for the temporary destruction of a few insects."[27]

Who, according to Carson, was to blame? Chemical companies with vested financial interests shared responsibility, as did simple ignorance on the part of pesticide users themselves. A more fundamental contributor was a larger cultural attitude of domination toward the nonhuman world, "born of the Neanderthal age of biology and philosophy, when it was supposed that nature exists for the convenience of man." But some of Carson's most important targets were government officials, bureaucrats, technicians, and scientists involved in federal pest-management programs, especially in the U.S. Department of Agriculture. Carson was certainly no political conservative or antistatist; as a Kennedy Democrat she had a liberal's faith in both the government's ability and its duty to protect its citizens, and *Silent Spring* was neither a paean to individual rights nor a jeremiad against the perils of state power. Nevertheless, she was keenly aware of the dangers of powerful and self-interested bureaucracies, and excoriated federal officials and management agencies again and again throughout *Silent Spring* for their gross disregard of civil rights.[28]

Government eradication programs threatened not only the health of songbirds and children, Carson argued, but also the individual's right to make decisions about her own bodily health as well as the larger community's right to preserve the ecological integrity of the environment. Common citizens were never consulted when a federal or state pest-control agency decided it was in the "public interest" to destroy insect pests with one chemical or another, nor were they protected when government spray planes doused them. They were not asked if insect control was worth the price paid by their bodies and those of their children, their pets, and the wildlife around them. Entomologists and other "control men in state and federal governments" were disposed by both training and temperament to ignore safety concerns, and to "steadfastly deny the facts reported by the biologists and declare they see little evidence of harm to wildlife" or people. They exemplified a scientific culture that took for granted the right of experts to play God with nature and human health, and if the citizenry complained, the experts patted them on the head and fed them "little tranquilizing pills of half-truth" or dismissed them as "fanatics and cultists . . . who are so perverse as to demand that their food be free of insect poisons."[29]

Government pest-control programs thus tainted the democratic process just as certainly as they did the human body, and for Carson the erosion of civil rights was one of the most important casualties of the quest to dominate nature. "Who has made the decision," she asked rhetorically, "that sets in motion these chains of poisonings, this ever-widening wave of death that spreads out, like ripples when a pebble is dropped into a still pond. . . . ? Who has decided—who has the *right* to decide—for the countless legions of people who were not consulted that the supreme value is a world without insects, even though it be also a sterile world ungraced by the curving wing of a bird in flight?" Such judgments were "[those] of an authoritarian temporarily entrusted with power." Carson's concern for civil rights came early in *Silent Spring*. "The crusade to create a chemically sterile, insect-free world," she wrote, twelve pages into the first chapter, "seems to have engendered a fanatic zeal on the part of many specialists and most of the so-called control agencies. On every hand there is evidence that those engaged in spraying operations exercise a ruthless power. . . . The most flagrant abuses go unchecked in both state and federal agencies . . . , [which] have subjected enormous numbers of people to contact with these poisons, without their consent and often without their knowledge." If "the Bill of Rights contains no guarantee that a citizen shall be secure against lethal poisons distributed either by private individuals or by public officials," she concluded, "it is surely because our forefathers, despite their considerable wisdom and foresight, could conceive of no such problem."[30]

Perhaps surprisingly, Carson never called for a complete ban on the new postwar pesticides, but instead urged their careful regulation paired with a strong emphasis on biological and cultural methods of control. She also argued for democratizating of the decision-making process concerning mass pesticide applications. "We urgently need an end to . . . the sugar coating of unpalatable facts," she wrote, for "it is the public that is being asked to assume the risks that the insect controllers calculate . . . , and it can only do so [fairly] when in full possession of the facts." The very fact of their humanity justified the public's knowledge of the risks. The "'obligation to endure,'" she concluded, quoting French biologist and writer Jean Rostand, "'gives us the right to know.'"[31]

Antis often made direct references to Carson and Silent Spring in their literature, and a number of them saw the crusade against fluoridation "as part of a broader movement" against chemical contamination. As one correspondent told her, "those [of us] opposed to . . . fluoride . . . draw an analogy to the use of fluoride chemicals and DDT." Like DDT in Silent Spring, sodium fluoride was no miracle for the antis. It was very dangerous, and whatever powers it might have to prevent cavities (which were debatable, in their opinion), fluoridation involved spiking public drinking water with a highly toxic substance and threatening the health of everyone. In short, sodium fluoride was "poison," a description that dominated anti literature. As early as 1953, for example, anti Fanchon Battelle was attacking profluoridationists as "poison peddlers." Fluoridation "injects deadly poisonous fluorides" into water supplies, wrote another critic in 1961, in the fiercely anticommunist newspaper Common Sense. M. C. Goldman, writing in Organic Gardening and Farming in 1954, called fluoridation "poison on tap." There were hundreds of similar examples.[32]

Unlike DDT, however, which was never intended to be anything other than a poison, sodium fluoride was supposed to be good for people. Thus it seemed especially ominous to the antis that sodium fluoride could also be used as a pesticide, and had long been employed to that end. Fluoridation supporters acknowledged that sodium fluoride was a pesticide, but only at very high concentrations. The standard dosage in fluoridated water was only one part per million, they noted, and at that low level it protected children's teeth without unhealthy side effects. But the idea that a substance could be lethal at one concentration yet beneficial to health at another struck the antis as an insult to logic and common sense. Poison was still poison, they reasoned, no matter how diluted it was, and no amount of scientific or medical rationalization was going to change that. "In small amounts," argued Rev. Lyle F. Sheen in *The Cross and the Flag* in October 1961, sodium fluoride was "still a small amount of poison." Since it took only a relatively small amount to kill insect and rodent pests, logic suggested that humans were similarly susceptible to the low levels found in fluoridated water.[33]

Profluoridationists scoffed at such rebuttals. They pointed out that in many places groundwater used for drinking contained high levels of naturally occurring fluorides—levels far higher than those used for artificial fluoridation—yet no one had been adversely affected, save for the mottling of their teeth. But for antis, one of the things that made the sodium fluoride used in fluoridation so dangerous was that it was profoundly "unnatural," a description with strong environmental overtones. Like accusations of "poison," charges of sodium fluoride's unnaturalness were a standard indictment in anti literature. A flyer from the Daughters of the American Revolution reproduced a letter from a dentist who claimed that "natural fluoride in food can be taken without damage. . . . But artificial fluoride placed in water may be dangerous." Another flyer, published in about 1960 by the Citizens Committee Against Fluoridation of LaCrosse, Wisconsin, and reproduced by a number of other anti groups, summed up the argument in more detail: "Are not naturally-fluoridated and artificially fluoridated waters the same? Absolutely not! The fluorides found naturally are usually organic calcium fluorides which are in combination with other natural elements serving to inhibit and neutralize the toxic effects of fluorine, and which can be assimilated by the body; the artificially fluoridated water is obtained with sodium fluoride, which is an inorganic, cumulative poison 85 times more toxic than calcium fluoride, and cannot be assimilated by the body."[34]

What, then, were the precise health problems caused by this "unnatural poison"? For the more passionate antis, there were virtually no health problems that fluoridation *didn't* cause, and to list them all would be an exercise in exhaustion. But one of the most commonly cited dangers of fluoride was its alleged effects on bodily enzymes, a topic that also loomed large in Carson's attacks on pesticides. Fanchon Battelle claimed that sodium fluoride was a cholinesterase inhibitor—much like DDT—and cited the *British Medical Journal* to back her claim. In a mid-1960s flyer, Nebraska antifluoridationist and medical doctor Robert Olney warned of sodium fluoride's predilection for "disturbing the vital enzymes in tissues" (exactly which enzymes, he did not say) because of its chemical "affinity of [sic] magnesium," one of the "vital elements in this enzyme reaction."

Elsewhere he claimed that "mental processes are seriously interfered with and nerve reactions throughout the body [are] depressed" by sodium fluoride's enzyme-inhibiting properties. *Organic Gardening and Farming* author M. C. Goldman indicted sodium fluoride for everything from fluorosis to kidney damage to harmful effects on the salivary glands. "Strong-arming its way into the critically balanced calcium-fluoride levels in the blood," wrote David O. Woodbury in the John Birch Society's *American Opinion* in 1968, "fluorine soon begins to cause havoc in the bone structure by interfering with the enzyme phosphatase. Damage to the enzyme system, the essential army of the body's catalytic agents, is a companion misfortune to mottling. There are hundreds of enzymes, each one essential to some phase of the life process. Some enzymes seem to be immune from [sic] fluoride poisoning; many are not." A decade later, one Dr. H. C. Moolenburgh claimed in *The Covenant Message* that his own research on sodium fluoride revealed an "inhibition of 35.5 per cent" in "cholinesterase activity."[35]

Many antis were not so specific, usually content to state simply that the sodium fluoride "inhibits a significant number of important enzymes." The supporting evidence for such claims was weak: a context-free sentence or two from a scientific journal or comments from individual medical doctors of varying and often tangential specialties. But whatever the evidence of its effects on enzymes, few summaries of sodium fluoride's dangers failed to mention them.[36] Meanwhile, antis laid the blame for a myriad of other health problems at sodium fluoride's doorstep, many of which echoed those discussed in *Silent Spring.* Cancer was one. "Cancerous growth [is] speeded up by the ingestion of fluoridated water," read a screed from 1960. Another in the mid-1970s claimed that in the United States there was one cancer death "every twenty minutes" from drinking it. Damage to the liver, the kidneys, and the nervous system were other commonly cited effects, not to mention a blizzard of other symptoms, the list of which varied from critic to critic.

In 1953, Fanchon Battelle accused fluoridated water of causing everything from an increase in polio death rates to abnormal coagulation of the blood. The conservative law-and-order periodical *Police Gazette* warned in 1962 of "an increase of mongoloid (imbecile) babies and various kidney, liver, and heart diseases." One anti, Ray L. Elliott, provided a long list of dangers in a 1962 editorial in the *Arizona Republic*: "Fluoride, in whatever quantity taken, increases the fragility of bones, develops allergies, helps hardening of the arteries, mottled teeth, causes gastro-intestinal disturbances, affects metabolism and lowers birth rates, damages brain and nerve cells, damages liver and thyroid glands, is injurious to the kidneys, causes dermatitis, is hard on the heart, speeds up cancer, etc." *The Cross and the Flag* in June 1967 told of "stiffness of the back ('poker back'), sores in the mouth, excessive thirst, digestive and urinary disturbances, hives, failing eyesight, and loss of limb control." An Aryan Nations anti writing in 1977 claimed that fluoridated water caused "bloody stools, vomiting, respiratory troubles, diarrhea, abdominal cramps, arthritis, and high blood cholesterol." He went on to observe with Strangelovian intensity that it also "killed" the "erection center" in the human male's brain, by which "the Jews the real promotors [*sic*] of Fluoride and Fluoridation have succeeded in making men impotent, in castrating them with chemicals; secretly and legally." And according to Robert Olney, not only was fluoride the culprit in "many diseases and degenerative and defective conditions for which doctors say the 'cause is unknown,'" it even harmed the teeth in a manner far beyond mere mottling, changing "the chemical structure of the living enamel of the tooth, making it a *dead* chalky substance" and causing "calcific plugs in the dentins [and] greatly disturbing the [tooth's] nutrition and circulation." The only thing missing from such lists, it seemed, was the common cold.[37]

Sodium fluoride's power to ruin human health was made all the worse by the fact that it was "cumulative," as antis often termed it. Like DDT, fluoride residues bioaccumulate, with trace amounts taking up residence in calcium-bearing tissues. This fact was not lost on antis, and their concerns connected closely with those in *Silent Spring* and reflected widespread postwar cultural unease about chemical contamination. "Fluorine is an insidious poison," cautioned a 1957 flyer from the National Defense Committee of the Daughters of the American Revolution, "which, when ingested even in small quantities, could accumulate in our body [*sic*] over the period of years," much as other "poisonous substances, including the deadly radioactive strontium 90, are stored and accumulated in the bones." Sodium fluoride is "a powerful, cumulative poison," warned another flyer from the early 1960s, which "accumulates in the bones and tissues, causing serious physical changes." Yet another pamphlet from the same era informed its readers that sodium fluoride "settles in the bones, teeth, and other tissues in the same way arsenic, lead, and other poisons do. The storage of fluoride in the body concentrates it, so that the body may be storing several thousand times that originally present in the fluoridated water that one drinks." "Did you know," asked the *Christian Vanguard* in 1972, "that Sodium Fluoride is accumulative? That is, it accumulates in the body . . . , [which] cannot get rid of it."[38]

In the issue of bioaccumulation, the links between antis and larger environmental concerns revealed themselves with little ambiguity. A particularly good example came when *Police Gazette* author George McGrath bemoaned sodium fluoride's cumulative properties in language reminiscent of *Silent Spring*. "For with the introduction of fluorides into our water supply," he lamented in 1962, the same year that Carson's book appeared,

> yet another poison has been added to the half dozen our bodies are trying to cope with. We are already fighting strontium 90 (from radioactive fallout), detergents, industrial waste and the numerous insecticides with which the food we eat has been sprayed. And at this moment fluorides may be completing the wrecking of your health that the other poisons have begun. . . . Already our bodies have begun to resemble banks for poisons. Almost everything we live on has been contaminated with some sort of chemical additive. The very air we breathe is fouled by a nightmarish variety of poisons—from industrial smog and diesel fumes to radioactive fallout. Don't let them add yet another item to the list.

There could hardly have been a better summation of the era's chemical anxieties.[39]

Closely related to worries about sodium fluoride's bioaccumulative tendencies were concerns about uncontrolled dosage levels. In *Silent Spring*, Carson criticized the casual, even careless overuse of pesticides in the mistaken belief that, used as directed, they were safe. Antis sounded similar themes, as fear of indiscriminate fluoridation and unavoidable exposure to excessive amounts were among their most common criticisms of the procedure. The problem was multifaceted. First, said the antis, fluoride's toxicity problems aside, public water systems were a rather blunt instrument for delivering a mere one ppm of the substance. Why not use more efficient means, like topical applications, toothpaste, or tablets? Most of the fluoridated water in a given public system would end up going down the drain, if nothing else a vast waste of taxpayers' money—"like using a 15-ton Mack

Truck," in the words of a Kansas City anti group, "to deliver a single aspirin tablet."[40]

More troublesome was the fact that if one part per million was the recommended "safe" amount of sodium fluoride for drinking water, how could anyone be sure that no one was getting too much? After all, individuals varied greatly in the amount of water they drank each day, depending on their personal habits, job environment, age, the local climate, and so on. Profluoridationists might refer to samplings and population studies and tolerance levels, but the antis replied that in the real world there was no such thing as an "average" fluoride consumer. It was people who mattered, not abstract "populations." "A physically active person in a hot dry climate may drink two gallons of water a day," wrote conservative commentator Dan Smoot in *The Dan Smoot Report*. "Other persons drink very little. Thus, even if a public water system is fluoridated *as recommended*, some people may consume eight times too much fluoride; others will consume practically none. Can a water system be fluoridated *as recommended*?" To ignore that question was to rationalize the poisoning of those unlucky enough to be susceptible, an echo of Carson's doubts about "safe" tolerance levels for pesticides.[41]

The problem was further complicated by other sources of fluoride other than drinking water, and there was no telling how much sodium fluoride a person might actually absorb in a lifetime. "Add to this sad situation," wrote science writer David Woodbury in 1971, "the fact that there are half a dozen other sources of fluoride competing for [a child's] teeth; many communities, as where auto traffic is heavy, have to breathe fluorine-polluted air, as do those which are near cement plants and other industrial establishments (aluminum, brick, etc.). Add still further the fluorides in food such as fish and tea, also in every drink that is mixed in the kitchen from the fluoridated faucet, plus most of the vegetables grown in the fluoridated garden. The fact is that a practice which is ballyhooed as a 'vital' step forward in nutrition is actually presenting itself to American communities without benefit of control; the famous 'parts per million' mean nothing."[42]

Having what they considered an abundance of evidence for the dangers of fluoridation, antis fumed at the curt dismissals they usually received from profluoridationists. They pushed back against accusations of irrationality and emotionalism, not unlike Carson and her scathing comments about "little tranquilizing pills of half-truth." Their resentment at being labeled kooks was palpable. "Who are [fluoridation's] opponents?" asked the Ohio Pure Water Association in 1959. Profluoridationists called them lunatics, shysters, and rubes, but the truth was different. "They are your neighbors," said the association, everyday people "concerned about children's teeth and the health and welfare of their nation. They think for themselves [and] do not accept the word of a federal agency." "Who opposes fluoridation?" echoed the Pure Water Association of America. Not kooks, it replied, but "responsible citizens . . . concerned about health and well being." For the antis, opposing fluoridation was not crazy or ignorant; it was a matter of life and death.[43]

Given its many dangers, the antis asked, who was responsible for forcing sodium fluoride on innocent American citizens, and why? Fantasies of fluoridation as a Soviet plan to tranquilize the American populace in advance of an invasion preoccupied certain antis during the intense Cold War days of the early to mid-1950s. Sodium fluoride had been used, they claimed, as a mind-control and pacification drug for prisoners by either the Soviets or the Nazis (or both) in the 1930s, and the Russians now had plans to use it to soften America's will to fight World War III. But such overt paranoia was never more than a subset of fluoridation fears, as Gretchen Ann Reilly has observed, and it had faded into the background by the time the 1950s ended. Thus when *Dr. Strangelove* appeared in 1964, General Jack Ripper was both a stereotype and an anachronism. In reality, most antis pointed the finger squarely at domestic foes, and in the process of laying blame, they revealed the extent to which antifluoridation sentiments blurred postwar ideological lines by melding environmental concerns with critiques of both corporate power and the power of the State.[44]

One common explanation for fluoridation focused on Big Aluminum. It ran roughly like this: stuck with thousands of tons of sodium fluoride as a by-product of the manufacturing process, aluminum companies like Alcoa concocted a story that the stuff could be added to drinking water to prevent cavities, thus creating market demand for it and driving up prices to absurd levels. They were aided in this scheme by a sympathetic medical establishment and "objective" scientific experts whose testimony about fluoridation's safety had been bought and paid for from the beginning. Meanwhile, corporate flunkies in government secured the political authority to approve fluoridation plans and the bureaucratic muscle to promote them, and the end result was a healthy profit for aluminum corporations at the expense of the public's health.

With its populist mistrust of concentrated capital, such an explanation echoed classic American fears of the rich and powerful, the bankers and railroad tycoons, the Morgans, Rockefellers, and Rothchilds who allegedly pulled the levers of the global financial and political machine (there was a healthy dose of paranoia in such anticorporate tales, but it is worth noting that they were not entirely without foundation; as coauthors Gerald Markowitz and David Rosner showed in *Deceit and Denial,* the lead and vinyl industries were both well aware of the health and environmental hazards of their products and deliberately suppressed evidence of the same, and lied repeatedly to the public for years about their safety). Such an explanation was also, with its emphasis on corporate influence on and alliance with government, reminiscent of contemporary New Left rhetoric, with the idea of scientists, corporate executives, and government bureaucrats as partners in crime sounding a bit like the Establishment. Fluoridation was a product of a culture and a world where the "right to make a dollar" by any means necessary, as Carson had written, went unquestioned.[45]

But many antis either relegated Big Aluminum to a secondary role or dispensed with it altogether in favor of blaming the federal government directly. It was not the Soviets or Red Chinese poisoning America's drinking water, they said, but Washington, D.C.'s own U.S. Public Health Service and a bureaucratic host of arrogant scientists and intrusive, know-it-all social planners. Criticism of fluoridation thus did two things for conservative antis: it expressed their fears of environmental pollution, which they shared with other antis, and it gave them a powerful rhetorical club with which to beat their "collectivist," big-government-loving enemies. Their concern about sodium fluoride, sincere in its own right, also carried water for their specific political critique.

For many antis, control of one's health, like control of private property, was a sacred individual right rooted in natural law and enshrined in the Constitution. What made fluoridation so hateful was not just that it poisoned drinking water but that it was government-mandated poisoning. Fluoridation supporters might claim that the procedure was a cheap and easy way to prevent cavities on a large scale, but for antis this was just a cover story for an attempt to socialize dental care. The individual's right to make his or her own choices about health care, to have a say about the chemicals and the procedures to which the government exposed them, thus fell victim to the USPHS's tyrannical drive toward state-controlled mass medication. Furthermore, fluoridation was only the USPHS's initial wedge in a much larger campaign to assume complete control of Americans' medical decisions.

This alone was enough to make fluoridation suspect, but the fact that the procedure was also highly dangerous made things that much worse. For more politically conservative antis, there was an unspoken assumption that the toxic character of sodium fluoride fit hand-in-glove with the political toxicity of socialized medicine. A poisoned ideology led to literally poisoned people; the second proceeded automatically from the first, and although they never said so in so many words, for conservative antis, mass poisoning was the logical and inevitable endpoint of liberal do-gooderism, welfare-state bureaucracy, and centralized social engineering. As with its pest control programs, the government never consulted the people on the receiving end of its crackpot fluoridation schemes to "protect" the public, and the people paid for it with their health and their rights. A 1976 headline from the Liberty Lobby's newspaper *The Spotlight* summed up these antis' feelings: "Uncle Sam Shoves It Down Your Throat Despite Experts And Evidence."[46]

Fear of authoritarian attack on individual rights saturated antifluoridation literature in general, especially that of more politically conservative antis, although it was by no means limited to them. To the Daughters of the American Revolution, in the late 1950s fluoridation was "an expression of socialized medicine . . . [and] a violation of our constitutional rights as citizens" by the USPHS, whose chief objective was "the application of government supervision to the details of our daily lives" and which had "camouflaged its activities" to that end. "We believe," declared Kansas City, Missouri's "Freedom Center" around the same time, that "every citizen" had the right to manage his or her own health, "instead of being subjected to mass medication regulated by some well-meaning bureaucratic official." For Vera Adams and the National Committee Against Fluoridation in 1962, the USPHS was an "octopus" whose big-government "tentacles . . . are reaching out into every activity in this country." The membership application form for the Pure Water Association of America's California Committee read, above the signature line, "I am opposed to mass medication by means of adding fluorides or any chemical compound to the public water supply for any intended preventative or curative medicinal effect it may have on my body. I wish to join in the united effort to recover our liberties and constitutional guarantees which I believe are violated by those who promote the addition of such poisonous chemical compounds to our water supplies."

In the early 1970s, anti Philip Zanfagna (who was among Carson's correspondents eight years earlier) defended the "right of every individual to determine what substance he or members of his family may take which will alter the physical or mental functions of the body. Fluoridation is synonymous with dictatorship. It gives government bureaucrats another excuse for taking over the responsibility of caring for our children."[47]

But even if it were perfectly safe, for many antis, fluoridation would still have been objectionable because it involved gross violations of individual rights. Dr. F. B. Exner told the readers of the John Birch Society's *American Opinion* in May 1962 that even though sodium fluoride's health risks were obvious to him, the "real issue" was one of mass medication and the defense of individual liberties. An unnamed anti group of the same era agreed, declaring that even if sodium fluoride delivered every benefit its supporters claimed for it with no adverse health affects, "a valid reason would still remain" for opposing it: "Any suggestion that [the] great principle of human liberty be violated by the totalitarian credo of individual subservience to the state is a frightening proposal."[48]

And why should the USPHS stop with fluoridation? Many antis saw the procedure as the leading edge of a more general governmental assault on individual "medical" rights. "If fluoride goes into water," warned Clive McKay in 1958, "the next demand may be for copper to prevent anemia, cobalt to prevent anemia and selenium to prevent liver necrosis. . . . Will the next step be to apply birth control methods to all because our population is getting too large, or to wipe smoking off the American continent in order to prevent individuals from getting lung cancer or to wipe out all consumption of alcoholic beverages because drunken drivers cause accident?" That same year *American Opinion* asked, "Shall we turn to Big Brother to cut down dental bills . . . ? If so, why not a daily glass of compulsory carrot juice to cope with the problem of defective eyesight? Why not get to the root of the matter and pass a law, making it illegal to sell candy to children and decreeing punishment for parents who permit excessive carbohydrates in their offspring's diet?" Ethel Dinning, head of the Northwest Safe Water Association, addressed the issue in 1974 with a sense of humor rare among antis. The fictional "A Plea from Inundation" told the story of a town of the same name that, having approved fluoridation, soon found itself assaulted by public health officials clamoring to add other chemicals. After sodium fluoride came "concentrated carrot juice" to improve eyesight, "bran concentrate to prevent gray hair," then lemon peels, sulfur, molasses, and finally castor oil "to make 'regular' socialists out of everybody in the city." The end result was water that "feels like eucalyptus leaves, looks like bilge, and smells like improperly tanned leather," a sharp rise in beer consumption, and the physical disintegration of the water system itself.[49]

Sixty years after fluoridation began, it remains a controversial topic, and its opponents still bear a close resemblance to their Cold War–era predecessors. DDT, endrin, dieldrin, aldrin, mirex, and the like may all have been banned for use in the United States, but health and environmental anxieties, particularly about pesticides and other toxic chemicals, remains strong. The Soviet Union may have fallen two decades ago, but fears about authoritarian "collectivist" government persist and, with the election of George W. Bush and the Tea Party movement, they show no signs of abating. Fear of fluoridation continues to link these two brands of anxiety together.

Resistance to fluoridation must be understood as an expression of anxieties about pollution, contamination, and bodily health, and particularly as a product of postwar environmentalism. Stereotypes portray fluoride fears as fringe sentiments, but placed alongside concerns about lead arsenate, fallout, thalidomide, aminotriazole, DDT, and within the context of the rising environmental movement of the 1950s, 1960s, and 1970s, they appear remarkably mainstream. The postwar antifluoridation movement also provides an example of the complex ways in which antistatist ideology and environmentalist sentiments intertwined with and reinforced one another. Although environmental issues were central to postwar American liberalism, resistance to fluoride reveals environmentalism's attractions for political conservatives and other ideological enemies of the State. They might not have been self-described "environmentalists," but in their anxieties about and criticisms of sodium fluoride, right-leaning antis were, like antis in general, not far removed from the growing green movement, and resistance to fluoridation thus offered an easy pathway into environmentalism because of the procedure's relationship to central government.

A close look at the anti movement suggests the limits of linking issues of bodily health and pollution exclusively to postwar liberalism and the left. Many environmental historians have argued that environmental histories too often focus on wilderness preservation and resource management, issues of only tangential importance for most Americans. They suggest that our narratives should instead place more emphasis on environmental justice, on race, class, and gender issues, particularly the exploration of problems affecting the nonwhite, the nonmale, and the nonelite: urban pollution, industrial safety, consumer safety, and health concerns in the places where we live and work. The protagonists in such new narratives are usually typical proponents of social justice: progressives, labor activists, feminists, African American and Latino/a activists, and so forth, and the unspoken assumption in "social justice" environmental history is that opposition to pollution and concerns about human health are the domain of nonwhites, progressives, and liberals. Opposition to fluoridation, however, complicates this assumption by suggesting that bodily health concerns and anxiety over pollution in the home and workplace could also be found among their staunchest enemies.[50]

One of the earliest antis was an enigmatic man named Emmanuel H. Bronner. If his resumé could be believed, Bronner's credentials were impressive; born in Germany in 1908, he claimed to be a research chemist, an escapee from a Soviet prison camp, a Holocaust survivor, an "Essene rabbi," and Albert Einstein's nephew. His critics countered that he was actually a veteran of a mental hospital and a man of continuing psychological instability. This was at least partly true, for Bronner had spent time in, and escaped from, an Illinois institution in 1946. Regardless of his mental health, Bronner also appeared to be a man of very conservative political leanings. In a 1952 letter to the *Catholic Mirror*, for example, he upbraided fluoridation supporters as "Godless 'intellectual' 'liberal' parasites," "internal enemies," and "traitors." But by the end of the 1950s, Bronner had seemingly disappeared.[51]

He might not have been heard from again had subsequent developments not intervened. Bronner was good at making soap, which had been his family's business in Germany before he immigrated to the United States in 1929. Dubbing himself "Doctor Bronner," in the 1950s he began marketing "Magic Soaps" made from natural oils and vegetable fats and free of artificial fragrances, colorings, or cleaning agents. The labels were often more interesting than the soaps themselves, as Bronner embellished them with philosophical observations on cleanliness and health, environmental protection, religion, and the unity of mankind. Some he sprinkled with conservative and antifluoridation sentiments: "Replace half-true Socialist-fluoride poison & tax slavery with full-truth, work speech-press, & profitsharing Socialaction! All-One! So, help build 4 billion Hannibal wind-power plants, charging 96 billion battery-banks, powering every car-factory-farm-home-monorail & pump, watering Babylon-roof-gardens & 800 billion Israel-Milorganite fruit trees." Sales were slow until the Earth Day–era counterculture took a shine to Bronner's mysticism and embraced him as an ecological seer. He went on to be a dedicated environmentalist and contributor to social justice and green causes, and today, more than a decade after his death, his soaps remain popular with neohippies, backpackers, and other devotees of a more natural lifestyle. It is unlikely, however, that many are aware of Bronner's links to postwar conservative antistatism or of the way his environmentalist sympathies intersected with his ideological leanings in his opposition to fluoridation. But as Bronner's example suggests, environmentalism's influence in postwar America can be found in some of the unlikeliest places.

Given their antistatist leanings, antis would never have much faith in the federal government's ability to protect environmental or human health, even during an era when large numbers of Americans insisted that it could and should do precisely that. One of the unlikeliest of these was Barry Goldwater. By the time of the first Earth Day, April 22, 1970, the senator from Arizona had begun to change his antistatist tune. He would never be a liberal, of course, but the nation's ecological problems were serious enough by the end of the 1960s that he had begun reevaluating his opinions about government regulation, at least when it came to the environment. Antis dismissed government as a source of environmental harm, but Goldwater began to see government as a shield against it. The sentiment would not last, but the senator's willingness to reconsider the most important tenant of postwar conservatism testifies to the power of the emerging environmental movement and the question of the State's role therein.

— 3 —

THE ENVIRONMENTAL CONSCIENCE OF A CONSERVATIVE

The Natural World of Barry Goldwater, Part II

> It is my belief that when pollution is found, it should be halted
> at the source, even if this requires stringent government action
> against important segments of our national economy.
> > —*Barry Goldwater, Conscience of a Majority, 1970*

> Regulations . . . have added hundreds of billions of dollars to the
> cost of our mineral products, highway construction, food, auto-
> mobiles, and housing. It almost seems as though the government
> regulators were determined we should all freeze to death in
> the dark.
> > —*Barry Goldwater, With No Apologies, 1979*

IN AUTUMN 1970, BACK IN WASHINGTON, D.C., AFTER RECLAIMING HIS SEN-
ate seat two years earlier, Barry Goldwater published the sequel to his ideological manifesto *The Conscience of a Conservative. The Conscience of a Majority*
had a breezier tone and a more contemporary focus than its ghostwritten
predecessor, but its targets were much the same: the media, labor unions, and
the perils of liberalism. But its penultimate chapter, which bore the attention-
getting title "Saving the Earth," was unlike anything in Goldwater's previous
oeuvre. There was "no doubt," he declared on its first page, that "we are in
trouble on the Earth in our continuing efforts to survive." The reason, he
concluded, was massive ecological decline. "It is difficult to visualize what will

be left of the Earth if our present rates of population and pollution expansion are maintained," he warned. The problem was so acute that "it is possible to credit the most exaggerated claims of the most hysterical alarmists." In light of the threat, "our job . . . is to prevent that lush orb known as Earth . . . from turning into a bleak and barren, dirty brown planet."[1]

Goldwater was just getting started. He cited Stanford biologist Paul Ehrlich on the threat of overpopulation and warned about increasing pollution with a passion equal to any doom-and-gloom environmental activist: "It is scarcely possible to claim that man's ability to destroy his environment has any serious limitations. There is no longer any reason to question whether the threat is real." He could see it in his own backyard; the man who had championed the Colorado River Storage Project (CRSP) in the mid-1950s now watched as Glen Canyon Dam destroyed the riparian ecology of the Grand Canyon downstream by preventing silt from replenishing its beaches. Meanwhile, ever-increasing numbers of tourists and river-runners overloaded the canyon with sewage and litter. Back in 1940 the Grand had abundant beaches, clean water, and no trash, but now "man [has] left his imprint," and it was not pretty. Goldwater even felt a creeping doubt about economic growth and progress. "In light of today's pollution," he mused, "one wonders at our former measuring rod of progress. . . . Is this the result people have worked and strived to achieve?"[2]

What was the Arizona senator's solution to pollution, overpopulation, limited resources, and ecological decline? He began by stressing personal responsibility. If Americans wanted a clean and healthy environment, they would have to choose what kind of lifestyle they wanted and what they were willing to give up. Hand-wringing and bumper-sticker slogans would not be enough. Nor should they "shrug off . . . personal responsibility on giant scapegoats" like industry. Applied science and high technology offered a solution, for they could clean up the environment while allowing Americans to maintain the consumer-based lifestyle to which they had grown accustomed. In that vein, the last few pages of "Saving the Earth" turned abruptly to the joys and benefits of space travel, the roundabout argument being that any society that could put a man on the moon could surely clean up its environmental messes. But the most surprising passage in "Saving the Earth" was about the role of government. "I happen to be one," wrote Goldwater,

> who has spent much of his public life defending the business community,
> the free enterprise system, and local governments from harassment and

encroachment from an outsized Federal bureaucracy. Thus it is that my attitude on the question of pollution seems to have caused more than customary interest. I am very frank about how I feel. I have discussed it with newspaper reporters, in speeches, and on nationally televised talk shows. I feel very definitely that the [Nixon] administration is absolutely correct in cracking down on companies and corporations and municipalities that continue to pollute the nation's air and water. While I am a great believer in the free competitive enterprise system and all that it entails, I am an even stronger believer in the right of our people to live in a clean and pollution-free environment. To this end, it is my belief that when pollution is found, it should be halted at the source, even if this requires stringent government action against important segments of our national economy.

It was a sure sign of changing times. Archconservative Barry Goldwater, perennial foe of Big Government, had not only become an environmentalist but also a defender of national environmental regulation.[3]

The senator's new federal-friendly environmentalism was not lost on political observers. The *Dallas Morning News* in January 1970 editorialized that "if [even] Barry Goldwater [now] favors tough government action against corporate and municipal offenders, those guilty of pollution can figure out how they stand with those who have always been hostile to business and local government." Former speechwriter Karl Hess was more critical, bashing his former employer for worshipping "corporatism" in *The Conscience of a Majority*'s first chapters only to attack it for its "radical zeal" in "Saving the Earth." Whatever their feelings about the book, readers on both the Right and the Left were asking a similar question: What had happened to Barry Goldwater? And would it last?[4]

Change was a constant in the 1960s, and the years between Goldwater's presidential defeat in November 1964 and his return to political office in January 1969 featured some of the most intense developments in modern American history. The New Left, the counterculture, the increasingly militant civil rights and Black Power movements, the antiwar movement, and the emerging feminist and gay-rights crusades all peaked together near the decade's end. In the meantime, Goldwater's fellow conservatives continued their own coalescence and growth, much of it in reaction to the era's left-leaning social and political turmoil. Republican presidential candidate Richard Nixon owed a large part of his own victory in the 1968 election to his appeal among voters who saw contemporary events as the rotten fruit of New Deal liberalism, and conservatives' organizing efforts would pay off handsomely as the liberal consensus began to fray with increasing speed during the 1970s.[5]

The rise of postwar American environmentalism, while less dramatic than its contemporaries, was no less important. Environmental concerns clearly predated the late 1960s, but a hallmark of the new movement was an increase in both concerns and adherents. Wilderness and recreation issues remained popular, but now mounting anxieties about air and water pollution, pesticides, overpopulation, urban sprawl, resource availability, and general quality of life joined them. The growing American middle class responded by demanding environmental "amenities." Meanwhile, personal experiences with the ecological consequences of urban contamination and suburban growth and broader qualms about nuclear fallout and pesticides added to the worry. The result was that by the close of the 1960s, environmentalism had become a major concern of citizens across the country, transcending political and cultural boundaries in a way that Black Power, the New Left, or counterculture sentiments did not. The number of participants in the first Earth Day underscored just how powerful and broad-based the new movement was. Millions of Americans—and many of their political leaders—gathered for rallies, teach-ins, litter cleanups, and a thousand other environmental events. In an era where a person could take his pick of fervent political causes, it seems clear that a significant shift in attitude had taken place.[6]

Although he may have been more ideologically extreme than most middle-class Americans in 1970, Barry Goldwater had a lot in common with them when it came to the environment. He too felt the influence of the nation's environmental awakening, and shared its concerns about pollution and air quality and mounting piles of garbage. As a suburbanite, he wanted environmental beauty, health, and permanence, just as so many others did. If "Saving the Earth" was any indication, Goldwater was willing, like them, to invoke the power of central government to make those things a reality. Over the next decade and a half, however, Goldwater's commitment to federally centered environmentalism would often founder on the rocks of his conservatism. Despite the warnings and sentiments in "Saving the Earth," Goldwater sometimes found himself at severe odds with the nation's environmental community. Within a decade of declaring the environment one of the most important issues in politics, he would be railing against some of the very environmental policies and organizations that he had once seen as indispensable. He would never entirely abandon the environmental movement or the concept of federal environmental regulation, but his ideological commitments would make their relationship a turbulent one.

For many Americans, concern for the environment grew out of personal experience, inspired by some disturbing thing they had seen, heard, smelled, or tasted in their water, air, local woodlot, pond, or stream. Adam Rome has argued that the loss of green space, erosion, and contaminated air and water that accompanied the postwar explosion of suburbia—malodorous foam in the tap water, septic-tank backups in the bathrooms, and bulldozed woodlots in the backyard—accentuated the middle-class desire for environmental amenities and were key inspirations for the environmentalism of the 1960s and 1970s. In late December 1969, in the skies over Phoenix, Barry Goldwater had one of his own ecological revelations. "On the day before Christmas I flew an Air Force T-29 into Arizona," he wrote to his friend Charles Orme,

> and never in all of my life in that State and with forty years of flying have
> I seen such a concentration of what I don't like to call smog but smust
> because we have no fog. You won't believe this, but at forty thousand feet
> I could see the white smoke coming out of the smelter in town and then I
> could see every smelter north plus the one in Mexico. In forty years of fly-
> ing in Arizona I had until that time made two instrument approaches into
> the valley but, believe it or not, I had to be vectored to radar to Luke Air
> Force Base and I didn't see it until I was on the downwind leg.

It was not the first time he had noticed a decline in the quality of the Arizona air. "I have long been exercised about this situation," he told Orme, and suggested that he had for some time been willing to "force" the state's smelters to clean up their emissions. Now his willingness had been reinvigorated. "I could go on and on about this, Charlie, because, as you can well imagine," Goldwater concluded, "the destruction of our clean air has me really concerned." Two years later, he confessed to Orme that, along with air pollution, he was also "terribly worried ... because as I fly around it [Arizona] and over it after prolonged absences, I see more and more gouging and cutting" from Phoenix and Tucson's inexorable suburban spread. Progress was becoming a problem, and "there should be some way to control it."[7]

Goldwater had another environmental epiphany in his beloved Grand

Canyon. In 1965 he floated the Colorado River through the canyon and found it a very different place than it had been in 1940. Glen Canyon Dam had eliminated both the seasonal floods and most of the silt in the river below it (as well as plunging the average water temperature below 50 degrees Fahrenheit), and the Grand Canyon's beaches had begun to erode away. Massive increases in the number of recreational trips through the canyon— thousands of people now ran that stretch of river in a single year—brought the consequences of overuse. By the early 1970s, both environmentalists and national park administrators were calling for strict limits on passenger numbers, and Goldwater found himself agreeing with them, a stark change for a man who had recently been fantasizing about eager crowds viewing the canyon from the surface of the Central Arizona Project's Bridge Canyon reservoir.

In a letter to Phoenix banker Gary Driggs in October 1972, Goldwater wrote: "Close to fourteen thousand people have gone through the River this year and it just can't stand it, Gary, and that's all there is to it. You have to remember the sanitation problem which is presently being taken care of, but you must remember that the beaches are not being replenished because there are no more floods. The danger of pollution of the River is grow-ing daily; insects are infesting the River banks, and because of these and other reasons, I think we have to reach a limit." Goldwater admitted that he was "probably spoiled by the fact that I was the seventieth person to ever go through," the canyon. "I can remember its beauty well," he wrote, "and when I compare what I saw then with what I see today it sickens me."[8]

There were other indications of Goldwater's increasing concerns in his voluminous correspondence with anxious citizens concerned about envi-ronmental issues. Much of it was in the form of semistandardized responses, some by staff writing under his name, but their sentiments were indicative of how Goldwater's attitudes were changing. In March 1970, for example, he agreed with a correspondent from Tucson: "It appears that some of the population explosion is finally catching up with Arizona," threatening the quality of life in the state. The next month, Goldwater assured another con-stituent that he had "long been an advocate of steps to conquer population growth before it conquers us" and that he was cosponsoring a bill to urge President Nixon to call a White House conference on the subject. He wrote another citizen that Arizona's air-pollution problems were "a matter of deep concern to me because one of our greatest natural resources has been the purity and clarity of our air." There were hundreds of similar letters.[9]

For Barry Goldwater, the reality of the nation's environmental problems had begun to hit home. Pollution and ecological degradation were no longer an abstraction, a problem for other people in other places; like so many other Americans, he was becoming more thoughtful about the environmental consequences of the national lifestyle. Unlike most of them, however, Goldwater was also in a position to translate his concerns into direct political action. He certainly recognized that "ecology" had become a permanent presence in political life—it was "very apparent," he told Charles Orme, "that what goes under the heading of environmental is going to become one of the great political issues in the coming year and I feel that we have . . . to keep pushing"—but for him it was a personal as well as a political issue. The "whole question of what's happening to our environment," Goldwater wrote a concerned Idaho fisherman in December 1969, "is one that gives the most concern of any issue before the Congress"—a significant endorsement from a Cold Warrior in the years before détente. Beginning in 1969, Goldwater would act on his concerns in a number of ways.[10]

Whatever his personal flaws, Richard Nixon was the most important "environmental president" since Teddy Roosevelt. Ironically, he was no environmentalist himself, privately dismissing the movement as a gaggle of leftist radicals and antimodernist kooks engaged in scare-mongering. Nature itself seemed scarcely to enter his mind at all, and the famous photograph of Nixon on the beach in dress clothes spoke volumes about his deeper feelings, or lack thereof, toward the natural world. Nevertheless, it was Nixon who first included environmental issues in a State of the Union address in January 1970, followed by an "environmental message" to Congress that presented an ambitious and unprecedented federal plan to fight water and air pollution and solid waste and to create park and recreation lands. That same month, Nixon signed the National Environmental Policy Act—landmark legislation that mandated environmental impact statements for all federal activities that had the potential to cause ecological damage. In December 1970 his administration created the Environmental Protection Agency (EPA). The president also placed his signature on the Clean Air Act (CAA), which set national mitigation standards for a variety of airborne pollutants. He also supported the Resource Recovery Act of 1970, an expanded Land and Water Conservation Fund, and initiatives addressing population issues, oil pollution, and endangered species. Nixon surrounded himself with a band of staffers for whom protecting the environment was a serious task: domestic affairs consultant John Whitaker, interior secretaries Walter Hickel and Rogers Morton, EPA directors William Ruckelshaus and Russell Train, and Watergate partner-in-crime John Erlichman.[11]

Goldwater showed more than passing interest in the president's green initiatives. He supported "each and every one" of the Clean Air Act's provisions, putting aside or at least muting his reservations about governmental regulation in the name of addressing serious ecological problems. "I have given my full support to bills such as the new Clean Air Act," Goldwater informed one correspondent, "which provides tough new regulation designed to purify the environment." He assured another that "air pollution is one [environmental problem] that must be tackled with the strongest laws we can devise. For this reason I was a sponsor of the stronger Senate version of the Clean Air Act, and you can be certain I will vote for it unchanged." He told a third that the "air pollution problem is getting to be a very serious situation," and if private initiatives and local government failed to address it, then "the Federal government may have to fill the gap to protect the atmosphere."[12]

Goldwater's support wasn't limited to clean air. "The newly formed Environmental Protection Agency," he claimed with pride to a Phoenix constituent, "resulted from legislation which I cosponsored." (The EPA was technically created by an executive reorganization subject to Senate oversight.) He told a correspondent from Bisbee in early 1971 that "I joined in sponsoring six or seven strong environmental bills" in 1970, and "in fact, I am a cosponsor of every one of the environmental proposals called for by President Nixon. Also, I have sounded off publicly to let big business know that keeping our natural resources clean and pure is going to have to be a cost of their operations or they might find themselves without any right to operate at all."[13]

These were not mere verbal palliatives. Goldwater's seriousness about such issues led him to sound off in private as well. In March 1971, the president of Phelps-Dodge, the copper-smelting corporate giant, wrote to Goldwater to complain about the Clean Air Act's threat to his company's economic health. The senator was sympathetic yet steadfast. "The urgency of accomplishing this goal [clean air] is . . . a clear objective," he replied. "It is easy to see why the expenditure you talk of could have serious effects on Arizona's economy but, to be perfectly honest with you, I think Arizona's entire economy and way of life will come before the difficulties of any setment [sic] of our economy." Goldwater was blunter with other correspondents. "Frankly, the [mining companies] are going to have to face up to the fact that efforts on their part to control pollution are going to have to be more positive," he wrote to a Phoenix bank president, "because if the State legislatures don't act, the Federal government will." Why "these large [companies] which could have easily afforded smoke abatement years ago have taken so many years to be awakened is beyond me," Goldwater grumbled to another Phoenix businessman about a Phelps Dodge pledge to curb its pollution in June 1970. "[Nobody] can say that the mines have suffered through the years." Goldwater also took public utilities to task, telling one executive that air pollution was a "far more serious issue . . . than most people in your business . . . are ready to admit," and that with growing public concern, "you can expect the government to move in." He attacked the auto industry as well, telling one auto dealer that "I am getting tired of Detroit shirking its responsibilities" to prevent air pollution, and "this doesn't come from a left wing liberal [but] a right wing conservative."[14]

Earth Day 1970 found the senator at Adelphi University in New York, where he gave an hourlong speech that summed up his new ecological turn. "Man is the cause" of ecological degradation, he pronounced, a sentiment reinforced by his helicopter flight to the campus from LaGuardia Airport, during which he was "astonished to see the number of junk piles in people's yards and vacant lots." He proceeded to castigate the copper and automotive industries for "pumping smoke into the air" and declared that clean air was more important than a healthy economy. He ended the talk with a plea for families to join Planned Parenthood in order to reduce the threat of overpopulation.[15] Yet when it came time to vote, Goldwater often failed to back up his words. In January 1970, for example, he cosponsored the Senate version of the Clean Air Act, yet did not vote on its final passage on September 22. In 1972 he was absent for both the initial Senate approval for the Clean Water Act and the congressional override of Nixon's veto, and he missed votes on land-use planning, toxic substances, and pesticides. The next year, he missed the vote on the Endangered Species Act. Given Goldwater's notoriously spotty Senate attendance record (regularly one of the worst in the body), missing these votes might be written off as a consequence of playing hooky, but it also suggests that in practice his commitment to federal environmentalism was not always as strong as his rhetoric.[16]

Goldwater understood the importance of offering a carrot as well as threatening with a club, and he embraced positive incentives as another means to environmental ends. He supported renewable energy, especially solar energy, and urged the federal government to fund research and development. In 1973 he cosponsored one bill to guarantee loans for commercial geothermal energy projects and another for a NASA-run commercial solar-heating demonstration project. In 1974 he cosponsored Democratic senator Alan Cranston's Solar Home Heating and Cooling Demonstration Act as well as another version of the NASA demonstration project. The next year he supported another geothermal bill, this time offering tax incentives for commercial development. Goldwater's renewable-energy inspirations involved more than simple environmentalism, of course. The 1973 oil embargo added a strong incentive for such projects; for the defense-minded Goldwater, the national security problems involved in dependence on foreign oil were unconscionable. Meanwhile, for a perennially sunny desert state like Arizona, solar-energy projects were an easy sell, and he enthusiastically pitched his home state as "the home of everything solar" and the perfect place to locate federal solar projects.[17]

Goldwater developed a more sympathetic view of federal wilderness as well. In 1969 he supported Senator Henry "Scoop" Jackson's proposal for three new wilderness areas in Arizona: Mount Baldy Wilderness in the east-central part of the state, Sycamore Canyon Wilderness near Flagstaff, and Pine Mountain Wilderness north of Phoenix. He told the Tucson Audubon Society that he would push the Senate Subcommittee on Public Lands to consider additional areas and showed no signs of being territorial about Jackson's interest. Four years later, he introduced legislation to repeal mining permits in several national monuments, including Organ Pipe in southern Arizona, where permits had been issued during World War II for potential defense needs. "The time is long overdue," proclaimed a press release from his office, to ban statutes allowing "bulldozers and drilling rigs to move about within [the Monument] with little restriction." On the Senate floor Goldwater grumbled that miners could legally "destroy and disturb vegetation" by virtue of permits that were "out-dated and unnecessary." Consequently he took a fair amount of flack from mining interests, but he stood firm. "Frankly," he told one critic in 1975, "I'm in disagreement with you on this one. . . . Any [mining] exploration will affect the cactus and this particular cactus [the organ pipe cactus] grows only in one area, and this is the one."[18]

Goldwater also took a new look at the Hells Canyon and the Snake River. In the 1950s he had stumped for the Idaho Power Company's proposed dams in the name of utilitarianism and progress. Now, in 1971, he reversed direction and cosponsored Oregon senator Robert Packwood's bill to establish the Hells Canyon–Snake National River, which would designate that section a "wild river" under the Wild and Scenic Rivers Act of 1968 and prohibit further dam-building projects. Goldwater attributed his endorsement to his new environmental sympathies. "As you know," he wrote the Sierra Club's southwestern representative in explanation, "I have a deep personal interest in seeing our people take greater steps to clean up or preserve the land we live in. For this reason, I told Senator Packwood that I would be glad to support his proposal."[19]

Goldwater's biggest environmental bombshell, however, was his about-face on Glen Canyon Dam. Before the dam was built, a handful of conservation activists, most notably David Brower, had begun to worry that the rising waters of Lake Powell would encroach on Rainbow Bridge National Monument, located on a small tributary of the Colorado. With that water, they said, would come not only another threat to the national park ideal, but also the danger that Rainbow Bridge itself, the giant natural stone arch that gave the area its name, might collapse as the rock beneath it eroded away. Some activists even suggested that the Bureau of Reclamation build a small dam to shield the arch from the reservoir. Like most reclamation boosters, Goldwater publicly rejected their concerns. A few years later, "Saving the Earth" made plain Goldwater's growing worries about the deteriorating riparian ecology of the Grand Canyon, and a close reading might have hinted at some doubts about Glen Canyon Dam itself. But there is little other evidence to suggest that he believed his support for the dam had been a mistake.[20]

But in the summer of 1976, however, during the Senate floor debate on amendments to the Wild and Scenic Rivers Act and their effect on a proposed dam on Virginia's New River, Goldwater revealed the extent to which his thinking about Glen Canyon had changed. "I rise to announce my opposition to this [New River] dam," he began, even though it "may sound funny coming from a man who was born and raised in the arid west." He went on: "Of all the votes I have cast in the 20-odd years I have been in this body, if there is one that stands out above all the others that I would change if I had the chance it was a vote I cast to construct Glen Canyon Dam on the Colorado. Today we can build nuclear power plants. We do not need to destroy running water." Although it was true that "Glen Canyon Dam has created the most beautiful lake in the world and has brought millions and millions of dollars into my State and the State of Utah," Goldwater admitted that,

"I think of that river as it was when I was a boy and that is the way I would like to see it again." He then voted to designate a twenty-six-mile stretch of the New River as Wild and Scenic and to invalidate all hydroelectric licenses on it.

It is hard to overestimate how much of a turnaround Goldwater's position in Glen Canyon represented. He had been as vigorous a cheerleader for dam-building as anyone in America and rarely met a reclamation project he didn't like. He had approved of Echo Park dam in Dinosaur National Park, supported Bridge Canyon Dam and excoriated its critics in public, and never had expressed any doubts about Glen Canyon Dam and its environmental costs. In 1976, in fact, there were few outside the world of committed environmental activists and hardcore wilderness lovers who questioned the flooding of Glen Canyon. Goldwater was now one of them.[21]

For the rest of his life, Goldwater maintained that voting for Glen Canyon Dam had been his biggest political mistake, a mea culpa that garnered him considerable respect among environmentalists and wilderness devotees. Much of his remorse stemmed from a combination of nostalgia and a sense of aesthetic loss. "The beauty of the canyons which are now covered by Lake Powell," he told one correspondent in 1982, "are etched forever in my memory, and it saddens me to think that my grandchildren will never see those magnificent creations of God. If I had to do it over, I would not support the construction of the Glen Canyon Dam." Ecological problems loomed large for him as well. He told Arizona State University law professor John Leshy that "I had no realization of what it [the dam] would do, not just to the beautiful canyon country surrounding the waters backed up by the dam, but also to the Grand Canyon which is just below it. . . . [We] no longer have the large floods that used to sweep the bottom clean, replace the beaches with new sand, and deposit thousands of acres of driftwood to be used for fires."[22]

He still struggled with his boosterish side, though. "Of course, one could argue that without the lake, literally millions of people would not have the opportunity of seeing those canyons," Goldwater mused to Leshy, "so, from the standpoint of opening up the country to people, my vote was right . . . [and] as history goes by, I suppose it will work out for the betterment of all the people." Nevertheless, from "the standpoint of keeping some parts of this country difficult to see, my vote was wrong," and "I would vote against it had I [another] chance." He concluded: "I guess I am somewhat of a stingy person who likes to think that there are parts of that state of mine that should be kept for people who don't mind working to see the beauty." It was another interesting reversal from a man who had long advocated "opening up" some of his home state's greatest wilderness areas. One imagines Goldwater's supporters shaking their heads, wondering how their Barry had become a wilderness elitist.[23]

Goldwater also worried increasingly about the Grand Canyon in the late 1960s and early 1970s. He assured a Phoenix constituent in 1969 of his opposition to a proposed hotel and tramway in Havasu Canyon, a beautiful side canyon of the Grand and home to perhaps the most stunning waterfall in the Southwest, and he continued to warn the public and Congress of the tourism threat to the canyon. But his most important contribution to the canyon's protection, and one of his crowning environmental moments, was his plan to enlarge Grand Canyon National Park.[24] On June 12, 1969, shortly after the park's fiftieth anniversary, Goldwater unveiled S. 2360, a bill "to build upon" America's national park tradition and "better preserve and protect one of nature's most magnificent creations." S. 2360 increased the size of Grand Canyon National Park by a third and doubled the river mileage inside it, mostly by absorbing Marble Canyon National Monument on its eastern end, the bulk of Grand Canyon National Monument to the west, and some fifty-two thousand acres from areas around Kanab Creek, Long Mesa, and a scenic buffer zone between the Marble Canyon area and the Navajo reservation. With those additions, the park's new total size would approach one million acres. The areas proposed for inclusion were insufficiently protected from development in their current state, Goldwater argued, and now was the time to change that. "With the demand on earth's resources becoming greater daily," he told the Senate, "it is none too soon to bar the door to any future pressures for the exploitation of the canyon area." At that moment, he observed, Arizona representative and liberal Democrat Morris Udall was introducing an identical bill in the House, "giving the legislation a bipartisan spirit that I hope will mark its future course."[25]

Little came of this first bill, but Goldwater and Udall tried again on March 20, 1973, with an even more ambitious piece of legislation. S. 1296 had been produced with prodigious input from the Sierra Club and the Wilderness Society as well as ranching, sporting, and Indian interests. Like the bill before it, S. 1296 absorbed the two national monuments bracketing the park, included the buffer zone, and made numerous other acreage additions, but it also added more land by extending the park's western boundary to the Grand Wash Cliffs. There were also some deletions of acreage, the largest of which involved the expansion of the five-hundred-acre Havasupai Indian reservation at the canyon's bottom. Goldwater had long championed the interests of Arizona's Native American population while in Washington, D.C., especially those from the Four Corners region—the Havasupai, the Hualapai, and the Navajo—and with S. 1296 he intended to come through for them again. Under the new bill the tiny Havasupai reservation would be expanded by 169,000 acres, allowing access to good grazing land. Approximately 113,000 of those acres would be transferred from the Kaibab National Forest on the rim, and the remaining 56,000 would come from the park itself. Finally, S. 1296 set aside 512,000 acres of the park as official wilderness and another 86,156 as "potential" wilderness to be reviewed by the interior secretary. With these changes, Grand Canyon Nation Park would encompass nearly 1.2 million acres, making it the fourth largest national park in the United States.[26]

Goldwater lauded his new bill as the best way to "effectively protect and secure for future generations that magnificent creation of God we call the Grand Canyon of Arizona." If "it is the last thing I do," he vowed on the Senate floor, "I want to find proper protection for the whole wonderful thing . . . , a protection that will guarantee it will not be molested and will remain forever as one of God's few practically untouched masterpieces." He was plainly proud of his proposal, especially that it reflected a satisfying compromise—or so he thought—among many competing interests. He assured Sierra Club president Raymond Sherwin that S. 1296 was a "model of protection," and it was a matter of great satisfaction when he eventually saw it signed (after some amendments) as the Grand Canyon Enlargement Act of 1975 by President Gerald Ford. But whatever the purity of his motivations, Goldwater's plan for saving the Grand Canyon would come at the expense of his bitter estrangement from the Sierra Club. The story of that estrangement opens a window into the limits of Goldwater's environmental conversion.[27]

The Sierra Club was not enthusiastic about Goldwater's Grand Canyon plan. Its leadership had no problem with enlarging the park, but they worried about the fifty-six-thousand-acre chunk that would be taken from the park and given to the Havasupai. Once again, they believed, the "national park principle" seemed under siege. If bills like Goldwater's could strip protection from national park land, then precedent assured that other parks could suffer the same fate, their land chipped away by a flood of hardship claims. While Goldwater's plan enlarged Grand Canyon National Park, the Sierra Club claimed, it actually reduced the National Park Service's total land area by some forty-seven-thousand acres. Having just seen the hated Bridge Canyon Dam go down to defeat, the Sierra Club was acutely aware of the political muscle it had gained and was in no mood to compromise. The proposed Havasupai deletions were "totally unacceptable," the Sierra Club's southwest regional representative John McComb wrote in the early summer of 1973. "This one factor alone is ample justification for opposing Senator Goldwater's bill." The other deletions were equally questionable, and the bill did not specifically exclude any future reclamation projects inside the park, a seeming prelude to Bridge Canyon redux. Thus the Sierra Club threw its support behind an alternative proposal offered by New Jersey Republican senator Clifford Case, which included no deletions and enlarged the park to 2.1 million total acres, a figure Goldwater dismissed as "conservation overkill."[28]

Goldwater was stung badly by the Sierra Club's rejection, and he lashed back with the fury of a man betrayed. He took to the Senate floor on August 2, 1973, to defend his plan and his honor against the "unsupported, misleading and downright erroneous propaganda" of his critics. Many of the provisions in S. 1296—the boundaries at Grand Wash Cliffs and Marble Canyon, the buffer zone, the proposed wilderness designations—were included, Goldwater said, at the suggestion of Sierra Club representatives whom he had included in discussions held in his own home. Now they had the audacity to criticize what they had helped to create. Meanwhile, he charged, the organization was spreading false rumors about the extent and detrimental effects of the deletions. Such devious behavior, Goldwater said, reminded him of the Bridge Canyon controversy, when the Sierra Club employed similar "propaganda tools" to spread fear about a flooded Grand Canyon, "quite a feat when one considers that there is not enough water in all the rivers in the entire world to flood [it]." In the end, he said, the Sierra Club had missed the larger point of his bill: "to put the Grand Canyon in the state of protection it is going to need in the future."[29]

He wasn't finished. On May 20, 1974, Goldwater again tore into the Sierra Club on the Senate floor, this time concerning the Havasupai. "I cannot understand," he said, "the persistent and unmovable resistance of the Sierra Club to the needs of this fine people. I cannot comprehend the vast ignorance and fundamental lack of understanding of the history and culture of the Havasupai which characterize a majority of the national leaders of the

Sierra Club. The only explanation, in my opinion, is the unfortunate fact that Sierra Club has become a closed society, a self-centered, selfish group, who care for nothing but ideas which they themselves originate and which fit only their personal conceptions of the way of life everyone else should be compelled to live." It was a vicious indictment. While Sierra Club leaders clearly placed the national park principle before the Havasupai's land issues, rightly or wrongly, they were hardly ignorant, cruel, or willfully selfish, and Goldwater had little grasp of just how tenuous the national park principle had been or how much the organization had contributed to its defense. For him, the Sierra Club simply demanded too much, and the damage to his relationship with them was irreparable. On July 12, 1973, Goldwater fired off a furious letter to Sierra Club president Raymond Sherwin that highlighted his sense of betrayal. He had given the Sierra Club everything it wanted in his proposal, he said, and yet that was not enough. "Frankly, I don't care to be associated with a group so uncertain of what they really want," he fumed, "so I am hereby submitting my resignation from the Sierra Club." Politics was compromise, and environmental politics was no exception. "While I know the Sierra Club would like about one-third of Arizona and a little bit of Utah and Nevada in the Grand Canyon National Park, it is not going to be that way."[30]

There was clearly a limit to Goldwater's support for green government. More than once in the 1970s, the senator would find himself at odds with environmental groups and their allies on major issues, a situation that grew directly from his visceral antistatism, high confidence in and love of technology, and his faith in capitalism. Cleaning up pollution, preserving wilderness, and pursuing alternative energy sources were all important to him, but so were freedom from excessive regulation, the preservation of states' rights, and the pursuit of economic growth.

An early example came with the controversy surrounding the proposed Supersonic Transport (SST) aircraft, which occurred as Goldwater's environmental sympathies were at their height. The SST was to be the American version of the Concorde, a needle-nosed, delta-winged airliner that would whisk between eighty and a hundred passengers through the sky at more than twice the speed of sound. Engineering advances in the 1950s made supersonic travel a technological possibility by the end of the decade, and President Kennedy, with the enthusiastic support of the aviation industry, initiated an SST prototype-development program in the early 1960s under the auspices of the Federal Aviation Administration. SST boosters argued that there was a built-in market for the plane, since passengers were always interested in reducing travel time. In addition, building a fleet of SSTs would generate thousands of well-paying jobs and produce innumerable other economic benefits. There were also patriotic interests involved. The era of supersonic travel was inevitable, and when vacationers boarded an SST in the future, boosters said, it should be an American product that delivered them to their destination. As the Anglo-French Concorde and the Soviet Union's Tupelov TU-144 indicated, if Americans failed to produce an SST, then other nations would fill the breach.[31]

The SST died in March 1971 when Congress refused to fund any further development of the prototype. Its cost, tremendous fuel consumption, relatively small passenger capacity, dubious job-creation effects, and the questionable vigor of consumer demand all suggested that an SST fleet would never even come close to breaking even, let alone turn a profit. Environmental considerations played a role as well, especially in the general public's substantial opposition to the project. One issue was the SST's sonic boom as it broke the sound barrier on both ends of a flight. A fleet of several hundred SSTs would produce such a banging, critics said, that a public nuisance was guaranteed and the potentially damaging effects on both human and animal health could be considerable. In addition, the water vapor, particulate matter, and other exhaust products generated by an SST fleet could have insidious and irreversible effects on the earth's atmosphere and climate, potentially destroying the ozone layer or inducing a massive greenhouse effect (or both). In retrospect, these fears were considerably overblown, but at the time they seemed serious enough that environmental and citizen-activist groups mobilized against the project, including the Sierra Club and the newly formed Friends of the Earth, led by David Brower.[32]

Goldwater never doubted the SST for a second; as a veteran pilot and Air Force reserve officer, he was a reliable champion of high-tech aviation projects. As he had with the Tennessee Valley Authority in the 1950s, he saturated the *Congressional Record* with commentary. He celebrated the SST's potential contributions to the nation's technological leadership, rejected any insinuations about its economic weaknesses, and pooh-poohed detractors who claimed that, like reclamation, the SST program was an improper subsidy to private industry. "It is an investment," he said, "an investment in the future, an investment in the beneficial dynamics of progress and change."[33]

Most of all, Goldwater savaged the SST's environmentalist critics with a ferocity that suggested he considered their opposition a personal affront.

He might have credited environmental concerns in "Saving the Earth," but when it came to the SST and other pet projects, those concerns became alarmism, extremism, and left-leaning claptrap. Sometimes he was merely dismissive, as in December 1969 when he joked that if the SST could indeed change the climate, then perhaps "it might even bring some water to Arizona." More often, he was vitriolic, as in the guest editorial he wrote for the New York Times excoriating SST opponents in a blaze of indignation. There was absolutely no evidence that the SST would have any economic or ecological ill effects, Goldwater declared confidently, and claims to the contrary were only "scare stories, myths, guesses, speculation, half-truths and downright lies" pushed by "an unusual combination of left-wing scientists, politicians, economists, and conservationists" in "a desperate attempt to channel ever more funds into social welfare programs." He told a constituent in September 1970 that "the claim of noise and air pollution" had simply "never been backed up by any expert testimony." Banning the SST would be a tragedy, he concluded: "If this country doesn't have the equipment to sell, other countries will, and I will do all that I can to prevent this from happening."[34]

Goldwater brushed off environmental concerns about the SST as "baloney" in December 1970, claiming that he had never heard "such wild assertions . . . [and] distortions" in his entire career. On March 1, 1971, he fumed that critics had "grossly distorted" the facts around the SST with "unsubstantiated and fantastic" suggestions about cancer, ozone depletion, and melting ice caps. Eight days later, he lamented the "concentrated and almost unending stream of charges concerning the SST and environmental pollution. At times it [seems] as though reason and fact . . . [are] given no weight in the consideration of this problem." On March 24, he invoked his own environmental credentials in defense of the SST. "Long before the words 'ecology' and 'pollution' became prominent," he huffed, "I was known in my State of Arizona as a nature lover . . . and I yield to no one . . . in my concern as a conservationist." Yet, he concluded, "I [will] vote for [the SST] with not a single qualm as to its possible effect on the earth's atmosphere. If there were even a question of a doubt I would be opposed to this program."[35]

Goldwater reserved special criticism for the Sierra Club. Its opposition to the SST bothered him particularly, he said, because he normally held the group in high regard. In the fight over Bridge Canyon Dam, it had unfortunately strayed into environmental extremism by "promoting the myth about flooding the Grand Canyon." Now the Sierra Club was doing it again with the SST. In July 1973, Goldwater told Sierra Club staffer Kermit Smith that he still felt "the whole presentation of the Sierra Club relative to the SST was about as mixed up as a subject could be. . . . I just retired from the Sierra Club because of similar actions in another field," he told Smith, "and it rather pains me to see an organization with such high ideals . . . sliding backward." It was a measure of Goldwater's anger that as late as 1976 he was still lambasting SST opponents in the *Congressional Record,* blasting the "anti-technology extremists of the environmental movement" for killing his supersonic dreams.[36]

Goldwater was an antistatist to the marrow, so it was not surprising that eventually he came to question the faith he had placed the federal government. But the events of the mid-1970s—energy crisis, inflation, economic stagnation, and the surge of conservative politics that brought Ronald Reagan to the presidency—clearly informed Goldwater's environmental doubts too. As a result, he often found himself at odds with some of the very federal environmental laws and enforcement agencies that he had initially embraced.

Goldwater had been fully supported the EPA when the Nixon administration created it in 1970, but a half-decade later he considered it a rogue bureaucracy more interested in wasting money, issuing orders, and hamstringing free enterprise rather than taking sensible measures to protect the environment. As early as May 1975, he voiced his growing disgust: "We [now] have . . . an Environmental Protection Agency that is slowly stopping building in this country. . . . I think it is time we stopped passing laws that create agencies to solve problems." In 1976 he wrote a constituent that he was "quite concerned that the Environmental Protection Agency has already gone beyond the original Congressional intent in issuing their various regulations." The agency existed "to promote cleaner air and water and to protect the environment in all feasible and reasonable ways," but it had moved beyond both feasibility and reason with its increasingly burdensome regulations. Goldwater was more frank with another constituent, a feedstore owner who wrote to complain about the EPA's concerns about chlordane and heptachlor. "I am not very happy with the way the Environmental Protection Agency . . . has exceeded the spirit of the law in issuing their regulations. It is time that this agency was brought into line and I am supporting legislation that would limit [its] authority." [37]

As the decade wore on, Goldwater's criticism of environmental regulation became even more pointed. When environmental regulation "goes too far," he told the Senate on August 8, 1978, "and when it gets to the point of impeding the progress of people and affecting the lives of people and the livelihood of people, then I think we have to have a reundertsanding [*sic*] of just what the environmental laws were intended to do and what they are doing now. I backed those laws [i.e., National Environmental Policy Act, the Clean Air Act, the Federal Water Pollution Control Act, etc.]. I thought they were good. I think they are being badly misused, badly used by organization people who really do not understand what they are supposed to do, nor what we intended them to do." What they were intended to do, Goldwater believed, was to protect the environment without hampering growth and development. "We who supported the Environmental [Protection] Act," Goldwater observed of himself and his fellow western politicians, "never dreamed that it would go this far, that it could, in effect, contest the erection of a post office or a bridge or a parking lot or a football stadium." Sensible federal environmental regulation had been hijacked by ecoradicals, he said, "nuts . . . who do not believe that people's lives are worth as much as a flowing stream or a tree." Things were so bad now, Goldwater told the president of the Phoenix group Proper Environmental Planning Inc., that "I would like to get rid of the EPA." He told another that the agency was "out of control" and needed to be stopped.[38]

Meanwhile, he was increasingly irritated by efforts to strengthen the Clean Air Act [CAA] as it came up for renewal. In 1976 the Senate considered so-called nondegradation amendments to the CAA, whose objective was to maintain air quality in "pristine" areas, mostly on public lands in the West, where air quality was high but could be easily degraded. Whatever his support for the CAA in 1970, Goldwater in 1977 was in no mood to see it strengthened, for it would place additional pollution-control burdens on places like Arizona. In March 1976 he complained to the state's governor Raul Castro that the EPA had gotten "way out of hand" with environmental regulations and that nondegradation provisions would make things worse. "These provisions spell out a program of federal zoning, federal control and federal land use. These proposals will substantially limit growth and severely hamper economic considerations in our state."[39]

In the Senate in July 1976 Goldwater attacked the nondegradation amendments again. "What impact," he asked rhetorically, "will these well intended and sweeping regulations have on our citizens, the economy, and our Nation's progress? Will they not contribute to the already escalating bureaucracy and the overwhelming entry of the Federal Government into the business of States, private companies, and the lives of the people? No one wants air pollution or the destruction of the beauty of our land—that is not the issue at hand. What we must do is protect the public health and welfare and set standards that will be fair to all segments of our population and not just benefit a few special interests." When it came time to vote, Goldwater cast his lot against nearly every amendment designed to strengthen the CAA, including provisions to protect air quality in national monuments over ten thousand acres, to regulate nonpoint sources in pristine areas, to enact stricter automobile emission standards, and to ban fluorocarbons. He also approved nearly every amendment to weaken the act and rejected the final version of the revised CAA.[40]

Why had Goldwater become so hesitant about federal environmental enforcement? To some extent, the senator suffered from an ideological version of buyer's remorse. Having embraced government help in the environmental battle, he was now having second thoughts about the wisdom of his actions, especially when he thought the government showed signs of going too far. But larger historical context played a role too. The early 1970s were wracked by the aftermath of Vietnam, social upheaval, and Watergate, and by the middle of the decade, inflation and stagflation, an unprecedented energy crisis, and general economic uncertainty added to the list, completing the recipe for the infamous malaise that seemed to grip the nation by decade's end. The oil embargo of 1973 exposed America's precarious dependence on foreign sources. Combined with broader anxieties about the extent of existing supplies, the result was the specter of energy shortage and economic privation. The popularity of American environmentalism rested largely on a foundation of economic growth, and when that growth was threatened, environmental commitment subsided accordingly; the maturing environmental movement foundered on "new economic realities," in the words of historian Hal Rothman. This seems to have been the case with Goldwater as well.[41]

During the 1970s the senator often parted company with environmental groups over energy and other resource issues. Always a believer in national military prowess, Goldwater saw vigorous energy and mineral exploration and development as key elements of preparedness in a Cold War world. But a more general fear of resource scarcity and economic collapse affected him as well, and he was intensely uncomfortable with the idea that environmental protection might adversely affect Americans' material quality of life. With that quality in seemingly dire straights in the 1970s, he was becoming less and less inclined to sacrifice even a small measure of industrial development in the service of ecological restraint. Now was not the time to hamstring industry with excessive regulations like the CAA or any other out-of-control EPA edicts.

The same went for other topics. Discomfort over scarcity and industrial decline motivated Goldwater's support for the proposed trans-Alaska oil pipeline, a major target of environmentalists who feared its effects on the state's wildlife and wilderness character. In July 1973 he grumbled "that so many people seem to think we have all the time in the world to study and debate and consider every conceivable argument" about the pipeline's potential ecological impact. But the looming oil crisis rendered such environmental concerns a luxury. "Frankly, we do not have the time," he warned, with more than a touch of the alarmism he accused environmentalists of harboring. Similar sentiments underlined his support of nuclear power. Conserving energy at home and work was a good thing, Goldwater told the Senate in November, as the oil embargo tightened, but it was "not an acceptable solution." Americans would never accept a permanent decline in their levels of consumption. "We must develop new sources of energy," he said, "or face drastically reduced standards of living. . . . Recent events in the Middle East underscore the urgency." Ideally such sources would be "pollution-free," which was why he supported solar and geothermal energy, but ultimately nuclear power was the best solution, and environmentalists would just have to accept that. "Without nuclear power," Goldwater claimed in 1979, five months after the Three Mile Island accident, the country could "just forget about the whole thing and go back to the days of the horse and buggy, steam and no advancement."[42]

Whenever environmental concerns ran up against resource development and scarcity issues in the mid- to late 1970s, Goldwater put environmental concerns aside. He voted to waive environmental impact statements on federal oil, gas, and geothermal leases in 1973, and the next year he voted against a bill providing for the "environmentally safe development" of offshore oil and natural gas deposits. In 1975 he supported waiving a ban on surface mining in national forests if the waiver served the nation's energy and mineral needs. The next year he voted against S. 2371, a bill that prohibited new mining claims in national parks and banned all mining by 1979. He endorsed an amendment allowing mining in parts of Glacier Bay National Monument, in direct opposition to his own mining-restriction bill three years earlier. In 1977 he rejected mandatory minimum standards for strip mining and reclamation of stripped lands, and he opposed an offshore-drilling bill that authorized seventy-five million dollars for environmental aid "for coastal and marine protection."[43]

As the 1970s merged into the 1980s, Goldwater continued his retreat from federal environmental regulation. He wasn't the only one. Deeply conservative westerners had been fuming about such regulation for years, their anger rooted not only in the malaise of the 1970s but also in their perception of environmentalism as an impediment to their unrestrained pursuit of wealth. Unwilling to express such motivations openly, they rationalized their position with a vision of themselves as a dying breed of rugged individualists who lived in a region exploited by greedy easterners. In this vision an old one in the rural West, environmentalists were only the latest version of know-it-all elitist outsiders who plagued the region. Recent federal regulations had given them unprecedented power to force their will upon the West with no consideration for its property rights or such traditions as ranching, mining, and logging. Two environmental-backlash movements, Wise Use and the Sagebrush Rebellion, took the rollback of environmental regulations and federal control of public lands as their central aim.[44]

The Wise Use movement coalesced in the early 1980s around activists Ron Arnold and Alan Gottlieb and the Center for the Defense of Free Enterprise. "Wise Users," as they were called, argued that nature existed to be utilized for individual profit. Any harm that nature might suffer in the process was unimportant as long as humans were not affected, and some even suggested that nature was essentially incapable of being damaged in any meaningful way. They also vehemently rejected government control and oversight of resource development and argued that unfettered free enterprise was morally and practically superior. It followed that environmental regulations were both unnecessary and unethical. Critics dismissed the Wise Use movement as a front for industry, despite considerable local-level support, and laughed off its advocacy for "free enterprise" as ideological cover for taxpayer-funded corporate exploitation of public lands. Arnold responded that his main goal was the destruction of the environmental movement.[45]

Goldwater was not a hardcore Wise User and had no interest in destroying the environmental movement, although he was certainly sympathetic to arguments about the morality of free enterprise, the utilitarian value of nature, and the excesses of federal regulation. At any rate, the influence of Wise Use peaked in the late 1980s and into the mid-1990s, well after he left political office. He had more in common with the architects of its immediate predecessor, the Sagebrush Rebellion, in the late 1970s and early 1980s. Like the Wise Use movement, the Sagebrush Rebellion drew on a long history of western antipathy to federal power and had its immediate genesis in regional grievances against environmental legislation. Its heart lay in the state legislatures of the intermountain West—Nevada, Utah, Idaho, Arizona, Colorado, and New Mexico—where its champions aimed to "liberate" lands under federal control and turn them over to the states and eventually private ownership. Western states, the Rebels said, had been forced to surrender large portions of their land as a condition of statehood. Now, draconian land-management bureaucracies and environment regulations like the Wilderness Act of 1964 and the Federal Land Policy and Management Act of 1976 (which essentially placed public lands under federal control in perpetuity) deprived the West of the opportunity to develop its economy fully. Eastern states labored under no such restrictions, and equity demanded the return of public lands to their rightful state owners. It was understood that "excessive" environmental regulation would not be part of the new state management.[46]

Goldwater had long complained about federal land management, and he was a fervent supporter of the Sagebrush movement. He helped to form one of its first umbrella organizations in 1978, a publicity group named LASER, or the League for the Advancement of States' Equal Rights. "All we want to do," he told an interviewer in October 1979, "is to see this [federal land] come under state control so that we can benefit from the money that's now going to the federal government." Local management of formerly public land would also be more efficient than federal oversight, he said; best of all, it would also be more environmentally sensitive. Environmentalists "have to realize," he declared, invoking a standard Sagebrush argument against federal environmental regulation, "that we who live on these western lands have a far, far greater respect and love for it than they can ever have, and that we will do a much better job than environmentalists can ever do. . . . I have a far deeper interest in the desert land that adjoins my boundary than some federal official . . . back here in Washington." Meanwhile, Goldwater read into the *Congressional Record* the Sagebrush-influenced Arizona House Concurrent Memorial 2004, which urged the federal government to convey "unreserved [and] unappropriated" lands to the state. He threw his support behind conveyance legislation and twice cosponsored a bill that limited presidential authority to set aside land under the Antiquities Act. For good measure, he also voted against S. 1009, a bill that created the 2.2-million-acre

River of No Return Wilderness in Idaho and added 125 miles of the Salmon River to the Wild and Scenic Rivers system.[47]

Environmentalists were not at all convinced about the West's ability to manage public lands properly. To them, the Sagebrush Rebellion was merely old-fashioned greed wrapped in an antifederalist banner, an attempt to gain unrestrained access to public lands by doing an end run around federal management. Especially ominous was that the Rebellion's arguments, taken to their logical conclusion, seemed to lead to the dismantling and conveyance to the states of national forests, wildlife refuges, wilderness areas, and even national parks. As a result, Goldwater soon found himself soothing constituents' concerns, telling them that their parks and wildernesses were safe and that it was mainly run-of-the-mill BLM lands and other superfluous federal holdings that interested the Sagebrush Rebels. "I see no reason why unneeded and unwanted Federal land and properties cannot be sold" to the states or private interests, he told a resident of Globe, Arizona, in September 1982. "Obviously we're not going to sell the Yellowstone Park, but we can sell some . . . land which the Federal Government does not need. Those restricted areas as refuges, national parks, and wilderness areas would be protected, and not subject to sale." He told another constituent that "wilderness areas, wildlife refuges, national monuments, national parks, recreation areas, Bureau of Reclamation projects, military reservations and federal building sites . . . will remain in federal hands." Forest Service lands were conspicuously absent from the list, although Goldwater assured a third correspondent that he supported President Reagan's proposed sale of surplus government property, including Forest Service parcels not deserving of the name. "I can think of literally thousands of acres of land in National Forests," he said, "that a person can't find a tree on." Such sentiments were unlikely to make environmentalists feel any better.[48]

It was probably no coincidence that the Sagebrush Rebellion caught fire during one of the biggest wilderness debates in America history: the Alaska wildlands controversy. Alaska was the holy grail for postwar America wilderness champions, a place both quantitatively and qualitatively different from the wild places of the Lower Forty-Eight. It had a tiny human population, massive mountain ranges, vast forests, entire river systems without dams, healthy ecosystems populated by grizzly bears and caribou, and millions upon millions of acres without any obvious signs of humans. In other words, it was as close to classic "untouched" wilderness as anywhere in America, although the people whose ancestors had lived there for thousands of years disputed that characterization as the mythical nostalgia of urban whites. Most wilderness areas in America were remnants of far vaster areas swallowed by westward expansion, often with a long history of intense exploitation. In the Alaska of the 1970s wilderness lovers saw, as historian Roderick Nash has written, the "last chance to do things right the first time."[49]

Environmentalists and their opponents soon battled over the Alaska National Interest Lands Conservation Act (ANLCA). The debate had all the hallmarks of earlier wilderness battles: charges of resource "lock-up" and federal land-management dictatorship on one side, celebrations of natural beauty, ecological integrity, and spiritual uplift, and charges of industrial greed on the other. When President Jimmy Carter signed the act into law on December 2, 1980, it was a stellar victory for lovers of wild land. ANCLA set aside some 104 million acres for protection, designating 56.7 million acres as official wilderness under the 1964 act, adding twenty-eight rivers to the Wild and Scenic River list, and doubling the size of the national park and national wildlife refuge systems. Goldwater had little nice to say about it. Publicly, he urged "a fair approach to the problem of the lands of Alaska," but in private he told an Arizona state senator that ANCLA was "the worst legislative foul up that I've seen in all of my years in the Senate." He voted against the final bill and supported every amendment to weaken it.[50]

By the early 1980s, the Sagebrush Rebellion had fizzled out, a victim of its narrow interest base, opposition from eastern politicians and urban westerners, and internal squabbling. Before its demise, however, the Rebels managed to gain a powerful federal ally in James G. Watt, President Ronald Reagan's secretary of the Interior. Watt was, to put it mildly, a lightning rod for environmentalist criticism. With deeply conservative political and religious views, he had impeccable Sagebrush-style credentials: former president of the fiercely antienvironmental Mountain States Legal Foundation, adviser to the U.S. Chamber of Commerce, a states' rights advocate, a supporter of reclamation, and a believer in the utilitarian stewardship of nature via "wise use." He was also opinionated and eager for a fight. Watt's tenure as secretary would be short, a mere two years. It ended with his resignation after a series of controversial comments including one cringe-inducing description of an advisory board: "a black . . . , a woman, two Jews and a cripple. And we have talent." But during his brief time on the job, Watt made no pretense of working with environmentalists, vocalizing his sympathy with resource interests, pushing for the "opening" of public lands to increased mining and logging, mocking the sentimentality of nature lovers, and feeling not the least bit guilty about it. On a trip he took through the Grand Canyon, for example, Watt said he was "praying for helicopters" to take him back to civilization. Environmentalists almost universally despised him. The Sierra Club organized a Dump Watt campaign, and "Out, Damned Watt!" graced bumper stickers across the nation.[51]

Goldwater loved him. Four times on the Senate floor Goldwater rose to praise the new secretary in a manner reminiscent of his defenses of Douglas McKay nearly three decades earlier. "This week more than 1 million signatures were presented by the Sierra Club and the Friends of the Earth ... urging the firing of Interior Secretary James Watt," he observed of the Dump Watt campaign on October 20, 1981. "All I have to say is, who cares?" Watt "is doing a tremendous job . . . , understands the importance of our natural resources and intends to provide the balance in our environmental policies that have been lacking under previous administrations." On August 11, 1982, Goldwater defended the "work of this concerned man" against "a lot of scurrilous press." The senator was equally supportive in correspondence. The best thing about Watt, he told a Tucson constituent in 1982, was that he was a westerner with a national vision. "There simply is not a 'wholesale rape' of public lands going on" under Watt's watch, he reassured the writer. "Watt is the first Secretary of the Interior that we have had in a long time who comes from the West who really understands not only the problems that we westerners face, but he also has a good insight into our nation's energy needs and our land conservation and preservation goals." He told another constituent that Watt "has been the most knowledgeable and understanding Secretary of our water problems that we have had in a long time" and "has bent over backward to . . . support the Central Arizona Project, and to assist us in other water problems which we are experiencing." Watt certainly appreciated Goldwater's praise, telling the senator upon his resignation that his "friendship and loyalty stand out as some of the most valued things that [I] take with [me] from this office."[52]

Goldwater continued to complain about resource scarcity and federal regulation throughout the late 1970s and early 1980s. He remained steadfast in supporting nuclear energy, coal, oil, and the search for vital minerals on public lands. He griped about the CAA and its effect on Arizona's copper industry, a big change from his get-tough attitude during the Nixon administration, and bewailed environmental restrictions on the proposed MX missile system. Ignoring environmentalist critics, he voted to exclude the controversial Tellico dam project in Tennessee from the Endangered

Species Act in 1979. And, as always, he stumped for reclamation, pushing the Central Arizona Project, working to ensure federally funded repair and maintenance of BuRec dams, urging the relaxation of acreage limits for BuRec clients, opposing both the Carter and Reagan administrations' threats to reduce reclamation funding, and suggesting the revival of the Bridge Canyon project (perhaps out of a lingering sense of spite) as an antidote to energy concerns.[53]

Goldwater's turnaround on environmental policy also affected his position on the management of his beloved Grand Canyon. Taking the side of commercial outfitters, he reversed his Nixon-era concerns about the effects of tourists in the park and opposed National Park Service restrictions on motorized river trips. "I can say without hesitancy," he declared in a November 1980 press release, "that there has been no environmental change in the bottom of the Grand Canyon as the result of thousands and thousands of Americans having gone down that river. I wish Americans would keep every campsite and every beautiful spot in this country as clean as the outfitters have kept this very remote area." "I would prefer to have no motors on the River, so that one could have a total wilderness experience," Goldwater told a correspondent two years later. "However, I do not feel that it is the right of the Federal Government to dictate the manner in which one travels down that River, since it has not been proven that the motors are ecologically damaging to the Canyon." He had not been nearly so certain about such things a decade before, and if there was better evidence that his environmental feelings had cooled, it was difficult to find.[54]

In the wake of the Sagebrush Rebellion, the Alaska wilderness debate, and his increasing frustrations with federal environmental regulation, had "Green Goldwater" been merely a flash in the pan in the wake of Earth Day? In many ways the answer was yes. Yet it is revealing to look again at the years after the mid-1970s and ask what environmental causes he *did* support and what concerns he shared with environmentalists during that time. Such a reappraisal shows that Goldwater could still make a place for environmental protection, even of the government variety.

For all his dissatisfaction with federal environmental protection, Goldwater never dismissed it out of hand. In 1976, for example, he voted to authorize some $570 million in federal aid to state and local waste management programs. In 1977 he voted to require federal employees to pay for their own parking, a measure intended to encourage carpooling and reduce fuel consumption. More significant, in 1978 he voted to extend the Endangered Species Act, much-hated among antienvironmentalists, and in 1980 he threw his support behind the famous "Superfund" bill, which authorized the federal government to clean up sites contaminated by toxics wastes, with funding taken from taxes on the petroleum and chemical industries. In 1982 he sponsored a Senate joint resolution urging continued federal funding for renewable energy. Indeed, he remained a determined champion of government-funded solar energy research and was loath to see it threatened, even by his ideological allies. He was all for reducing government spending, he told the chairman of the Arizona Senate Finance Committee in 1984, for example, but when it came to balancing the official budget, "I don't think solar energy is exactly the place to start." Finally, in 1985 and 1986, Goldwater joined his Senate colleagues in voting unanimously to renew, over President Reagan's objections, the Clean Water Act of 1972.[55]

But it was a flurry of wilderness legislation in the early 1980s which really suggested that Goldwater's environmentalist streak was still discernible. On April 29, 1982, the senator introduced S. 2458, a bill to give Arizona's Aravaipa Canyon, then a Bureau of Land Management "primitive area," permanent protection as the Aravaipa Canyon Wilderness. It would be only a small addition to the national wilderness system—6,670 acres—but in the case of Aravaipa Canyon, small was also beautiful. "Its . . . multicolored cliffs rise as high as 1,000 feet" above the canyon floor, Goldwater said as he described the proposal to the Senate. "In the bottom of the canyon," he went on,

one finds the Aravaipa Creek, a perennial stream which travels for about 15 miles. It not only supports a lush green vegetation, it also provides water for wildlife and for 12 fish species, two of which are threatened and endangered. In the canyon one can find more than 158 species of bird and also bighorn sheep, mule deer, fox, mountain lion, coyote, bobcats, javelina, and other small animals. This scenic canyon is not only a haven for naturalists, but it offers many recreational opportunities such as backpacking, hiking, horseback riding, hunting outside canyon bottoms, mountain and rock climbing, bird watching, photography, and sightseeing.

Goldwater noted in conclusion that his bill was "a very simple [one] which attempts to preserve and protect a magnificent desert sanctuary." It had been a long time since he had waxed so enthusiastic about a federally managed wilderness.[56]

Normally there was nothing unusual about a wilderness bill such as this, but what made it interesting was historical context. In 1982 the smoke was still rising from the ashes of the Sagebrush Rebellion, and James Watt occupied the Interior secretary's chair. Yet here was Goldwater, one of their most prominent allies, proposing to cede land permanently to the hated Feds. It was sign of the proposal's incongruousness that the senator, with a hint of defensiveness, felt compelled to note that "in no way would the wilderness of the Aravaipa Canyon area result in any adverse impacts on the Nation's security, mineral needs, or economic well-being. I am very cognizant of the sensitivity of the mineral issue on potential wilderness land."[57]

But the Aravaipa bill paled in comparison to another, S. 2242, that Goldwater introduced in February 1984. The Arizona National Forest Wilderness Act of 1984 designated twenty-eight areas inside national forest land, some 752,000 acres in all, as Wildernesses under the 1964 act (including Aravaipa Canyon Wilderness, which was absorbed into the bill), proposed 61,000 more acres for further study, and added fifty miles of the Verde River in central Arizona to the Wild and Scenic River system. As with his Grand Canyon bill a decade earlier, Goldwater held up S. 2242 as a model of healthy moderation. Cosponsored in the House by liberal Morris Udall, it set aside 250,000 more acres as wilderness than did comparable proposals from resource-friendly groups, the senator observed, yet was smaller than the Arizona Wilderness Coalition's unreasonable suggestion of 1.6 million acres. It was not ideal, he conceded, but it split the differences among competing interests with commendable evenhandedness. "My office and I have worked with individual ranchers, mining groups, the timber industry, utility groups, environmentalists, Native Americans, the Forest Service, the Bureau of Land Management, local, and State governments, you name it," Goldwater told the Senate in August 1984. "[We] tried to work with everyone. I do not think everyone will be happy with the results. There will always be people who want more, and some who want less. But, I think we have a bill that the people of Arizona can live with."[58]

Certainly Goldwater's motives were not all environmental sunshine and goodness. In 1979 the U.S. Forest Service had completed the second version of the Roadless Area Review and Evaluation program, known shorthand as RARE II (the similar RARE I had occurred in the early 1970s), which surveyed its lands to assess their wilderness qualities and their potential for inclusion in the national wilderness system. The Forest Service had recommended that only fifteen million acres be designated as official wilderness, and a fierce debate erupted in the early 1980s over RARE II's exclusions, the fate of lands targeted for "further study," and the program's larger flaws and biases. An unspoken motivation for the fairly generous sweep of Goldwater's Arizona Wilderness proposal was to head off even more generous proposals from wilderness advocacy groups in the event of a "RARE III" survey. "If we do not get some sort of forest wilderness legislation," Goldwater warned, "the State of Arizona faces the certainty of a RARE III study process which would take years to complete and would be a waste of taxpayers' money. This wilderness issue is not going to go away, and the sooner we handle this, the better off all parties will be." Better to mollify wilderness lovers now, he might have added, than to risk a proposal like that of the Arizona Wilderness Coalition becoming a reality later.[59]

Nevertheless, such pragmatism does not detract from the larger significance of Goldwater's bill, and as with Aravaipa, historical context brings that significance into relief. When President Reagan, no environmentalist himself, signed the Arizona Wilderness Act of 1984 into law on August 28, 1984, the legislation he was approving had been championed, with the help of a liberal Democrat, by a devout Sagebrush Rebel and advocate of James Watt who only four years earlier had voted against the Alaska wilderness bill, clashed with wilderness advocates over the Grand Canyon in the early 1970s, and in 1964 rejected the very fountainhead of federal wilderness protection, the Wilderness Act. Viewed in this light, the turnaround was notable, even if it was redolent of political expediency.

In the larger context of Goldwater's life, however, the Arizona Wilderness Act is less surprising. As we have seen, the deserts of his home state were strong threads in the fabric of his life, and despite his opposition to things like ANCLA, his passion for Arizona's wilderness meant that he could and often did see a place for government in its protection. His actions in the early 1970s had confirmed that, and the Arizona Wilderness Act of 1984 was thus only a later manifestation of a longer trend. Meanwhile, only two years away from retirement, Goldwater was likely considering his broader environmental legacy. His identity as the nation's conservative godfather was secure, but his long association with Arizona's natural environment suggests that he was thinking about his lasting influence there as well. Enlarging Grand Canyon National Park had been one important step in defining that legacy. The Arizona Wilderness Act of 1984 was the follow-through.

In November 1986, at seventy-seven years of age, Goldwater left the Senate for the second and final time. As often happens when stalwarts retire from that body, in the days before his departure a number of senators took to the floor to offer tributes to their departing colleague. On August 9, 1986, Republican senator William Cohen of Maine rose to deliver his own. "I know he is known as the Godfather of Conservative Politics in this country, a man who has never believed in moderation on the pursuit and defense of freedom," Cohen observed of the gentleman from Arizona. "I know many recognize him as an aviator . . . [and there] are a few who know about his deep feelings and commitment to the American Indian, to their culture and way of life, and the need to see . . . that we do not forsake them in the face of expediency." But, Cohen went on, "I know Barry Goldwater as more than all of these things—I know him as a great naturalist—a man who has a profound love of nature and the wilderness; an explorer, an adventurer who believes that 'the running streams of this country should not be let out of the possession of the people.'" Most people knew about Goldwater's *Conscience of a Conservative*, Cohen continued, but few had heard of *Delightful Journey down the Green and Colorado Rivers*. Cohen then read a short passage, and declared that "these are the words of a man who has had a long love affair with life—here in the Senate, but especially out amongst the canyons, rapids and stars."[60]

In his retirement, Goldwater became famous for an increasingly irascible libertarianism, as he vocally supported abortion rights and gay rights, including the right to military service, expressed an unambiguous mistrust of the religious Right, and offered words of support for Democratic president William Clinton, to name only a few prominent examples. Some observers speculated that Goldwater had actually become a liberal. It was not really true, of course, and there was never much danger that anyone would mistake him for a Kennedy. Nor was Cohen entirely correct in saying that few people knew of Goldwater's love of nature. Such was his status as godfather of postwar conservatism that he could appear to be a creature of pure ideology and little else. But his association with the Arizona desert, especially the Grand Canyon and the Colorado River, have still made their way into popular consciousness, albeit with little nuance. When the topic of "conservative environmentalism" comes up in casual conversation today, two names inevitably pop up, even among nonenvironmentalists: Richard Nixon and Barry Goldwater.[61]

Goldwater was indeed an environmentalist. The tougher question to answer is, what kind of environmentalist? In his definitive biography, historian Robert Goldberg notes that in recent years "liberals have welcomed

Barry Goldwater into their fold" because his take on abortion, gay rights, and so on "validates their own beliefs." But there is a danger here, because "the liberal embrace is possible only by ignoring the Arizonan's enduring conservatism." The same might be said for Goldwater as an environmentalist. In the mid-1990s he was given an honorary membership in Republicans for Environmental Protection (REP), an advocacy group that celebrated the GOP's historical accomplishments in conservation and environmental protection and simultaneously criticized the current party's Reaganesque rejection of environmentalism as a whole and federal environmental regulation in particular. Goldwater's inclusion in the REP certainly suggested that, as with abortion, gay rights, and religion, he was none too happy with the GOP's current environmental stance. Yet, as Goldberg writes, the "environmentalist and booster instincts of Barry Goldwater . . . coexist[ed] in tension." For every instance that he agreed with environmentalists and environmental groups, for every concern that he shared with them and every issue for which he gained their support, there was another on which they disagreed, where he dismissed their concerns, rejected their arguments, and read them the conservative riot act.[62]

When all is said and done, we might be tempted to write the senator off as a fair-weather environmentalist or even a hypocrite, green on the outside but brown within. Hypocrisy would be an overly harsh judgment, but Goldwater did seem perennially incapable of a consistent environmentalism, a firm set of enduring principles and ideas to guide his thinking about the natural world and the human role in using and protecting it. He seemed to be whipped about by history, bobbing back and forth between the powerful historical currents of his time without finding a balance between them. But then this was not much different from many Americans' feelings about environmentalism. If Samuel Hays has claimed that the rise of postwar environmentalism represented a sea change in Americans' attitudes about the value of nature, Hal Rothman has countered that that sea was never very deep. Most postwar Americans, Rothman has argued, wanted to use nature and have it too—to enjoy pristine wilderness, beautiful scenery, and clean air and water, all without any real restrictions on their consumption levels, their ecologically destructive habits, or the capitalist economy that made them possible. It is a description that seems to fit the senator from Arizona to a tee. Like so many postwar Americans, and especially his fellow middle-class suburbanites, Barry Goldwater was a sincere environmentalist, one who cherished nature and worried about its fate. But he was many other sincere things as well, and so it comes as no surprise that his conservative and environmental consciences had a lifelong rivalry.[63]

Barry Goldwater's waxing and waning environmental sympathies were in large measure a product of the times, but they also reflected the lack of a well-constructed philosophy that could accommodate both his desire for the protection of nature and his mistrust of government. He was neither a rigorous thinker nor prone to intellectual self-examination, so he tended to vacillate in his opinions about the environmental management state, now embracing it, now pushing it away, depending on circumstance and desire. While he struggled with his ambivalence, a small group of economists, political scientists, and resource managers with strong libertarian leanings began sketching the contours of what would become known, by the 1990s, as "free-market environmentalism." Its philosophy was simple: government is profoundly unable to protect the environment and is often its biggest source of harm. Yet mainstream environmentalists continue to invoke government while rejecting the very thing best suited to saving the planet—laissez-faire capitalism. Just as it efficiently delivers goods and services, capitalism can also deliver environmental goods. Only when Americans have been released from regulatory interference, armed with clear property rights and the incentive of capital accumulation, and given the freedom to negotiate in an unfettered market, will they find effective, comprehensive, and fair methods of environmental protection. In short, free-market environmentalism proposed to turn the Progressive conservation ethic on its head.

— 4 —

TENDING NATURE WITH
THE INVISIBLE HAND

The Free-Market Environmentalists

Combining the spark of innovative ideas with the fuel of
individual entrepreneurship gives us hope that we can break
the regulatory fist of command and control and replace it with
a greener invisible hand.

—*Terry Anderson and Donald Leal, 2001*

OUT OF THE 1960S CAME SOME OF THE FIRST ATTEMPTS AT AN ANTI-
statist-friendly environmental philosophy. Stewart Brand was a counterculture wunderkind with graduate training in ecology, a strong libertarian
streak, and a penchant for grand visions, and his environmentalism was
decidedly different from the old-school agenda of conservation and preservation. For the enigmatic Brand—an anticommunist ex-serviceman who
supported the war in Vietnam as well as a counterculture activist—government could not be trusted to save the environment or improve the lives of
its residents. Instead, he put his faith in a grassroots do-it-yourself ethic that
eagerly embraced small-scale technology and regarded things like wilderness preservation as secondary goals at best and misanthropic distractions
at worst. Inspired by figures like E. F. Schumacher and Buckminster Fuller,
Brand established the Point Foundation and published the legendary *Whole
Earth Catalog* to spread the gospel of appropriate technology, mindful consumption, and individual, not governmental, responsibility for living light
on the planet.[1]

Historian Ted Steinberg links the current-day "green capitalism" of Paul

Hawken, Amory Lovins, Thomas Friedman, and the like to Brand and the *Whole Earth Catalog*, but they are only part of its parentage. A century ago in Chicago, urban activists argued that the city's waste and pollution problems should be solved by methods as profitable to local businesses as they were rational, a view challenged by others who argued that such reform ought to put people before profits. In the 1950s Resources For the Future was among the first groups to explore the potential of market incentives in protecting scarce resources, and today "green capitalism" quickens the pulse of many a business-minded environmentalist. The rise of free-market environmentalism in the 1970s, however, marked the first attempt to forge a broad environmental philosophy consistent with American conservative/ libertarian political principles. How successful it has been, or ever can be, is a matter of debate, to put it mildly. Critics have hammered it mercilessly, most of its prescriptions have never been tested against real-world environmental ills, and its advocates remain at the fringes of American environmental politics. But, effective or not, like Barry Goldwater and conservative antifluoridationists, free-market environmentalists exemplify the fascinating ways in which antistatism and environmentalism affected each other in postwar America.[2]

Fundamental to free-market environmentalism is the idea that regulatory approaches to environmental problems have been a disaster, not only by failing to protect the environment but also by wasting taxpayers' money, alienating those subject to regulations, and unduly restricting their rights. The federal government has been especially bad at managing public lands, so it follows that both taxpayers and the environment alike would be better served by an approach that abandons "command and control" regulation and government management as much as possible and replaces them with well-defined, defensible, and transferable property rights, market incentives, and common law.[3]

Human beings are inherently selfish, free-marketers argue, and are motivated primarily by what they perceive to be their own interests, which are usually financial in nature. They also act based on the relative quality of "information" they acquire about the choices before them; how they act is a function of their perceived interests weighed against the discernible costs and benefits of their various options. The best way to acquire information on costs and benefits is in the marketplace, where prices serve as an objective yardstick for self-interested humans to decide which activity, action, or resource would best serve them. In other words, incentives and information are what matter for altering human behavior, and the problem with government is that it tries to play the role of an objective good guy acting in the name of the public welfare. Because government operates outside the market and rarely suffers directly from the consequences of its decisions, as a private individual or company would, its incentives are "distorted." Thus government necessarily makes all kinds of environmental decisions that are neither economically rational nor environmentally sound. Instead, it is among individuals in the free market where incentives, information, and environmental values will best be aligned, and to recognize this, say free-market advocates, is to see the future of environmental protection.

Take public lands, for example. Progressive conservationists argued that unrestrained markets were the root cause of environmental destruction because they encouraged speculation, "cut and run" mentalities, and an overall emphasis on immediate economic self-interest. This was especially true on public lands, which were subject to tremendous damage by short-sighted private enterprises that became rich by exploiting resources while leaving the citizenry to deal with the aftermath. The solution was for government to manage the public lands using politically neutral trained experts, a plan that was part and parcel of the larger Progressive mission to rationalize American society. Such management, the argument went, would minimize ecological damage to public lands while ensuring their full and efficient economic use. Thus were born the U.S. Forest Service (USFS), the Bureau of Land Management (BLM), and the Bureau of Reclamation (BuRec)—bureaucracies staffed by experts charged with managing the nation's public land resources for the public good.[4]

These assumptions and this approach continue to inform public-lands management today. But, free-market advocates charge, the government's management of public lands has failed. A century after the Progressive Era, national forests are vastly overlogged, federal rangelands are badly overgrazed, national parks suffer from an overabundance of visitors and a lack of funds, and water resources are heavily damaged and misallocated by financially disastrous reclamation projects. Blame lies squarely with conservation's reliance on the State. "The Progressive Era experiment featured centralized planning by green Platonic despots," wrote economist John Baden, one of the movement's founders, in the *Seattle Times* in 1997. It "focused on capitalism's flaws, often characterizing private-sector entrepreneurs as inherently venal and short-sighted. In prescribing a dominant planning and coordinating role for government, Progressives demonstrated great naiveté. They believed benevolent bureaucrats would exercise intelligence and foster the public good, not their own or that of constituents." In the end, although "the Progressives did us a service by calling attention to real problems" in land management, "their favored solution was fundamentally flawed." Other free-market advocates have been even harsher, claiming, for example, that federal land policy "encouraged [the] fraud and theft" by private interests that it was supposed to prevent.[5]

The U.S. Forest Service is one of free-market environmentalists' favorite examples of Progressivism's ecological irrationality. Its problems, they argue, have been many. While reportedly managing national forests for "multiple use," the Forest Service's real emphasis has been on logging and road building, and massive environmental damage—erosion from roads, logging in ecologically sensitive areas, clear-cutting, and so on—has been the result. It almost always loses money on its timber sales as well, selling its trees "below cost" and often below market value. This happens because the agency absorbs most of the associated costs, such as sale preparation, road building, replanting, herbicide application, and payments to county governments for lost tax revenue without adjusting its timber prices to cover them. To make things even worse, the timber is often next to worthless economically because wood is not a scarce commodity; such sales do little more than depress prices to the detriment of private producers. Meanwhile, faulty and even fraudulent accounting practices obscure huge financial losses. Finally, free-market environmentalists point out, most public recreation on Forest Service land is virtually free—recreation which, if the agency charged even a small fee for it, would often bring in far more money than timber sales.[6]

The USFS overlogs, damages its land, and loses money in the process, free-market environmentalists conclude, because of the incentives its managers have. Forest Service bureaucrats are not bad people, but their bureaucracy is structured in such a way that its managers are not "disciplined" to do the right thing—that is, manage forests in an ecologically and financially healthy way. Like people in general, free-marketers argue, bureaucrats are self-interested, but profit is not their motivation. What they want is to increase their agency's budgets, and that is the root cause of mismanagement. Take, for example, the Knutson-Vandenberg Act of 1930, which allows national forests to keep most of the receipts from timber sales. Because of the act, much of a given national forest's budget comes from harvesting its trees; thus there is a strong incentive to harvest willy-nilly in order to get more receipts. Meanwhile, congressional appropriations, the other major source of the Forest Service's budget, are usually tied to board-feet quotas that Congress sets, which are always very high because representatives from timber-producing areas force them upward to keep their industrial constituents happy (meeting the board-feet quotas is also a means to promotion within the Forest Service itself). Finally, the timber industry has a strong "client relationship" with the Forest Service. The industry benefits greatly from access to cheap USFS timber and therefore sinks a lot of effort into cultivating close relationships with forest managers, who in turn want to keep their "clients" happy.[7]

For many free-market environmentalists, the ideal solution to this problem is to privatize the national forests. Others, recognizing that privatization may not be politically realistic, propose major reforms to "get the incentives right," to find ways to make bureaucratic motivations correlate with ecological and financial goals. For the Forest Service this means "marketizing" it, in the words of policy analyst Randal O'Toole—that is, basing its funding on net income from its forests, not gross income or appropriations, instituting recreation and other user fees, eliminating bad funding rules like the Knutson-Vandenberg Act, and so forth. Still others have suggested turning national forest management over to private trusts that would then be subject to incentives for proper husbandry. Either way, by separating USFS funding from timber-cutting and the associated incentives and appropriations, the idea is that motivations for overcutting will disappear, taking their ecological effects with them. Forest ecology will benefit, and the Forest Service will stop losing money. In fact, with most of their revenues coming from the user fees of campers, hikers, hunters, and the like, forest managers will actively promote and practice ecologically sensitive management to keep their new "clients" happy and their own budgets high.[8]

Free-market environmentalists offer similar criticisms of the Bureau of Land Management (BLM), the Bureau of Reclamation (BuRec), the National Park Service, and other resource agencies. The BLM, for example, issues grazing permits below cost, which not only subsidizes permitees but also contributes little beef to the economy and harms private ranchers. Meanwhile, ill-conceived rules concerning base-acreage requirements and permit transfers prevent the development of an efficient market where permits might be bought, sold, or traded by environmental groups to protect sensitive areas. Free-marketers also argue that BuRec water projects in the West constitute a massive federal subsidy that destroys free-flowing rivers for the benefit of agricultural interests, the electricity market, and the members of Congress who deliver the pork. National parks lose money, meanwhile, by undercharging entrants and suffer from the usual economic inefficiencies and bad incentives resulting from funding via federal appropriation. The solutions to these problems are similar to those for the USFS: eliminate appropriations, along with the rules and procedures that encourage mismanagement, and create new incentives that encourage ecologically sensitive management.[9]

Often, however, free-market advocates go even further in their criticism. Government has not only botched the management of public lands, they argue, but also its management of private land and activities. It has failed to protect environmental quality while wasting huge sums of money and has alienated private citizens with hamhanded and sometimes dictatorial regulations, violating individual rights in the process. This is most unfortunate, say free-marketers, because private citizens operating in a free market are the key to environmental protection. Many environmental problems are "commons" problems. Natural resources without ownership—air, water, wildlife, and so on—are inevitably subject to damage because, with no rules or authority to manage them, everyone who uses the "commons" has every incentive to use it as much as possible before someone else does. Further, any damages to the resource will be, as economists say, "externalized": costs will be shared by everyone using the resource while most of the benefits flow to the initial users.

Government management and regulation has been the typical solution to this dilemma. Sometimes, as with forests or grazing land, the government assumes direct managerial control. More often, it uses regulations and statutes to control private use and minimize damage (the Clean Air Act is a typical example). A power plant or factory could dump its waste into the atmosphere or nearby lakes and streams, allowing it to reap the benefits of free waste disposal while passing the cost on to the breathing and drinking public. But the government steps in to prevent this behavior through its power to punish via regulations, rules, and mandates. If regulations prohibit such behavior, the theory goes, then it will not happen. But things seldom go as planned, say free-market environmentalists, and often they go horribly wrong. First, some of the problems regulated by government may be more imagined than real. Regulatory agencies, like land management bureaucracies, have incentives to increase budgets, maintain power and prestige, and so forth, and the tendency of groups like the Environmental

Protection Agency is to regulate the tiniest of problems to gain those things. Second, regulations dealing with legitimate environmental problems have a tendency to become labyrinthine to the point of madness, reflecting the general micromanaging tendencies of regulatory bureaucracies and the fact that they are not subject to the costs imposed by their decisions.

Free-market environmentalists also argue that "command and control" alienates the regulated with draconian demands and abuses of power, allowing regulators to violate property rights with excessive use restrictions and takings, to dismiss local people's knowledge about and efforts to ameliorate problems, and avoid considering the costs involved in regulation. In other words, regulators and their champions demand maximum regulation because they gain benefits without having to bear any costs. Such regulation can even produce unintended consequences that border on the absurd. Certain requirements in the Endangered Species Act, free-market advocates claim, push some landowners to destroy habitat in order to avoid the burdens that would come if a protected animal took up residence on their land. Meanwhile, others try to avoid regulations strenuously, sometimes illegally, because the costs of compliance are often so high.[10]

A better approach, free-market environmentalists advise, is to abandon most or all environmental regulation and replace it with a combination of private property, economic incentives, markets, and tort law. Ideally this would involve the extensive, if not complete, privatization of resources. The argument is that privatization internalizes all benefits and costs, which is important not only for libertarian ideological reasons but also for behavior management. Property owners, the argument goes, have economic interests in their property. Generally they want wealth from it and will do what they can to get it. Thus owners will be less likely to clear-cut forested land, for example, if they will lose money by doing so, or if it lowers the long-term value of the land. Ranchers will not overgraze their lands if the costs exceed the benefits realized, farmers will not overuse their groundwater, and so forth. Full ownership forces users to consider the full costs of their actions, something with which government resource managers never have to contend. Without the incentive-distorting benefits of subsidies like below-cost grazing permits or timber sales, rational economic behavior will be environmentally sensitive behavior to boot.

Free-market environmentalists realize, however, that ownership might not be enough to foster environmentally sensitive behavior. Consider a timber owner's clear-cutting, which results in massive flooding, erosion, and water-quality problems for neighbors. What will prevent such things if there is no regulation of harvesting methods, water quality, and so on? Enter the courts, one of the few realms of legitimate government for free-market environmentalists. To work, advocates say, property rights must be well defined and secure; that is, they must entail clear rights and protections. One is the right to be free of "nuisance"—that is, subjected unwillingly to the detrimental effects of the activities of others and thus unable to fully utilize one's own property and rights. The government plays a vital role in the protection of these rights, and tort law and the court system are the mechanisms it should use. Thus, in an ideal free-market system, the victims of the erosion and flooding "nuisances," aided by strong laws defining their rights, take the offending clear-cutter to court for a cessation of the activity and sufficient compensation. Other timber owners, seeing the effectiveness of such lawsuits, will then have an incentive to avoid any kind of harvesting activities that might harm their neighbors and land them in court as well.

Free-marketers also recognize that even tort law and well-defined property rights might not always be enough. Many resources are not easily "decommonized" or clearly definable as private property. Factories releasing their wastes into the atmosphere or rivers, lakes, or the ocean might be clearly responsible for polluting the environment and creating a nuisance, but defining who owns the air or water, and therefore whose property rights are being violated, is a real problem. The fluid nature of some resources makes them difficult to privatize fully. In situations like these, free-marketers argue for "marketizing" the problem as much as possible. For air and water pollution, for example, they often suggest cap-and-trade approaches, wherein polluters must possess government-issued pollution permits equal to the levels of pollutants they currently release and which can be bought or sold. Polluters who reduce emissions will be able to sell unneeded permits to polluters who do not wish to make such reductions, generating financial incentives for lower emissions overall with a flexibility and sensitivity unavailable to "command and control" approaches.[11]

Free-market environmentalism takes as its foundation the idea that government is singularly ill-equipped to manage environmental problems. The cure must come instead from the invisible hand, from the information obtained from market prices, the incentives inherent in property rights and profits, and the common-law system that backs them up. Whether that cure can be effective is another question, of course, and free-market approaches have come under serious fire as a result. What is certain, however, is that free-market environmentalism is a product of specific postwar historical trends.

It is easy to assume that free-market environmentalism is primarily a product of the Wise Use and Sagebrush Rebellion movements of 1980s, which peaked at about the time that free-market approaches were first maturing. The three were ideological cousins, to be sure, chanting the mantra of individual rights, private property, and free markets, sharing a suspicion of government that bordered on contempt and an equally intense criticism of mainstream environmentalism. And there is no doubt that when free-market environmentalism began to gain an audience in the 1980s, the era's conservative political context was essential. There were a number of differences among the three, however, and it is important to recognize that the free-market approach was not simply an alternate version of the others. The roots of free-market environmentalism go deeper, and its analysis is much more sophisticated. It was a child of academic economics, born of debates over common-property resource management and the problem of externalities.

Environmental problems have long been a concern for economists. The twin specters of resource scarcity and overpopulation, with their potential to terminate economic growth and induce human misery, caught the attention of heavyweights like David Ricardo, John Stuart Mill, and, most famously, Thomas Malthus some two centuries ago. In the twentieth century, specialists like Kenneth Boulding, Harold Barnett, and Chandler Morse and groups like Resources For the Future and the Club of Rome brought scarcity concerns up to date with writings like "The Economics of the Coming Spaceship Earth," (1966), *Scarcity and Growth* (1962), and *The Limits to Growth* (1972). Economists, starting mainly with Arthur Pigou in the 1930s, began to take an interest in pollution; after World War II such interest increased significantly as massive environmental problems accompanied fantastic economic growth.[12]

A common characteristic of this new environmental interest was a healthy suspicion of free markets. Perhaps the best postwar example was K. William Kapp's 1950 book *The Social Costs of Private Enterprise*. Kapp, a German-born economist who spent his professional life in the United States, was deeply interested in externalities, the idea that costs associated with private enterprise are shifted to someone other than the person or entity to whom the benefits accrue, or to the public at large. Such externalization, he argued, was a hallmark of modern capitalism. Sometimes it was deliberate, but often it was simply inherent in the free-enterprise system itself, disguised by an a priori assumption that market economies function rationally and all costs of production are covered by "entrepreneurial outlays." Pollution of air and water, workplace exposure to toxic substances, soil erosion, deforestation, and depletion of coal reserves were particularly troubling examples of such externalities, and were at the core of Kapp's analysis of the problem. "Capitalism must be regarded as an economy of unpaid costs," he wrote acerbically toward the end of the book, and assumptions about its abilities to cover its costs fairly were ultimately "an institutionalized cover. . . [for] a form of large-scale spoliation which transcends everything the early socialists had in mind when they spoke of the exploitation of man by man."[13]

Often, accompanying suspicion of the free market among environmentally minded economists was a preference for state-centered approaches to solving the externality problem. Kapp's own faith in state-centered solutions was not great; even strong regulations, he argued, offered only limited amelioration, and what was needed was a wholesale rethinking of basic Western assumptions about economics. But other economists, such as Pigou, envisioned a major role for governmental tools, particularly taxation, subsidies, and legislation, in preventing externalities (the economist Ehrun Kula has called them "the interventionist school"). In the United States such an approach harkened back to the statist philosophy of Progressive conservation, and in the New Deal–influenced postwar economic climate, redolent of John Maynard Keynes and John Kenneth Galbraith, it had an obvious appeal to liberals and even some conservatives, as many of Barry Goldwater's sentiments suggested.

From such critiques would emerge, in the 1960s and 1970s, the field of "ecological economics." Led by figures like Herman Daly, this new branch of the discipline argued for the inclusion of biological and ecological realities in economic thinking. Nature matters, said ecological economists, but all too often the study of economics took unlimited natural resources and bottomless sinks for waste and pollution as givens, resulting in an irrational belief that economic growth was both inherently good and essentially endless. Free-market thinking has been particularly prone to such delusions, they argued, and the creation of an environmentally sustainable economic system will require considerable revamping of private enterprise.[14]

Free-market environmentalism emerged as a part of the larger postwar concern about environmental externalities, but its conclusions were worlds apart from the likes of Kapp and Daly. Deeply influenced by the so-called Austrian school of neoclassical economics and its American proponents at the University of Chicago, free-market environmentalists positioned themselves deliberately against the prevailing interventionist sentiment. Unlike some of the more fervent Wise Users, most free-marketers predicted no green road to serfdom as a result of command-and-control environmentalism. Nevertheless, they numbered among their influences economists and philosophers with less than sanguine opinions about the state and doubts about the alleged costs of private enterprise.[15]

Free-market environmentalism's intellectual foundations rest heavily on the work of certain postwar economists, not all of them of a particularly libertarian bent. Its focus on commons, for example, drew on the work of H. Scott Gordon, who in the 1950s was one of the first in the field to deal in detail with commons problems. In an influential 1954 article, he argued that ocean fisheries, as unmanaged common-property resources, gave fishermen a number of powerful incentives to overfish. A decade and a half later, ecologist Garrett Hardin would make this argument famous, but it was Gordon who did much of the analytical detail work, and free-marketers still cite him with regularity. Their take on tradable permits, meanwhile, reflected the influence of work on the topic by economists John Dales and T. D. Crocker (and others) in the 1960s.[16]

But the free-market movement had more direct roots, both intellectual and ideological, in the University of Chicago economics department, which was famous for its coterie of critics of Keynesianism and its spirited defense of neoclassical laissez-faire economics. While ideologically marginalized among its contemporaries, the libertarian-leaning "Chicago school" was also a hotbed of intellectual ferment and daring, garnering an impressive collection of Nobel Prizes and hosting some of the most famous names in twentieth-century economics. English-born Chicagoan Ronald Coase, for example, won the Nobel Prize in 1991 for his lifetime work, particularly for his 1960 article, "The Problem of Social Cost," which (it is claimed) is the most-cited article in economics. Coase rejected "interventionist" solutions to pollution and argued that such problems are best handled through bargaining between offender and offended when both possess well-defined property rights. Another Chicago economist, Harold Demsetz, took up Coase's idea and argued that the private-property approach could apply to a whole host of social problems. Free-market environmentalists seized on both and placed them at the center of their analysis. Coase was the single most important intellectual influence on the free-market movement, rivaled only by fellow Chicagoans Milton Friedman and Frederick Hayek.[17]

The Austrian-born Hayek, who would become a legend in conservative circles for his 1944 anti-collectivist book *The Road to Serfdom*, contributed significantly to the notion of government's inability to manage resources due to "incomplete information." He argued in a 1945 article, "The Use of Knowledge in Society," that the problem with central planning is that it cannot account for all the information necessary to make correct management decisions. Complete information on supply and demand is spread throughout society, he observed, with a little given to each member while the total remains elusive. The advantage of the market—Hayek called it a "marvel"—is that accumulated decisions of each "man on the spot," acting in his own interest and with what little information he possessed, could achieve what central planning could not: a nearly ideal distribution of resources. Free-marketers drew deeply on this idea in their criticism of government's "one size fits all" regulatory approach, its dismissal of local concerns and knowledge, and its insensitivity to regional characteristics. Friedman, meanwhile, generally had little to say about environmental issues, but as defender of free enterprise he offered the free-marketers a significant ideological inspiration.[18]

But another important intellectual influence on free-market environmentalism came not from economics but from the philosophizing ecologist Garrett Hardin. In 1968 he published one of the most famous pieces in the history of environmentalism, "The Tragedy of the Commons." It made a mighty splash, crossing over into a myriad of disciplines and launching a tidal wave of articles and books dealing with all aspects of the "commons problem." The essay dovetailed nicely with the work of economists like Gordon and appealed especially to Chicago-style economists, for it confirmed for them the drawbacks of a lack of property rights in the effort to protect nature. Hardin argued that commons inevitably suffer ecological damage from human use because there is no incentive or authority to manage their use. They force users to seize as much of a commonly held resource as they can as quickly as possible, each user knowing that if they don't, someone else will. Meanwhile, any associated costs are spread among all users while the benefits come mainly to those who succeed in grabbing them first. So powerful was this "commons effect" that it was tragic in the classic sense. "Each man," Hardin wrote, "is locked into a system that compels him to increase [his use of the commons] without limit—in a world that is limited. Ruin is the destination toward which all men rush, each pursuing his own best interest in a society that believes in the freedom of the commons. Freedom in a common brings ruin to all." Ecologically, this meant unstoppable depletion and destruction of the common resource.[19]

Hardin wasn't specific about a remedy beyond what he famously called "mutual coercion, mutually agreed upon" among resource users. He suggested privatization as one of several ways to achieve this, though his endorsement was lukewarm; privatization was inherently "unjust," but "injustice is preferable to total ruin," for the "alternative of the [unregulated] commons" was "too horrifying to contemplate." For neoliberal economists interested in the issue, however, privatization was the ideal form of mutual coercion precisely because it *wasn't* unjust. On the contrary, it respected individual rights and choices while simultaneously bringing the necessary management to the commons problem.[20] Shortly after Hardin's article was published, the first recognizable works of free-market environmentalism appeared in economics and political science journals. They were often densely intellectual works, tough to grasp fully without training, and at first there was little interest in them outside libertarian circles. Also, amid the Nixon-era florescence of the environmental-management state, few people seemed eager to suggest that this might be a questionable approach, especially before the jury was in on its effectiveness. By the decade's end, however, the "new resource economics" (as free-market environmentalism was sometimes called) would gain a hearing among other academics, analysts, journalists and, significantly, a number of politicians.

John A. Baden, a political economist who spent much of his professional life in Bozeman, Montana, would become the free-market movement's most important figure, as founder of two of its most important think tanks and a veritable one-man publishing house of "new resource" texts. Born and raised in the rural West, Baden took his PhD at Indiana University in 1969 and the next year published the first in a cascade of free-market analyses of environmental issues. With "a quick grin beneath his bushy mustache," Baden was a "vocal and enthusiastic" promoter of free-market ideals (he once wrote, tongue only halfway in his cheek, that Milton Friedman should be canonized, and was a member of Hayek's famous Mont. Pelerin Society)." He was a former logger, small-scale rancher, and outdoor enthusiast, and he chafed at the very idea of commons resources, especially their management by a government so obviously incapable of environmental sensitivity, efficiency, or respect for individual rights. Between 1970 and 1977 he wrote ten pieces on environmental topics, from water rights to recreation.[21]

In 1977, Baden and Hardin edited *Managing the Commons*, which centered on Hardin's famous "Tragedy" essay, outlined its history, and suggested potential solutions to the commons problem. Within a year or so, the "new resource economics" movement had its first official organization, the Center for Political Economy and Natural Resources at Montana State University in Bozeman, founded by Baden and his colleague Richard Stroup. Baden was the center's center, and his "abundance of energy and entrepreneurial drive," as a UC–Santa Barbara review board described his style in 1982, was one of its most crucial assets. He gathered a small but committed group of scholars who shared the neoliberal dedication to rights and markets and an aversion to central government. Many of them would go on to prominence in the free-market movement in later years, especially Richard Stroup, Terry Anderson, and Chicago-trained economic historian Peter J. Hill.[22]

For several years the center was the movement's institutional heart, and like most think tanks it hosted seminars and published articles and reports to spread its gospel to the wider world. Its most important product was the 1982 book *Bureaucracy vs. Environment: The Environmental Costs of Bureaucratic Governance,* which explored governmental failures in everything from forestry to grazing policy to reclamation and offered a spirited argument in favor of market-based alternatives. Meanwhile, the center began to attract funding from private sources such as the Carthage Foundation, the Liberty Fund, the Sarah Scaife Foundation, and the Mountain Fuel Supply Company (prompting critics of later free-market groups to accuse them of being thinly veiled covers for corporate interests and the conservative wing of the Republican Party). In 1982, Baden left to found the Bozeman-based Property and Environment Resource Center (PERC) with Anderson and Stroup, which remains the largest and best-known free-market environmental think tank in American environmentalism. Three years later, Baden left PERC to form the Foundation for Research on Economics and the Environment (FREE), where he remains as director. He continued to produce free-market literature at an impressive rate, writing, cowriting, or editing a small flood of books, articles, and commentaries.[23]

The early 1980s saw more free-market environmentalist writings, not just from Baden but from a widening pool of other authors and groups. One especially important venue was the Pacific Institute for Policy Research, which focused much of its energies on environmental issues and published a large amount of free-market literature. Many of its authors also did intellectual spadework in well-known think-tank publications like the libertarian Cato Institute's *Cato Journal* and *Regulation* magazine and the more traditionally conservative *Policy Review*, published by the Heritage Foundation. Think tanks were hardly a new development on the American political scene, but pointedly ideological ones were, particularly of the conservative and libertarian variety. They formed for a variety of reasons: as a general response to social ferment of the 1960s, to serve as counterweights to the perceived excesses of liberal think tanks like the Brookings Foundation, to give antistatism a firmer intellectual grounding (or just a veneer, their critics might have countered), and, most important, to mobilize, organize, and direct conservative political activities in an era when conservatives were struggling in elections. Free-market environmentalism was a natural fit with them, and vice versa; PERC and FREE were essentially issue-specific versions of the Cato Institute, and by the early 1980s it was becoming difficult to disentangle the free-market movement from conservatism and libertarianism writ large. The lines between them blurred further as free-market ideas gained traction with the number of Reaganites who were in a position to implement them.[24]

The growing popularity of free-market environmentalism paralleled a broader intellectual backlash against environmentalism embodied by Julian L. Simon. A professor of business at the University of Illinois with a doctorate from the University of Chicago, Simon was not a free-market environmentalist per se but shared its faith in the marketplace. He wrote extensively on environmental issues, especially resource scarcity and overpopulation, which he claimed were not actually problems at all. He was best known to environmentalists for his winning 1980 wager with ecologist Paul Ehrlich that the price of metals would decline over the next decade, which, he said, gave the lie to environmentalists' claims of an impending resource crisis. In books like 1981's *The Ultimate Resource*, Simon argued that population growth, because it generates increased social capital, actually reduces resource scarcity, lowers pollution levels, and increases overall quality of life, especially when paired with a market economy. Environmentalists and their allies in academia were scathing in their dismissals, but for the movement's critics, especially those of the free-market stripe, Simon's work gave them both intellectual ammunition and moral inspiration.[25]

The most thorough free-market critique on the U.S. Forest Service appeared in 1988, when Randal O'Toole, an economist and environmental consultant, published *Reforming the Forest Service*. The book was a ripsaw attack on Forest Service mismanagement, full of stinging criticisms of the ecological ravages and economic damage wrought by USFS bureaucrats. O'Toole argued that the USFS functioned mainly in the interest of maximizing its budget, with results devastating for both the environment and the taxpayer, although from the perspective of the Forest Service itself, such actions made perfect sense. The agency logged too much and charged too little for the resulting timber, built highly overengineered roads without recouping costs or considering need, placed itself at the service of narrow timber interests, and rationalized it all with propagandistic threats of "timber famine," twisted logic about the benefits of logging and road building, and unorthodox, faulty, even fraudulent accounting practices. In the process, it gained more timber-receipt funding, its managers got promoted, its congressional appropriations stayed high, and its clients in the timber industry remained happy. And until outside interests forced major rearrangements in the bureaucratic structure, none of this would change. "The Forest Service," O'Toole declared, "cannot reform itself."[26]

The remedy was the "marketization" of USFS practices to bring its incentives in line with environmentally and fiscally responsible actions: no more below-cost timber sales or subsidized road building, funding from net income, a focus on user fees instead of timber receipts, decentralization of forest planning and management, and so on. It was a measure of the growing popularity of at least some free-market environmental ideas that *Reforming the Forest Service* was the product of a mainstream publishing house, not a think tank, and that its sentiments would be embraced by many mainstream environmental groups (O'Toole himself would form the Thoreau Institute in the 1990s, a free-market environmental group based in Oregon, where he remains today).[27]

But 1991 was a banner year for free-market environmentalism, when Terry Anderson and Donald Leal published *Free Market Environmentalism*, the first single-volume synopsis of the movement's philosophies, arguments, and proposals. The book laid out the entire free-market argument: the role of incentives and information and the importance of property rights in using them properly, the government's long history of environmental and fiscal mismanagement, and the advantages of free-market alternatives to command and control. Individual chapters dealt with particular issues— national forests, reclamation, air and water pollution, and the like—and the resulting whole was a ringing indictment of traditional environmentalism and a call to arms for free-market approaches. It remains the most comprehensive treatment of free-market environmentalism available.[28]

With Anderson and Leal's book the free-market approach broke out of its small circle of champions and caught the attention of mainstream environmentalism. Recent policy developments gave free-marketers some reason to believe that their ideas might catch on. As early as the mid-1970s, the Environmental Protection Agency had adopted a tradable-permit approach to phasing out leaded gasoline, a result of its recognition of the economic burdens inherent in its regulatory approach. In the 1980s the Montreal Protocol on Substances That Deplete the Ozone Layer used a permit scheme to eliminate ozone-depleting CFCs, and the Clean Air Act of 1990 used permits to reduce acid rain–inducing sulfur emissions from coal plants. Some of the movement's champions had even gained the ear of powerful people in Washington, D.C. Interior Secretary James Watt, for example, tapped Richard Stroup as an adviser in the early days of the Reagan administration. Perhaps the best evidence of free-market environmentalism's coming out was the interest of outsiders, some of whom saw much to admire and others who dismissed it as "snake oil."[29]

Some of the strongest criticisms came from legal specialists, who took exception to what they considered the superficial and naïve invocation of common law and "environmentalism by tort." Such an approach, they argued, would require a massive increase in legal structure—more courts, lawyers, judges, experts, and so on—which, at the very least, would clash with the free-market mission to maximize efficiency and minimize bureaucracy and at worst create an endless nightmare of private lawsuits for every conceivable violation of environmental property rights. Furthermore, financial costs would likely be prohibitive for less affluent plaintiffs, and class action suits no guarantee of getting around the problem. Most industrial polluters would be able to hire more and better lawyers and experts who would only need to show reasonable doubt to emerge victorious. Powerful polluters might also pressure government into defining "rights" and "harm" in their favor, similar to the ways in which business interests lean on regulatory agencies to place their interests first. In the end, many lawyers, sensing the difficulties, would likely refuse to take on an environmental tort case at all, and, as law professor Edward Brunet noted, "for numerous private-property holders, the concept of 'free market' enforcement so zealously advocated [by free-marketers] is, in reality, no enforcement at all."[30]

Other critics, including not only lawyers but environmental activists and ecological economists, expanded the critique. Even free-market approaches with a proven track record like cap-and-trade, they argued, presented difficulties. First, there was the question of initial allocation: who would get allowances at the beginning of any trading scheme, and how many would they get? Experience in the 1970s and 1980s had resulted in some tweaking of later programs, but problems remained. Second, who would set the "cap" under which future programs would take place? Free-market advocates often argued that the cap should be set by bargaining among traders themselves and not by government regulators; critics countered that this would eliminate input from ecologists and biologists with a far better understanding of what constituted an environmentally safe capping level. Meanwhile, even if government regulators did set the cap, there would again be the problem of affected-party pressure for favorable levels. Third, there were equity issues. Cap-and-trade approaches aimed to reduce overall pollution in a given area, but within that area communities with limited political power—poor, nonwhite, or both—could be subject to disproportionate levels.[31]

Critics also attacked the free-market movement for its larger assumptions. Consider, they said, the argument that the state management is inherently myopic, self-interested, and wasteful. Rather than doing rigorous side-by-side comparisons of private and public approaches in particular situations, free-market environmentalists only offered caricatures of bureaucracy and anecdotes about government messes and free-market triumphs. In the real world, critics said, the significant transaction costs involved in coordinating large-scale environmental issues among a myriad of private owners, or those involved in tort-based enforcement of property rights, are often made *more* manageable by central agencies and regulations. Free-market environmentalists assume that humans are "rational economic animals," but critics asked whether economic interests alone were strong enough to induce ecologically sound behavior. Short-term economic needs—a chance for big profits, financial stresses caused by debt, and so forth—could trump any long-term incentive to manage in an environmentally sensitive way. The Dust Bowl region in the 1930s, argued law professor Eric Freyfogle, was almost a perfect anti-commons, its agricultural lands "divided into securely owned tracts" with clearly defined rights and economic incentives to take care of it. Market forces generated by World War I and later by the Depression, however, inspired a headlong rush to plow up the grasslands and plant crops, first to make a profit and later to avoid bankruptcy, with "results that half the continent could see": the great dust storms that would give the area its name.[32]

What do "secure property rights" really entail, asked the critics? Do they give owners near-absolute power to do what they want, as free-marketers seemed to suggest, subject only to nuisance-type laws? Or are property rights imbedded in a larger social context, upon which they are reliant for existence and to which they have certain obligations to limit their scope? Free-market environmentalism assumed a nineteenth-century vision of property as "eternal" and "absolute," critics said, with few to no community obligations attached, ignoring older conceptions of property rights that placed them firmly inside a larger context of community well-being and authority to manage private affairs to assure it. America's legal history gave little hope for the free-market approach. Before industrialism, American common law's emphasis on community rights served as a brake on environmental damage, preventing (for example) things like the flooding of both private and common riparian areas by milldam builders in New England. But under pressure from advocates of industrialization, common law gave way to a more industry-friendly, instrumentalist legal system that overlooked such damage, granted property owners wide latitude in the use of their property, and limited compensation for damages in the name of economic growth as the "greater good." This was the kind of private-property regime that free-marketers now took as an eternal given, and it was unlikely that free-market environmentalism could protect either nature or the public interest, critics concluded, when it relied on definitions so stacked in favor of economic exploitation.[33]

Critics also argued that there are more options for environmental protection than relying on either government or private enterprise. A historically informed look at the commons problem revealed that many communities had worked out arrangements to protect commons without capitalist-style property rights and wealth incentives. In other words, privatization was not the only answer. This particular critique was especially effective. In the revised 2001 edition of *Free Market Environmentalism*, Anderson and Leal devoted a chapter to the efficacy of communal management, which, they conceded, had considerable historical evidence backing it up.[34] Finally, critics hammered on the "liquidity" problem. Can certain parts of nature be privatized in any meaningful way? How does one privatize air? The ocean? Wildlife? Recognizing the problem early on, Terry Anderson and Peter Hill attempted to address the issue in a 1975 article titled "The Evolution of Property Rights: A Study of the American West," wherein they argued that the invention of cheap barbed-wire fencing made possible the privatization of the increasingly crowded and overgrazed open range. Inspired, other free-marketers concluded that other kinds of "fences" would follow in the future. "Advances in technology may yet allow the establishment of enforceable rights to schools of whales in the ocean, migratory birds in the air, and—who knows?—even the ozone layer," wrote Richard Stroup. "Such is the hope of free-market environmentalism."[35]

Herman Daly summed up the critical response nicely, and is worth quoting fully. We are told by free-market environmentalists, he writes, that

> all environmental problems can be solved by some high-tech analogue to the fencing of land or the branding of cattle. These new property-defining technologies will evolve in the future, just as fencing and branding. . . to give property-rights solutions to environmental problems. Wolves can be "fenced" with a radio-activated collar. . . that injects the animal with a tranquilizer when it crosses an electronic barrier so that it may be returned to its designated habitat (presumably the habitat owned or rented by its owner). Whales can be "branded" by genetic prints and monitored by satellites that would establish a mechanism for enforcing property rights in whales. If you want to save the whales you can buy some—and then spend all of your time and money in court enforcing your property right against whoever damages your whales with pollutants that have also been chemically "branded" and rendered traceable. Perhaps you could even sue another whale owner over custody of offspring. Litigation to establish the property rights of whale owners relative to [those of] krill owners will certainly enrich the lawyers. . . . [But] barbed wire fence was a cheap fencing material, not a conceptual breakthrough.

"Even with lasiometrics," he concluded, "apportioning the atmosphere remains unfathomable to anyone who tries to think it through."[36]

Since the 1990s, relatively little has changed for either free-market environmentalists or their critics. Free-market advocates—among them Karl Hess Jr. of the Thoreau Institute, the son of Goldwater speechwriter Karl Hess—continued to produce prodigious numbers of books and articles. With the 2000 election of President George W. Bush, who tapped both Hess and Terry Anderson as advisers, some advocates saw a glimmer of hope, but the Bush administration proved disappointing in its mere lip service to free-market principles and, in some cases, its outright rejection of them. Meanwhile, critics railed against the movement's coziness with conservative think tanks and its funding from right-wing foundations, extractive industries, and other corporations. Free-marketers responded that corporate sponsorship in particular was hardly limited to them, as a glance at the advertisements in *Sierra* or *Wilderness* would attest. In the early 2000s John Baden took heat for the seminars that FREE offered to federal judges, his critics arguing that they were an unethical attempt to manipulate judicial oversight of environmental regulation. But, overall, free-market environmentalism remained a fringe idea, an ideological pet project of libertarians and conservatives.[37]

The general feeling among mainstream environmentalists has been that the free-market movement is not "real" environmentalism, or even legitimate "green capitalism," but simply an intellectual veneer for a cruder antienvironmentalism not unlike the "intelligent design" movement's relationship to creationism. While its potential effectiveness is most certainly up for debate, it would be a mistake to equate free-market environmentalism with the Sagebrush Rebellion or the Wise Use movement, their ideological similarities notwithstanding. Parallels in rhetoric should not be taken as evidence of alliance. Hating the government gives many Americans common cause, but it takes more than that to keep them together, and the differences between free-marketers and antienvironmentalists can be significant. Take, for example, free-marketers' objections to below-cost USFS timber sales, BLM grazing permits, and federal reclamation as prime examples of government-subsidized environmental destruction. For the Wise Use movement, protecting those same subsidies was primary concern, and to suggest that they represented unfair payments to special interests was to risk a set of broken teeth. Also, free-market environmentalists have been far more nuanced in their analyses of opponents, blaming bureaucratic structures and incentives, and not caricatures of tree huggers, lunatics, communists, or jackbooted federal thugs for the ineffectiveness of regulatory environmentalism (although at times their morally loaded language—"green despots," "sylvan socialism," "environmental feudalism"—could undercut their sophistication).[38]

Instead of being simple antienvironmentalists, free-market advocates exemplify Samuel Hays's thesis about postwar American environmentalism as a product of middle-class status. Firmly rooted in the conditions and characteristics necessary for environmental sentiments—educated, financially well-off, and decidedly consumerist in their approach to quality of life—they are environmentalists in the Hays mold. Their disagreements with other environmental activists have been profound, to be sure, but they all have valued environmental protection. Their differences lay in their answers to the questions of what exactly needs protection, and who or what is best suited to provide it. Free-market environmentalism, in other words, is a strongly conservative/libertarian variation on Hays's middle-class environmentalist theme.

The movement's future seems unclear, however, for it is fraught with deep tensions and contradictions. As historian William Cronon has suggested in his *Changes in the Land,* since colonial times Americans have believed that "wilderness should turn a mart" and have striven to transform the natural world into a land of fields and fences by the use of property rights, legal structure, and free enterprise. Over three centuries the costs have been enormous—the nation's environmental history suggests strongly that the free market has been its single biggest source of environmental harm—but the "marketizing" mission has remained powerfully attractive. Free-market environmentalism has been alluring because it suggests that one can have one's capitalist cake and eat it too, as it were, offering a whiggish environmentalism that relies on, even celebrates, familiar American ideals while avoiding tough questions about their implications.[39]

Despite their wider embrace of free enterprise and consumerism, relatively few Americans have been entirely comfortable with the idea that the cure for environmental ills is more and better capitalism. The postwar environmental movement may have been rooted in affluence, but its members sometimes asked uncomfortable questions, setting themselves against the ethic of human dominance over nature that they believed was inherent in American capitalism. For them, in other words, the environmental crisis was a cultural crisis. But for free-market adherents, the "system" is fundamentally sound and environmental degradation merely an indication of its imperfect function, easily solved by some institutional tweaking: removing a regulatory burr, tightening a legal screw, replacing a faulty bureaucratic part. Nothing in capitalism's deeper assumptions about property and profit warrants much reflection, criticism, or change. For free-market environmentalists it is *only* through privatizing nature that it can be best protected. The tension inherent in placing nature in the care of an institution that has played such an important role in its destruction goes unmentioned. While the free market may augment command-and-control approaches, it seems hard to imagine that it will supplant them anytime soon.

A deep irony in free-market environmentalism is that it shares a great deal with the Progressive conservation movement that it explicitly rejects. Like conservationists before them, for example, free-market advocates viewed nature as a collection of resources for human use and little else, with no moral obligations to protect it for its own sake or even to take its needs into consideration. Ecologically derived limits on human behavior had no relevance outside their role in producing goods for the market, and to suggest otherwise was to be accused of taking an "emotional" or even "religious" approach, as both conservationists and free-market environmentalists prided themselves on their cool, detached, objective (and decidedly masculine) rationality. Unlike bird watchers and tree huggers, they congratulated themselves for thinking with their heads, not their hearts.

The similarities ran deeper, however. In his 1998 book *Seeing Like a State*, political scientist James Scott offers a withering indictment of central government. Life at the "vernacular level," as Scott calls it, is an immensely complicated business, in which common people develop intricate local worlds of law, custom, and language that seem enigmatic and "opaque" to outsiders. Such opacity has been an especially thorny problem for large ruling bodies, and traditionally they have responded by attempting to standardize local worlds in order to render them easier to manage, using standard weights and measures, cadastral maps, surnames, legal codes, and even architecture. Scott calls the twentieth-century version of this "high modernism"—an amalgamation of science, bureaucracy, and faith in rational social planning by trained experts. Whatever the name, the end result has usually been failure. Central planning cannot perceive, let alone control, the complexities of local worlds, Scott argues, and in its attempts to do so, it has often run roughshod over democratic rights and valuable local "unscientific" knowledge, usually engendering considerable resistance in the process.[40]

This all sounds familiar to free-market environmentalists, especially when Scott ventures into the issue of central-state management of nature. For him, such management serves as metaphor for the larger ills of centralized planning as a whole. As his example, he uses nineteenth-century German scientific forestry, the forerunner and inspiration for American Progressive conservation. The German government, Scott argues, viewed its forests as merely timber. Revenue was the only thing that it wanted from them. It could see nothing else in them, and employed scientific management that radically simplified forest ecology in order to extract it: monocultures, even-aged stands, scheduled rotations, and pesticide applications.

But after initial successes, the forests' ecological health, and therefore yield, declined precipitously. Conservation forestry's Achilles heel was that it destroyed the ecological characteristics of the forest outside those related to timber yield. In creating a forest to serve narrow economic ends, it devalued any other functions and in the end impoverished the whole resource. "The utilitarian state," Scott writes, "could not see the real, existing forest for the (commercial) trees."[41]

One can almost hear the cheers of vindication from free-market environmentalists, and not without good reason. The free-market interpretation has much to offer American environmentalism about the pitfalls of central-state management. Its sophisticated critique of bureaucratic structure, lack of good information, and incentives suggest, as Scott does, that command-and-control approaches can sometimes be alarmingly ill-suited to the job of protecting both natural and social diversity—a judgment that American environmental history confirms. In the same vein, the free-marketers' stress on local interests and knowledge complements Scott's praise for indigenous modes of life and production, recognizing the importance of decisions made in situ. After deep reading in free-market literature, it is difficult to embrace state environmental management without at least a hint of apprehension.

But on the other hand, free-market environmentalists have missed an equally important if subtle point in Scott's argument. Conservatives and libertarians often "forget or ignore the fact," he wrote, "that in order to do its work, the market requires its own vast simplifications in treating land (nature) and labor (people) as factors of production (commodities). This, in turn, can and has been profoundly destructive of human communities and of nature." In the final analysis this may be free-market environmentalism's most fundamental flaw: the inability to see the similarities between itself and the command-and-control system it has so passionately opposed. The ideological commitment to property and profits can be, in the end, as blind to ecological complexity as any government-centered management scheme. Put another way, the free-market represents another version of "high modernism." It also sees like a state, and tomorrow's free-market environmentalists might do well to ask how their vision of the environmental future will, in the end, look much different.[42]

For free-market environmentalists, government was the enemy of both private interest and environmental health. Edward Abbey would have agreed, but only in a general way. He easily matched them—far outstripped them, in fact—in his disdain for the state. But he had even less faith in capitalism than he did in government. For him, the two were partners in exploitation, and preserving human freedom and the nonhuman environment involved not keeping business safe from the state but keeping nature safe from either. To Abbey's fascinating views on the relationship between wilderness and corporate/state tyranny, we turn next.

— 5 —

LIKE A SCARLET THREAD

Into the Political Wilderness with Edward Abbey

No undertakers wanted; no embalming (for godsake!); no
coffin. . . . Wrap my body in my anarch's flag. But bury me if
possible; I want my body to help fertilize the growth of a cactus,
or cliffrose, or sagebrush, or tree, etc. Disregard all state laws
regarding burials.
                              —*Edward Abbey's funeral instructions, 1981*

IN 1888 JOURNALIST EDWARD BELLAMY PUBLISHED A SMALL NOVEL
called *Looking Backward, 2000–1887*. Its protagonist, Julian West, was a conservative middle-class Bostonian who had fallen asleep in his basement
chamber in 1887 and awoken 113 years later to find himself in the midst of
a high-tech socialist Eden. The ruthless industrial capitalism of his own
day had evolved into a cooperative commonwealth where citizens labored
together, shared the resulting bounty, and enjoyed cradle-to-grave health
care and room and board. War, crime, and corruption had been extermi-
nated. Education and the arts flourished. Technology enriched life in a million ways—from live music piped into homes to automated awnings that
covered the sidewalks when it rained. Watching over it all was the American government, organized and staffed by specialists who had society's best
interests at heart, a paragon of benevolent social engineering to which the
citizenry submitted willfully, thankfully, and completely. In an era frayed
by labor strife, urban blight, and garish displays of robber-baron wealth,
Looking Backward proved wildly popular.[1]

Whatever other attractions Bellamy's utopia might have had, close
physical or spiritual contact with nature was not one of them. The world of

Looking Backward was a thoroughly humanized one where nature, if it was visible at all, deferred to rational planning as surely as the people did. West's new companions were shocked to hear, for example, that nineteenth-century Boston had no sidewalk awnings, and considered it "an extraordinary imbecility to permit the weather to have any effect on the social movements of the people." No one gave a thought to the countryside outside Boston or even expressed a desire to escape the city. Such was not the case, however, in the twentieth century's two best-known novels about technocratic central states, Aldous Huxley's *Brave New World* and George Orwell's *1984*. There the natural world offered a counterweight to authoritarian state control. *Brave New World*'s John the Savage was the only authentic human being in an otherwise rigidly engineered society, his New Mexico reservation home a strange, myth-haunted wildland nonetheless preferable to Soma-doped "civilization." In *1984*, Winston Smith found momentary relief from Big Brother in a secluded glade in the English countryside, entranced by the song of a thrush. In the end the State triumphed, of course, but the natural world offered escape for a while.[2]

Edward Paul Abbey was more confident in nature's benefaction. Known primarily as an essayist, in 1980 he tried his hand at futuristic fiction with *Good News*. That book was no Bellamyesque tale of socially engineered paradise. It opened with a world where state, military, and corporate power had combined to create a regime less intensively authoritarian than *1984* or *Brave New World* but no less pervasive, a techno-dystopia of broken familial and social bonds, soulless work, and meaningless leisure, its anxieties medicated by television, rock music, and consumerism. "Not so much unbearable as unreal," as Abbey described it in setting the scene, "not a nightmare of horror but a nightmare of dreariness, a routine and customary tedium." But in *Good News* the central state did not triumph. Wracked by pollution, overpopulation, and scarcity, its cities collapsed in a spasm of starvation and war. Meanwhile, deliverance waited in the wild country beyond, where scattered survivors pulled together to "rebuild the simple farming and pastoral economy that had been destroyed by the triumph of the city, trying to re-create a small society of friends in a community of mutual aid and shared ownership of land." The bulk of the novel revolved around the conflict between those survivors and the remaining technocrats and militarists who sought to reconstitute what had been lost. Abbey was vague about the eventual outcome, but it was clear where his sympathies lay. For Bellamy, nature didn't seem to exist, and for Huxley and Orwell, it was overshadowed by tyranny. In *Good News* nature was the preservation of the world.[3]

So it was in reality as well. To Abbey, the threat of tyrannical social engineering by a powerful high-tech government was no mere plot device. "The central conflict" of the twentieth century, he once wrote, was the story of "individuals, families [and] communities" struggling "to preserve their freedom [and] integrity against the overwhelming power of . . . modern techno-industrial military superstates," and the future was likely to bring more of the same. "I do believe we live in real danger," he warned in 1972, "of having a technocratic technotronic totalitarianism forced upon us . . . , a nightmare world in which Mao Tse-Tung Jr. writes the official philosophy, in which [Buckminster] Fuller builds geodesic domes over the cities . . . [and] in which somebody like Richard Nixon explains that it's all for the best and is only temporary." Such a world had the potential to make "Orwell's *1984* . . . look like the last phases of the Golden Age."[4]

But there was an avenue of escape: the wilderness. For Abbey, wilderness was not just land as Nature had made it, unpopulated and untouched. It was also a symbolic and a literal refuge from the tyranny of the state, and a crucible for the creation of a democratic, decentralized, agrarian alternative. Environmental protection was thus never "a question merely of preserving forests and rivers, wildlife and wilderness," he wrote in 1979, "but also of keeping alive a certain way of human life. . . . If we can draw the line against the industrial machine in America, and make it hold, then perhaps in decades to come we can gradually force industrialism underground, where it belongs, and restore to all citizens of our nation their rightful heritage of breathable air, drinkable water, open space, family-farm agriculture, a truly democratic political economy." Every "square mile of range and desert saved from the strip miners, every river saved from the dam builders, every forest saved from the loggers, every swamp saved from the land speculators, means another square mile saved for the play of human freedom."[5]

Among the most renowned American nature writers of the twentieth century, Edward Abbey liked to deny that he was one at all. "I am not a naturalist," he insisted in the introduction to his 1977 essay collection *The Journey Home*. "The only Latin I know is *omnia vincit amor*—and *in vino veritas*. . . . The only birds I can recognize without hesitation are the turkey vulture, the fried chicken, and the rosy-bottomed skinny dipper." Such statements came with tongue planted firmly in cheek, but there was a grain of truth in them, for

Abbey bore little resemblance to the genre's archetypal member. Over a thirty-five-year career that produced twenty-one books and a mass of articles, reviews, and essays, he trafficked in the same themes as Muir and Thoreau: the beauty and value of wild land, the superiority of pastoral life, the venality of modern urban civilization, and the urge to escape it.

There the similarities ended. His blunt writing style was in sharp contrast to the filigreed prose of Thoreau, and his favorite landscapes—the slickrock canyons of Utah, the Sonoran desert of Arizona, the tablelands of New Mexico—were not the usual haunts of most forest- and mountain-writers. And Abbey was earthy in ways few naturalists were—a vigorous boozer and a relentless philanderer who felt little need to conceal his lustful side (it is hard to imagine Thoreau or Muir, for example, penning explicit verses about their sex lives, as Abbey did in the poems "I Wish" and "Two Profane Love Songs"). Nevertheless, his 1968 *Desert Solitaire,* a collection of essays about his experiences as a ranger at Arches National Monument, became a classic of environmentalist literature in the vein of *Walden* and *My First Summer in the Sierra.* By the time of his death in 1989, Abbey was something of a minor legend.[6]

He was an intensely political writer. Perhaps no author in the environmental genre was more outspoken in criticizing government, or more zealous in his distrust of centralized power and manipulative bureaucracy. Few railed against the State's obsession with economic growth and high-technology with such eloquent fury. Few, excepting Wendell Berry, argued for agrarianism with as much passion. And few, if any, linked the destruction of nature to the domination of humans as tightly as Abbey did. For him, preserving human freedom went hand-in-hand with protecting the environment. The first could not survive without the second, and the key to limiting the power of the technoindustrial state was to deny its ability to control nature. Abbey's literary mission, then, involved more than celebrating the natural world or moaning about its destruction. He put pen to paper, he believed, to defend individual freedom and community integrity against the expansion of state power. "Most of my writing," he once observed, "has been . . . [about] the traditional conflict between our instinctive urge toward fraternity, community, and freedom, and the opposing demands of discipline and the state. . . . That theme, like a scarlet thread, runs through everything I have written, binding it together into whatever unity it may have." In "A Writer's Credo," he declared: "I write to . . . oppose, resist and sabotage the contemporary drift toward a global technocratic police state, whatever its ideological coloration. I write to oppose injustice, to defy power, and to speak for the voiceless."[7]

Certainly Abbey's bluntness could make him hard to like—historian Patricia Nelson Limerick once noted wryly that he was blessed with "freedom from politeness"—as could his rampant sexism. He claimed that his opposition to Latino immigration was a result of his cultural preferences, but the line between "culturalism" and racism in Abbey's writings was often perilously thin; when he celebrated agrarian life, it was a particularly white Anglo-Saxon version that he held up. Environmental historians, however, have been wary of him mainly because of his association with wilderness. Far from being untouched and timeless when Europeans arrived, the American "virgin" wilderness was home to millions of Native people and had been for thousands of years, shaped extensively by their farming, hunting, and burning. Nevertheless, advocates of wilderness preservation have traditionally perpetuated the virgin myth with talk of escaping civilization for the purity of the wild, a "flight from history" (in William Cronon's words) that avoids both historical reality and social responsibility. Because few writers have been as closely aligned with wilderness preservation as Abbey, historians have tended to dismiss him accordingly. Limerick has argued that "when it came to the basic conceptual problems of wilderness advocacy, Abbey carried a full set," and historian Elliott West has called him "the modern master of the adolescent male escape fantasy."[8]

Such critiques bring a welcome sophistication to our understanding of the wilderness idea, but as historian Paul Sutter has argued in *Driven Wild*, for wilderness (as for everything else) historical context is essential; how people define "wilderness" depends on the specific social, cultural, and political circumstances in which they live. Sutter shows how the interwar advocacy group The Wilderness Society formed in response to specific resource-management issues to the 1920s and 1930s, such as the rise of the automobile, the growing popularity of auto-centered recreation and a consumerist approach to nature, and the explosion of road building in U.S. Forest Service lands. Virgin-wilderness myths may have had an influence on the group, but they were hardly paramount.

So it was for Edward Abbey. His "wilderness" was not a rehash of the virgin myth but a sophisticated concept lashed tightly to some of the most important developments in twentieth-century American history. He grew up in rural Appalachia, and the region's history of human and ecological exploitation at the hands of timber and coal companies and their allies in government colored his later ideas about nature, agrarian life, and democracy. He served as a military policeman after World War II, which reinforced his antistatist tendencies, and went on to live in the postwar American West, where the growing presence of the federal government coincided with the era's conservative backlash. Both would leave a deep mark on his thinking and writing. His work also echoed the antiauthoritarian and antistatist critiques coming from the New Left, the counterculture, and their descendants. These diverse circumstances and influences combined to shape Abbey's definition of wilderness into an explicitly late-twentieth-century political one. Whatever else they might have been, Abbey's thoughts on the relationship among wilderness, human freedom, and the State were not simply flights from history. On the contrary, they were a creation of and a reaction to it.[9]

Abbey spent his formative years in western Pennsylvania, and we must begin there if we are to analyze him as a product of history. From his birth in 1927 to his departure for the U.S. Army in 1945 (and briefly again after the war), Abbey lived among the small towns, farms, forests, and mines of the Allegheny mountains east-southeast of Pittsburgh, and these places were vital to the development of his adult ideas and attitudes. His most thorough and sensitive biographer, James Calahan, lays particular emphasis on his Appalachian childhood. Few readers grasp the significance of the region to Abbey's development as a writer, Calahan has argued, highlighting Abbey's use of names, places, and events from his youth in his fiction. But Appalachia's influence went far beyond place-names and pastoral memories. The region's social and cultural history bore directly on Abbey's later convictions about politics, power, and the natural world. The broad outlines of his "political wilderness" formed amid a natural environment battered by a half-century of boom-and-bust logging and mining and a social world stripped of its agrarian roots. It was there that he first learned to fear the state, and to see life on the land as the key to freedom.[10]

    Appalachian Wilderness, one of his first books after *Desert Solitaire*, was full of admiration for mountain life and reminiscences of his youth. Sometimes he could tend to the maudlin on such topics—"my deepest emotions," he observed mistily in a 1982 essay, "those so deep they lie closer to music than words - were formed . . . by intimate association with in childhood with the woods on the hill, the stream that flowed through the pasture, the oaken timbers of the barn, the well, the springhouse, the sugar maples, the hayfields." Similar references peppered such essays as "Blood Sport" and "Shadows from the Big Woods." Abbey even claimed that he was born in a cabin by candlelight and raised on a farm near the tiny agricultural community of Home, Pennsylvania. He actually came into the world like most other twentieth-century Americans, in the local hospital beneath electric lights and with medical staff in attendance; he did not live on a farm until he was fourteen. Nevertheless, he was a legitimate son of lower-class rural Appalachia. His family was not destitute or without education, but they were hardly elitists. His father, Paul, labored in blue-collar jobs for most of his life, and his mother, Mildred, was a schoolteacher born to a family of local businessmen. The couple's farm, purchased during Abbey's adolescence, was never more than a shade above hardscrabble. He did his share of chores there, although in contrast to his praise of farm life as an adult, as a teen he was not especially fond of pitching manure and mending fences.[11]

Abbey often identified less with southwestern Pennsylvania than nearby eastern Kentucky and West Virginia. His thinly disguised autobiographical novel *The Fool's Progress* featured the journey of a dying man from urban Arizona back to the fictional "Stump Crick, West Virginia," suggesting that he longed for more southern roots. It also suggested the degree to which that region's history shaped three important themes that would surface later in his writings: the coarse but honest self-sufficiency of farm life, its connection to the land, and the collusion of Big Government and Big Business in its destruction.[12]

"Few areas of the United States in the late nineteenth century," wrote historian Ronald Eller in 1982, "more closely exemplified Thomas Jefferson's vision of a democratic society than did the agricultural communities of southern Appalachia." To be sure, the area was never a pure bastion of pre-capitalist values or a backward region passed over by history. Many mountaineers participated enthusiastically in the market revolution, especially with cattle and timber, and the region's river-valley towns were home to elites whose visions of economic progress and prosperity differed little from boosters elsewhere. Similarly, speculation and absentee land ownership were common even in the remotest backcountry. Still, that backcountry was among the last places in the East to be transformed by industrialization, and its social and cultural makeup revealed the relatively light touch of the market's hand. It was also largely free of government influences beyond local politics, circuit courts, and the postal system, as few roads or rails linked it to larger centers of power until near the end of the century. Mountain folk often had little use for outside authority. Western Pennsylvania was the locus of the famous 1794 Whiskey Rebellion, for example, and it is easy to imagine Abbey, who hated government as much as he loved whiskey, hoisting his musket among the rebels had he lived then. "Scattered, loosely integrated, and self-sufficient island communities" defined the region's social geography, and together its residents wrote the rules that governed life there.[13]

Most backcountry Appalachians before the early 1900s lived on farms clustered along bottomlands, from which they met most of their needs save for manufactured goods. Biological diversity was a hallmark, and a typical farm consisted of fields of corn, a garden, orchard, beehive, pasture, streams, and woodland. Dogs, chickens, and geese ran in the yards, and pigs and cattle roamed the nearby forest. Horses, mules, and dairy cows supplied muscle power and milk, and sheep grazing the hillsides provided wool for clothing and blankets. What the farm could not produce could be found in the adjoining forest or purchased in the nearest town or from itinerant peddlers. Life on a backcountry farm required intense labor and a capacity to endure isolation, especially for women, who not only shouldered many of the physical burdens of farm life but the patriarchal ones as well. Yet it was for many mountaineers an honest, rewarding, and familiar lifestyle.[14]

Agrarian self-sufficiency precluded the rise of complex social and cultural organization in the mountains. In turn, the "absence of highly structured communities and formal social institutions contributed," Eller writes, "to the evolution of a comparatively open and democratic social order in the mountains" and "the emergence of strong egalitarian attitudes and beliefs" among the mountaineers, as well as a sense of being one's own master—all of which Abbey would have in spades. "'I'm as good as you are' and 'I'm as good as he is' were stock expressions recorded in almost every account of premodern mountain life," notes Eller, indicative of the area's profound "democratic ethos." Individualism existed within a larger context of social ties, however. Strong nuclear families and kin networks united the mountaineers and defined their responsibilities. Worship brought them together in rustic Baptist and Methodist churches and camp meetings, as did births, weddings, and funerals, court cases, and campaign speeches. Cooperative labor brought them together as well, for barn raisings, clearing land, harvesting, road maintenance, and so forth. Of course, some individuals were more free and independent than others, for Appalachia was strongly patriarchal and cloven along class lines like the rest of rural America. Yet there were few better real-world models for Abbey's later agrarian leanings.[15]

Appalachia not only provided Abbey an ideal—and idealized—social model, it also supplied him with a template for threats to it. From the end of the nineteenth century to the 1920s, the backcountry would be drawn into the American industrial orbit by lumber and coal industries and their allies in government, and that landscape and way of life would be devastated in the process. Farming life would be replaced, at least partially, by wage dependency, poverty, and the vagaries of the market. Community and family bonds would dissolve, shift, or at least weaken, and the land itself would be shaven clean by loggers and disemboweled by miners, its wealth flowing to faraway centers of capital. By the time of Abbey's birth in 1927, traditional backcountry Appalachia was largely a thing of the past.

Timber interests came first to the mountains, followed by coal, motivated by the spirit of enterprise and the invitation of local and state governments. These industries were assisted immensely by the spread of the railroads. In the wake of the Civil War, local boosters trumpeted the region's natural wealth—much of which they held title to—in an effort to attract outside investment. State governments did likewise, sensing vast economic potential in an era of rapid industrialization. Meanwhile, urban intellectuals pushed economic modernization as a way to redeem the region's reputation as a place populated by backward hillbillies. Industry needed little encouragement, though, as it was already well aware of Appalachia's natural riches. By the 1880s a bundle of new rail lines threaded the region, and soon it swarmed with land agents and speculators of both local and alien origin, intent on securing mineral and timber rights.[16]

With little cash and a shrinking land base due to population growth, many mountaineer families saw few reasons not to sign over rights to resources they might never use. Their inexperience with industrial capitalism and its legal mechanisms, however, put them at a disadvantage. Some gave away vast resources for a few dollars, a good mule, or a rifle. Others willingly signed the notorious broad form deed, which gave the lessee unlimited access to a parcel's timber or coal and which allowed any method of extraction, no matter what the effects on the land. Those mountaineers who were unwilling to sign—their numbers increased as the enormity of modernization became clear—could be forced to knuckle under through legal pressure or simple subterfuge. In some mountain counties, outsiders eventually controlled between 50 and 90 percent of the resource-bearing land.[17]

The result was a sweeping severance of the mountaineer community from its traditional way of life. Mountaineers were now shackled to the fortunes of the market, dependent for their welfare, and even survival, on economic forces beyond their control. Many departed their farms for dangerous and low-paying jobs in mining and manufacturing, exchanging the insecurities of agrarianism for those of wage labor in a volatile economic sector. After the day's work they retired to ugly and unsanitary company towns, their behavior tightly policed by guards and overseers. Meanwhile, Appalachia's natural wealth migrated into the hands of entrepreneurs from the nation's investment capitols, and the land lay cut-over, eroded, and dotted by tailings that leached chemicals into nearby streams and rivers.[18]

By the 1920s, as Eller writes, the mountaineers had become miners and millhands, bereft of the rough independence that had characterized their lives. Their limited attempts to defend their interests—organizing, unionizing, striking—would be struck down harshly by their employers. They had few friends in officialdom, for in the new Appalachia the line between private capitalism and public government was porous. Corporate influence on state and local government was a nationwide hallmark of the Gilded Age, but it was all the more intense in the mountains. Coal companies dominated state politics from the county courthouses to governors' mansions. "Some counties" in Appalachia, Eller writes, "were little more than industrial autocracies," where company representatives and political officeholders were the same people. The entire state of West Virginia was essentially a fin de siècle coal-baron fiefdom, where both political parties and the legislature largely served the interests of the companies. Coal companies worked hard to kill labor, safety, and antipollution laws, prevent the implementation of progressive tax schemes, avoid compensation payments to injured workers, and secure government help in suppressing labor unrest. Sometimes they even usurped local government services, staffing and paying county sheriff posts and police forces and "assisting" miners in "proper" voting at election times. Should the workers prove too rowdy, management could count on the state militia to restore order.[19]

When it was all over in the late 1920s, rural Appalachia was a shell of what it has been. "By then," writes historian Ronald Lewis, "entire ecosystems had been destroyed, the backcountry had been tied to the market system, independent farmers had become wage hands, and the political system had been transformed into a mechanism for the protection of capital." Timber and coal companies "had never expressed a deep concern for the mountain people," Eller observes, and "came into the region for the sole purpose of extracting the natural resources . . . as quickly and as profitably as possible." An alliance of government and business had turned Appalachia's nature into economic and political power and its agrarian backcountry citizens into subjects.[20]

The mountaineers' traditional independence and the bitterness many of them felt toward industrial capitalism deeply colored Abbey's early years. His father, Paul, for example, spent part of his own childhood on an Allegheny farm and dropped out of school at an early age to go to work. By twenty-six he had earned his blue-collar credentials in various mills, working for wages like so many other rural highlanders. He eventually left the mills—going on strike, he called it—and spent the rest of his life working in real estate, selling magazines, farming, driving a bus, and cutting pit props for the local coal mines. By all accounts, he was a well-read, hardheaded, intensely opinionated man who detested the rich and powerful—"one man's as good as another," Paul would tell his sons, in Appalachian style, "if not a damned sight better." Abbey's brother Howard characterized their father as "anti-capitalistic, anti-religion, anti-prevailing opinion, anti-booze, anti-war and anti-anyone who didn't agree with him." Young Edward would grow up to be a lot like his father, save for the teetotaling.[21]

Unlike his son, however, Paul retained faith in the power of government until he died. His particular choice grew out of his experiences in Appalachia's mills. He was a self-described socialist/Marxist who read *Soviet Life* religiously, idolized Eugene V. Debs and supported Norman Thomas for president. Paul's Marxism was never doctrinaire or even particularly well-formed. In letters to his son, he fulminated against wealthy politicians of both parties but never talked of modes of production, superstructure, or dictatorships of the proletariat. Nor did he seem troubled by Communist-bloc authoritarianism or poverty. Paul's letters from a trip to Cuba, for example, have a rose-colored tint: "I've never seen so many happy people [or] such comradship [sic] . . . [as on] the most beautiful and inspiring Isle of Youth." He also despaired that his son would never see the political light. "I wish you could see as I do," Paul told his son in 1987, "how necessary communism is to 90% of the world's population." As a teenager, Abbey wore Norman Thomas campaign buttons to school, but as an adult, his visceral mistrust of industrialism, collectivism, and powerful government pushed him away from the Left. His father's broader influence on him, however, is clear.[22]

The same can be said of the industrialization of backcountry Appalachia.

By the time Edward Abbey was born, the region had been fully industrial-ized, but the remnants of its older ways informed his view of life. His heroes and villains in the postwar Southwest bore a close resemblance to the mountaineers and the corporate/government combines that so profoundly shaped the land and society of his youth. He wasn't always specific about their influence, but he knew it was there. In a 1973 letter to the *New York Review of Books* (which was never printed; Abbey bitterly scrawled the word "suppressed" in dark ink across the top), he drew the connection. True qual-ity of life could not be found in "the endless production of junk," he fumed, but in "breathable air and edible bread . . . and freedom from more and more technological tyranny. . . . Industrialism, beyond the optimal point, which we passed about seventy years ago, tends to impoverish, not enrich our lives. . . . Ask any Appalachian. Ask me."[23]

Abbey got his first real taste of the government he would grow to despise during World War II. In the summer of 1945, eighteen years old and newly drafted, he left the family farm and shipped off to basic training. He arrived in Italy in December and served as a military policeman until his discharge in February 1947. Years later the irony of a self-styled anarchist and sworn enemy of bureaucracy working as a uniformed governmental authority delighted him. In "My Life as a P.I.G., or, the True Adventures of Smoky the Cop," he worked it for laughs. "Some sergeant put a black and white Nazi-like armband on my sleeve, a white helmet liner on my head, a nifty red scarf around my neck, and a .45 automatic in my hands," he reminisced about his first days on the job. "At once I began to feel mean, brutal, arbitrary, righ-teous. 'Let's stop coddling criminals,' I wrote home to mother, that first night in Napoli; 'let's put father in jail where he belongs.'" During his long career as a Forest Service and National Park Service seasonal employee, Abbey reprised his law-enforcement role a number of times, his sense of irony intact and his antiauthoritarianism undimmed. "An odd part to play, you might think, for one who fancies himself a libertarian, an anarchist, a dedicated scofflaw," he later observed. "Perhaps not. I've never known a serious policeman who had much respect for the law; in any well-organized society the police constitute the most lawless element."[24]

Upon his discharge, Abbey enrolled at Indiana State Teachers Col-lege in Pennsylvania and promptly drew attention to himself by posting an antidraft letter around campus that set the tone for the rest of his career. "Send your draft card with an explanatory letter to the President," he urged.

"He'll greatly appreciate it, I'm sure." The FBI was not so appreciative. In the heated atmosphere of the Cold War, such sentiments caught their attention, and for the next twenty years they monitored Abbey's activities and interviewed associates about his lifestyle, habits, and beliefs. By 1967 they had scraped together a small file before ceasing their observation. When he finally saw the file in 1983, he was sorely disappointed. "I haven't the slightest doubt," he had written in the 1970s, "that the FBI, the NSA, the CIA, and the local cops have dossiers on me a yard thick. If they didn't, I'd be insulted." In reality, they had about an inch's worth.[25]

Abbey first traveled in the West in 1944, while hitchhiking his way around the country, and the austere beauty of the landscape made a powerful impression on him. In "Hallelujah on the Bum," he remembered himself as a "bold, stupid, sun-dazzled kid" of seventeen when he laid eyes on the Front Range of the Rocky Mountains. Conditioned by countless pulp novels and cowboy movies, he saw them as "a magical vision, a legend come true." Inspired, he left both Indiana State Teacher's College and Appalachia in the late 1940s to take up undergraduate work at the University of New Mexico. The desert landscape made as strong an impression on him as had the mountains: "purple crags, lavender cliffs, long blue slopes of cholla and agave—I had never before even dreamed of such things." He would never live permanently in the East again.[26]

The 1950s were hectic years for Abbey. From 1948 to 1951 he took classes at the university, wrote for its literary magazine, and met and married the first of his five wives. He then studied in Scotland on a Fulbright scholarship, published his first two novels, began work on a third, and divorced to marry art student Rita Deanin. In the meantime, he explored the New Mexico backcountry and, for the first time, ventured into the Four Corners region of Utah and Arizona. After ping-ponging around the country, Abbey and Deanin returned to Albuquerque in 1954 so he could work on his master's degree in philosophy. For the rest of the decade he split his time among school, writing fiction, and scratching out a living. In the late 1950s he spent two seasons as a ranger at Arches National Monument in southeastern Utah, living in a house trailer near Balanced Rock. It was a seminal experience, as the fantastic slickrock landscape of the Arches area cemented Abbey's passion for the Four Corners region. It was not so seminal for Deanin or the couple's son Josh, however. The area's rustic solitude and Abbey's frequent absences intensified the pressure on an already-shaky marriage, and the two would finally divorce in 1965. But Abbey loved the outdoor life, and for years he would take seasonal work as a ranger and fire lookout for both the Park Service and the Forest Service.[27]

It was during this period that his political convictions began to mature. Like his father, the youthful Abbey was an antiauthoritarian, and not overly systematic in his grievances. But he was also more of a thinker than Paul and early on recognized the need for a stronger intellectual basis for his instinctive antistatism. In his journal entries, Abbey began to work out the philosophical details. In 1959 he submitted his master's thesis, titled "Anarchism and the Morality of Violence," which included studies of Mikhail Bakunin, Pierre-Joseph Proudhon, Peter Kropotkin, William Godwin, Georges Sorel, and Emma Goldman. Abbey would later dismiss it—"bristling with footnotes," it had earned him a master's degree, which "means absolutely nothing"—but the thesis revealed his familiarity with and deft grasp of theoretical anarchism. Theory, however, never appealed much to Abbey, whose anarchism, philosophy professor Harold Alderman has argued, was "gut-level."[28]

Abbey's mistrust of the state resonated more with his immediate experience, and for someone looking for concrete manifestations of government power, there was no better place to find them than his new home, the American West. Spawned by the New Deal and World War II, and nourished by the Cold War, government-centered development exploded across the region in the 1950s. The urban population soared as new residents were drawn westward by the blossoming electronics, aircraft, and other defense-related industries. The expanding infrastructure that accompanied that growth was all the more noticeable in the region's open landscape: massive dams and reservoirs, power plants and high-tension lines, highways and subdivisions, airports, aqueducts, factories, mills, and mines. And it was impossible to miss the growing presence of the U.S. military, especially in the Southwest, as new bases, artillery and bombing ranges, proving grounds, and missile silos dotted the land and sonic booms reverberated off the mountains. If Abbey had been attracted to the West for its libertarian possibilities, the changes that occurred in the region during the 1950s offered a lesson in futility.[29]

Abbey's third novel, published in 1962, drew direct inspiration from the federal government's growing western presence. The protagonist in *Fire on the Mountain* is New Mexico rancher John Vogelin. Like Abbey's Appalachian ancestors, Vogelin lives in close working contact with his own patch of land. His "Box V" ranch is small, isolated, and unprofitable in the capitalist sense, but Vogelin is more interested in his way of life than his lifestyle. He has no electricity and few conveniences save for a butane-powered refrigerator and an old pickup truck, and he is profoundly suspicious of modern technology and modern government. He soon finds his independence threatened by the U.S. Air Force, which plans to annex his ranch for use as bombing range. One-sided negotiations ensue—Vogelin declines all offers from the Air Force to buy the land, and frustrated military officials condemn the ranch. Holing up with a shotgun in his house, he forces the local police to flush him out with teargas. Confined to his daughter's home, he flees to the mountains above the Box V, where he dies of a heart attack in an old cabin. The novel ends with the discovery of his body by his grandson (the narrator) and a hired hand, who soak the cabin in kerosene and turn it into Vogelin's funeral pyre.[30]

Fire on the Mountain categorically linked government power to the decline of individual freedom and the demise of the agrarian lifestyle that, for Abbey, made such freedom possible. He had been circling around that theme for some time in his journal, toying with the connections among land, democracy, and power, and speculating about an antiauthoritarian novel focused on "the everyday ordinary hardworking . . . small southwestern rancher with his starved cows, pickup, kids, windmill." He had touched on the idea in *The Brave Cowboy*, his second novel, which revolved around the futile efforts of an anachronistic, antisocial cowboy to break a draft-dodging friend out of prison. Hunted by the authorities, he meets an ignominious and symbolic demise by being run over a truck full of toilets. In *Fire on the Mountain*, Abbey finally brought his belief in agrarian independence and hostility to government together in explicit fashion.[31]

Fire on the Mountain also resonated with the rising antistatism of both the region and the era. Abbey's critique of an arrogant and antidemocratic military would have sounded familiar to the New Left, then gathering to write the Port Huron Statement and begin its assault on The Establishment. Vogelin's independent life on the land also bore a close resemblance to the coming countercultural fascination with living "off the grid" and its libertarian do-it-yourself ethic. Meanwhile, postwar conservatism's coalescence was well under way in 1962, especially in the Southwest, home to the movement's unofficial leader, Barry Goldwater. Abbey's celebration of rugged individualism and property rights in *Fire on the Mountain* paired well with its philosophical agenda too, and the similarity between Vogelin's complaints against the Air Force and later Sagebrush Rebellion and Wise Use criticisms of government "takings" is striking. The conservatism of *Fire on the Mountain* was perhaps more akin to the Nashville Agrarians, important ancestors of postwar conservatives and severe critics of industrial capitalism, consumerism, high-technology, and the federal government. One of the book's biggest fans was the agrarian philosopher Wendell Berry, who told Abbey, when he read the book a decade later, that he admired Abbey's "old-fashioned head" and didn't know "when I've read a book that moved me more."[32]

It was in the same year that *Fire on the Mountain* appeared that Rachel Carson sprung *Silent Spring* on the world. Abbey agreed with Carson that environmentalism was about more than just clean air and water or any other middle-class amenities; it was also about democracy and freedom. Like her, he saw environmental issues as inseparable from issues of political power. By the end of the 1960s Abbey had come to believe that it was primarily through the domination of nature, made possible by high-technology, that the state attempted to dominate people. From that point on his writing became significantly more political. Particularly in the speeches and lectures he was now delivering with regularity, he outlined the connections between environmental destruction, economic and technological development, and the increasingly authoritarian power of government. It was these connections that provided the grounding for his defenses of wilderness preservation and agrarian independence.

Historical context is vital to understanding Abbey's critique. Conservatives, of course, had been railing against Big Government since the New Deal and consolidating their power during the 1950s, and Lyndon Johnson's Great Society programs and civil rights legislation only reinforced their ire. But the New Left offered its own particular indictments of the government. Liberalism, they said, was a wolf in sheep's clothing. Liberals paid lip service to reform, while tolerating and even encouraging corporate influence and bureaucratic corruption in government. They served as enablers and apologists for a banal suburban middle-class "affluence," turned a blind eye to poverty and racial injustice and, above all, prosecuted an immoral and illegal war in Vietnam. Thus Washington, D.C., was under an ideological assault from both sides, and Abbey drew from them both as he described the decline of freedom and democracy. He knew who threatened the people, why and how they threatened them, and what some of the necessary steps were to turn things around, and he was never hesitant to state his positions in plain terms. He was not a systematic anarchist philosopher or political scientist, but his personal experience and concrete historical context came together to make his brand of environmentalism more complex, and certainly more contingent, than many have given him credit for.

Abbey's life during the 1960s unfolded much as it had before. He divorced again, and remarried again, and fathered two more children. His work life was similarly erratic, as he bounced around from job to job and from place to place: technical writer and welfare case work in Hoboken; ranger at Sunset Crater, Canyonlands, the Everglades, Lassen and Organ Pipe National Parks; and a short, unhappy stint as a writing instructor at Western Carolina University. He continued writing, and in 1968 his fortunes began to turn with the publication of *Desert Solitaire*. By the dawn of the new decade, his tenure as an obscure regional novelist was over for good.[33]

Subtitled *A Season in the Wilderness*, Abbey's *Desert Solitaire* was a collection of essays centered on his experiences in Utah's Arches National Monument. Like other works in its genre, *Desert Solitaire* described its natural setting in exultant detail, glorying in the beauty and spiritual purity of the nonhuman world. Woven into the rhapsody were some great stories: an encounter with a wild horse named Moon-eye, a death-march cattle roundup in the heat of summer, a search for a lost hiker, and a detailed account of Abbey's 1959 raft trip through the doomed Glen Canyon. Released to little notice initially, *Desert Solitaire*'s popularity skyrocketed in the wake of Earth Day 1970, and it remains one of the most popular books in the history of environmental literature.[34]

One of the things that made *Desert Solitaire* an interesting book was its sense of political outrage, as Abbey's antigovernment sentiments bubble up in the stream of his prose. In an early chapter he tells of hoisting his red bandana, a set of Chinese windbells, and the Stars and Stripes up a flagpole— "damn both houses and *pox vobiscum*"—and by the fifth chapter he is in high dudgeon over the ineptitude of federal land management. "Polemic: Industrial Tourism and the National Parks" depicts him arguing forcefully and humorously against the National Park Service's automobile-friendly "Mission 66" developments and its penchant for bureaucratic blundering in the name of park improvement. "Rocks" muses on the greed and social corrosion that accompanied the uranium rush of the 1950s, as speculators fanned out across the slickrock to get rich off the military's insatiable desire for weapons-grade ore. Throughout the book Abbey keeps up a steady stream of short jabs and one-liners against the federal powers-that-be.[35]

Things get more serious with *Desert Solitaire*'s defense of wilderness as an escape vehicle from totalitarianism. Wild land should be preserved for "political reasons" as well as environmental ones, Abbey declares in "The Heat of Noon." "We may need it someday," he warns, as "a refuge from authoritarian government, from political oppression. Grand Canyon, Big Bend, Yellowstone, and the High Sierras may be required to function as bases for guerilla warfare against tyranny. What reason have we Americans to think that our own society will necessarily escape the worldwide drift toward totalitarian organization of men and institutions?" The argument might sound outlandish, he admits, but history demonstrates that "personal liberty is a rare and precious thing," and that "all societies tend toward the absolute until attack from without or collapse from within breaks up the social machine and makes freedom and innovation again possible. Technology adds a new dimension to the process by providing modern despots with instruments far more efficient than any available to their classical counterparts. Surely it is no accident that the most thorough of tyrannies appeared in Europe's most thoroughly scientific and industrialized nation." He predicts: "If we allow our own country to become as densely populated, overdeveloped, and technically unified as modern Germany, we may face a similar fate."[36]

What exactly would be required to impose a dictatorial regime on America? First, the populace would need to be concentrated in "megalopolitian masses" to make them easier to monitor and, if necessary, bomb and shoot into submission "with a minimum of expense and waste." All agriculture would have to be mechanized, "thus forcing most of the scattered farm and ranching population into the cities," where they and other "self-sufficient types" could be more easily managed. Gun control, military conscription, and imperialist wars would follow—"nothing excels military training for creating in young men an attitude of prompt, cheerful obedience to officially constituted authority." Next would come a "finely reticulated network of communications, airlines, and interstate autobahns" to facilitate the physical deployment of state power. The final step would be to "*raze the wilderness.* Dam the rivers, flood the canyons, drain the swamps, log the forests, stripmine the hills, bulldoze the mountains, irrigate the deserts and improve the national parks into national parking lots." With that, the final escape route would be cut off. But there was yet hope. Urban revolts in Budapest and Santo Domingo were easily crushed because "an urban environment gives the advantage to the power with the technological equipment," but in rural countries like Cuba, Algeria, and Vietnam, resistance movements thrived in "mountain, desert and jungle hinterlands," supported by a thinly spread population and hidden in broad expanses of undeveloped land, which negated the advantage of high-tech weaponry. Thus the necessity of preserving wilderness in America—"the city, which should be the symbol and center of civilization, can also be made to function as a concentration camp."[37]

The politics of 1968 were all over passages like these. With a war raging in Vietnam, police and protestors battling in the streets of Chicago, riots across Europe, the Soviet crackdown in Prague, and the frenzy of Mao's Cultural Revolution, Abbey's preoccupation with excessive state power was understandable if not always believable. Meanwhile, broader antiauthoritarian attitudes drawn from both the Right and the Left informed the book. Its suspicion of high-technology, celebration of independent agriculture, and portrayal of the natural world as the antidote to the human one resonated with the contemporary counterculture's back-to-the-land sentiments and its penchant for rural do-it-yourself communal living. They also resonated with certain elements of the survivalist Right; there was at least a dash of Robert DePugh and The Minutemen in Abbey's appeal to the freedom of the hills.

Abbey's next three books—*Appalachian Wilderness* (1970), *Black Sun* (1971), and *Cactus Country* (1973)—were not as overtly political, although they too abounded with cheerfully nasty swipes at government and industry. But it was mainly in his lectures, reviews, essays, editorials, and letters that his increasingly politicized environmentalism began to take shape, and they reveal how Abbey was influenced by the important social and cultural trends of his era. In Abbey's political hell, the ninth level was home to the devil of collectivization. "Evil lies not in individual humans," he claimed in the late 1970s, in a nod to political theorist Hannah Arendt, "but in the mob, the conglomerate, the institution. Men in groups, thru [sic] institutions, commit crimes that no single person, or small band of persons, would ever be capable of doing, or even think of doing. . . . The really monstrous crimes of modern times . . . have been committed by committee." There seemed to be no way around the problem. "There is," he wrote in 1976, simply "something in the character of large-scale organization itself which is qualitatively different" from the individuals within it. To organize human beings in any such way was thus to risk tyranny.[38]

For the anarchistic Abbey there was no better embodiment of that risk than the state. He had been suspicious of state power for most of his adult life, and books like *Fire on the Mountain* were strong if somewhat indirect expressions of that feeling. Now, in the 1970s and 1980s, he named the beast with little equivocation. "Of all modern institutions," Abbey informed a University of Colorado audience in 1978, "none is more brutal, more cruel, more blind, more aggressive and expansionistic than the contemporary nation-state. The function of the state is not to organize but to dominate human society . . . , [and] it tends to expand to the limits of its powers." He told an interviewer in 1984 that the state was "a grotesque distortion of human community," and in the essay "Theory of Anarchy" from that same decade he put it more succinctly: the function of government is nothing more than "coercion through monopoly of power."[39]

Such statements were redolent of postwar conservative rhetoric, and Abbey's specific political views in those years closely matched many of those in the conservative movement. Like them, he lamented the growth of government in the years after the New Deal and World War II, especially its increasing role as a regulator of social behavior and an agent of reform. Given its coercive function, he argued, government could hardly be counted on to resolve social ills à la The Great Society. "One thing we should all have learned by now," he wrote in 1976, "is that we cannot rely on government to solve problems. . . . Give the people a chance [to] get government off their backs . . . and ordinary citizens . . . will not only survive but thrive. . . . I have absolutely no faith in government." He was also a rabid supporter of another conservative cause: the right of individual citizens to keep and bear arms. "Rifles and handguns are the weapons of democracy," he told *Playboy* magazine in 1988. "If we allow them to be taken from us [by the government] we retreat one more big step back from the great American tradition of self-reliance and decentralized power." He also opposed welfare programs, dismissing them as a "subsidy for baby production" and suggesting that welfare benefits be tied to "birth control and tubal ligatures." Welfare also underlay poverty on Indian reservations, he argued, whose residents needed "more than anything else . . . the strong tonic of self-reliance." Nor did he have much use for affirmative action programs—"a policy of favoring blacks, Hispanics and other Official Minority members with special favors at the expense of whites, Jews, Orientals, etc."—or immigration from Latin America, a "cheap cause" for "doctrinaire liberals" who ignored its social and cultural implications. "I am opposed to all forms of government including good government," he told an interviewer in 1983, a declaration sure to make conservatives smile. "Especially good government."[40]

But Abbey quickly took his antistatism into areas guaranteed to make most conservatives uncomfortable. If rifles and handguns were the weapons of democracy, then "the tank, the B-52, the fighter-bomber, the state-controlled police and military are the weapons of dictatorship," employed to intimidate the citizenry as much as to defend them from outside threats. Similarly, America's war in Vietnam—which he called "criminal, cowardly, atrocious, dishonorable"—and its support for right-wing governments in Latin American were not noble fights against Communism but acts of state-sponsored aggression. Then there were his pro-choice views ("a woman's womb is not the property of the State") and opposition to the death penalty ("I suspect that [its] true purpose and meaning is to instill in the hearts of the people an indelible fear, awe, and terror of the state"). He especially parted company with conservatives in his view of capitalism. "Everything I see that is dangerous in the power of the state," he told an audience in 1978, "I see as equally dangerous in the concentration of economic & industrial power. They all go together—Big Biz & Big Gov't are interdependent, they need and feed each other, they prop each other up, they engage in a continual exchange of ideas, money (most of our tax money goes to subsidize big biz in one form or another) and personnel. Today's Sec. of State will be tomorrow's chairman of the board at Chase Manhattan. Today's Pres. of General Foods will be tomorrow's Sec. of Agriculture. We see this going on all the time."[41]

Such sentiments also revealed the influence of the contemporary political Left as well as the Right on Abbey's antistatist thinking. He was a decade too old to have been a member of the New Left, but his criticisms of the corporate state in the 1970s and 1980s sounded a lot like that movement's attacks on the Establishment. Listening more closely, one could pick up the arguments of books that had influenced the New Left directly, like Herbert Marcuse's *One Dimensional Man* and C. Wright Mills's *The Power Elite*, along with echoes of Lewis Mumford, E. F. Shumaker, Theodore Roszak, and others. Such a mishmash likely explains the confusion among his audience concerning his place on the ideological scale. Leftist anarchist Murray Bookchin called Abbey an "ecofascist," an odd charge in light of his disdain for militarism and corporate power, and one angry reader referred to him as a "half-baked, uninformed, phoney [sic] liberal." Another called Abbey a "New Left acid freak recycled as an ecologist." Abbey couldn't even describe himself consistently, referring to himself by turns as "a liberal democrat," a "wild conservative," a "liberal and a libertarian," and a "Jeffersonian agrarian anarchist."[42]

Whatever the ambiguity of his political identity, Abbey was sure about who his enemies were. He had a name for them: the Power Combine (sometimes rendered in a variant form, the Greedhead Combine). The Combine, close cousin to Mills's similarly named power elite, consisted "of the interlocking corporate monopolies of oil, coal, the energy industries, the road & plant construction companies, the land speculators and developers, the Chambers of Commerce . . . , Big Business in general—all those, in short, who tend to get very emotional where making money is concerned. The Power Combine also includes those public agencies and public officials who serve it, who are indeed indentured servants of it—i.e., the Depts of Interior & Agriculture, the Corps of Engineers, the Bureau of [Reclamation], the state highway depts, most of our state legislators, most of our [governors] & senators & congressmen . . . [who are] much too closely entwined with, almost identical with, big business and big industry." Such sentiments drew on a long anticapitalist tradition on the political Left, but one also sees here the legacy of Abbey's Appalachian upbringing, especially in his vitriol for oil, coal, and energy companies and their government allies.[43]

So far, this critique was much like a hundred others before it, but now Abbey began to head off into less familiar directions. He had identified the members of the Power Combine, but what did it want? The answer was apparent in its name. It wanted power, over both its own citizens and other nations, and it attempted to get that power through a ruthless dedication to economic growth based on the massive exploitation of natural resources. Thus the government took a keen interest in logging, mining, large-scale agriculture, reclamation projects, highways, and so on. Few if any of the government bureaucracies dedicated to land management and development—the U.S. Forest Service, the Bureau of Land Management, the Bureau of Reclamation, the U.S. Army Corps of Engineers—were benign "conservation" organizations dedicated to improving Americans' lives. Instead, they were the first stations on the assembly line of authoritarianism, providing the natural grist for the Combine's efforts to dominate the citizenry.[44]

The domination of nature was crucial to the domination of people. "There is a purpose behind this drive toward complete commercial-industrial exploitation of all natural resources," Abbey explained to an Arizona audience in 1981. "And that purpose is power. . . . And whether or not you care about nature, we humans are a part of it; the domination of nature leads to the domination of human beings. An expanding industrialism is not compatible w/ [sic] democracy." "The great drive by the power institutions to transform our land, our planet," he told another audience, " . . . is also a war on people. Tyranny over nature will lead to tyranny over human beings. [It] is already doing so." But precisely how did the domination of nature lead to the domination of humans? To begin, he suggested, economic growth itself was fundamentally undemocratic because the wealth of nature was never distributed widely or fairly. No matter how big the economic pie, too many people—usually those who labored most directly to create it—got too little, and even that came mainly in the form of consumer trinkets and a lack of basic amenities "which [even] the most humble Bushman or Amazonian tribe [manages to give] its own members," like clean food and water.[45]

A more dangerous consequence of economic growth was that the population increases accompanying it generated an ever-increasing need for centralized social control—which was the Power Combine's ultimate goal. "If you have more and more people," Abbey told *Mother Earth News* in 1984, "you also have more and more need for regulation in the form of government, laws, police, [and] prisons." A "crowded society," he wrote elsewhere that same year, "is a restrictive society; an overcrowded society becomes an authoritarian, repressive and murderous society." Postwar Arizona offered a vivid example. "The best evidence of economic growth" there, he told a Scottsdale audience in 1980, "is the need . . . to build another prison." And in the end, "that's what industrial growth really means, in our society: more prisons. More prisons, and more freeways, and more laws and taxes and regulation . . . , more IBM [the giant technology corporation International Business Machines] invading our lives, and more police, more Big Brother helicopters in the evening sky, keeping watch over our patio picnics and swimming pool parties . . . , more drugs, and more assaults, rapes, murders, and more prisons." Soon the entire nation would be "one gigantic prison of walls and fences and streets and guards and police and laws and regulations covering America from sea to sea, from the Atlantic to the Pacific." Thus he opposed Latin American immigration not for racial or cultural reasons but for social and political ones. "Mass immigration, legal or illegal, whatever the source," he wrote to *Mother Jones* in 1983, "is a threat . . . to our democratic traditions and aspirations; dense populations lead to centralized, authoritarian, police states, with or without a façade of civil liberties. And if this amounts to 'cultural bias,' what's wrong with that?"[46]

High technology was crucial for both the extraction of natural resources and for keeping large populations under control. "Technology gives the few the means, the instruments to dominate the many," he observed in an interview in *Mother Earth News*. Its "tendency is to encourage and pro-mote hierarchical, authoritarian social structures equipped with tyranni-cal tools," especially of the military and law-enforcement variety. "Soon . . . there will be no refuge anywhere, no escape possible from the techno-crats." Technology also had a parallel tendency to make citizens reliant upon it for their basic needs—jobs, wages, clothing, food, water, and shelter—and thus reinforcing the Combine's control over them. "The truth is," Abbey avowed, that because of high-technology

> we are all becoming slaves. If slavery can be characterized as a state of utter
> dependency on another, or on a system or institution of some kind, then it
> is surely true . . . [that we] are all—or nearly all—helpless dependents upon
> the great social-industrial mega-machine that our technicians & engineers
> & scientists & politicians and managerial entrepreneurs have built around
> us. Around us: we are not only dependent on the industrial machine for
> survival—there are too many of us to live directly on and from the land—
> even if we knew how—not only are we dependent but we are enclosed by
> the machine. We are surrounded and trapped by an intricate web, a cob-
> web, of wires, walls, cables, freeways, dams, canals, highways, fences, laws,
> regulations, taxes, strange people in sinister uniforms, snarling boys.

Meanwhile, the consumer "amenities" that technology made possible—automobiles, computers, television, rock music—only distracted people from the reality of their own enslavement.[47]

Abbey had particular contempt for the scientists and engineers who supplied the Combine with its technological tools. Nuclear physicists, for example, created "the most advanced form yet of centralized power, anony-mous authority, [and] techno-industrial tyranny," and he offered his services to antinuclear protests in the 1970s and 1980s. Federal hydrologists were another favorite target, their reclamation projects literal monuments to the Power Combine's authoritarianism. He also gleefully attacked the inventor and futurist R. Buckminster Fuller, who was best known as the origina-tor of the geodesic dome, which embodied his belief that a super-efficient, environmentally sustainable high-tech lifestyle was the planet's best hope for long-term survival. Fuller was famous for coining the term "Spaceship Earth," a reflection of his view of the natural world as a complex machine amenable to human management and control. He was also supremely self-confident, even arrogant, and legendary for inventing complicated terms (for example, "dymaxion," a portmanteau of the phrase "dynamic maximum tension") to correct the inefficiencies and inaccuracies he perceived in standard English. As such, Fuller was ripe for lampooning by the likes of Abbey, who was merciless.[48]

Fuller was particularly popular among libertarian-tinged counterculture environmentalists of the 1960s and 1970s, such as Stewart Brand and the readers of his *Whole Earth Catalog,* who, unlike many members of the environmental movement, had both a firm faith in small-scale technological solutions to environmental problems and a lack of faith in large governmental remedies. The 1975 science-fiction novel *Ecotopia* was the best known fictional description of a Fuller-Brandian-*Whole Earth* society. Its twenty-first-century citizens combined high-technology with a low-impact ethic to create an environmentally sustainable world of peace, health, close-knit egalitarianism, and personal fulfillment. While he would have appreciated both Ecotopia's communal vibe and its respect for individualism (and certainly its abundant casual sex), Abbey had little use for its patron saint. Fuller was an "earnest old crackpot" and a "totalitarian ideologist" whose ideas, whatever their pretense to democracy and progress, reduced both nature and humanity to mere things and rendered them more easily controllable by the Power Combine.

"He doesn't answer questions," Abbey complained in the University of Arizona's newspaper in 1973, "he delivers monologues. His books read as if written by a computer; the prose clanks forward like the treads of a tractor. This is important because style reveals the nature of the man. Unintelligible jargon self-invented is the traditional smokescreen of the bureaucrat, the high priest, the witch-doctor. . . . Centralized power thrives on secretive, esoteric and exclusive code-systems known only to the inner circle." Fuller's readers, Abbey concluded, "will search in vain . . . for any sympathetic discussion of such concerns as personal freedom, variety and diversity in social arrangements, the preservation of wilderness, a healthy balance between rural and urban ways of life," and a slew of other moral, nontechnical concerns.[49]

Put it all together—the inherent authoritarianism of the state; the consolidating schemes of the Power Combine; the technological handcuffs fashioned by scientists, engineers, and other apologists for tyranny—and you had, Abbey concluded, the makings of dictatorship, not just in America but across the globe. The aim of highly centralized and technologically intensive states was the same everywhere. The United States and the Soviet Union, while "by no means morally equivalent," pursued the same goals of "nationalism, militarism, industrialism, technology, science, organized sport and, above all, the religion of growth—of endless expansion in numbers, wealth, power, time and space." Whether led by capitalists or communists, humanity was "drift[ing] toward the technological superstate . . . , densely populated, nuclear-powered, computer-directed, centrally-controlled, and *very firmly policed*." Evidence for this was everywhere: dams, highways, urban sprawl, military bases, power plants, computers, the proposed SST supersonic airliner, police helicopters ("one more significant step toward an authoritarian police state"), firearm registration, "domestic surveillance, fingerprint files, data centers, personnel records," and Social Security numbers, which Abbey jokingly referred as "my superstate IBM number." Even the campaign for adopting the metric system was an ominous sign, for it was intended to supplant traditional English measurements for "the convenience of technology and technicians." The potential end was "life in the Totally-Integrated Society of the 21st century," when "each and every worker-unit will spend his/her/its allotted time-span pushing buttons and scanning a video screen within its assigned self-sufficient living capsule inside its designated tier and cellblock in the great universal technocratic Beehive of the Future," the same "ultimate techno-tyranny that some of our better science fiction writers have prophesied."[50]

Nature would be similarly enslaved. "What we must expect is a planet where the entire surface . . . is subjected to intensive exploitation." Abbey predicted. "The sea will be farmed, all deserts irrigated, whole mountains pulverized, the last forests turned to pulpwood plantations, in order to satisfy the ever-growing needs . . . of a human population much larger than present." Over it all, he continued in an echo of Lewis Mumford, would be "a ruling priesthood of administrators and technicians still trying . . . to build a pyramid of power up to the stars. And this pyramid, like those of Egypt, will be based on the subjugation of human beings." More "industrialism & technology, more crowding, more loss of the natural world, more loss of freedom. . . . These evils go together. They reinforce each other." Each time "we allow the extinction of a species," he warned in 1978, "each time we allow the obliteration of a little more wilderness, each time we witness the displacement of another farmer, rancher, fisherman, native hunter, independent craftsman or family-sized enterprise of any kind . . . , we are watching the closing off of diversity, the spread of uniformity, the dying of possibility."[51]

How was it possible to avoid such a future? Abbey's first suggestion was to avoid forming large, organized groups to counter the state and its allies—a favorite tactic of American reformers throughout the nation's history—because they automatically tended to authoritarianism and conformity. Any communist movement was clearly out of the question. All Marxist utopias, "especially those worked out in detail, with blueprints, strike me as autocratic, arrogant, essentially authoritarian, anti-human," he declared. "My Maoist friends tell me that [in] China . . . a revolutionary utopia has been achieved—but I am . . . repelled by any society where all . . . read the same little red book; where all think alike, no one thinks much; where one man is elevated to the rank of a god, all the rest are . . . slaves." Nor "would [I] want to be ruled," Abbey told a group in 1971, by any American radicals like "Jerry Rubin or Bobby Seale anymore than I enjoy being taxed & supervised by Nixon, Mitchell, Laird & Co." Anarchist that he was, Abbey's ideal solution was encapsulated in one word: decentralization.[52]

"Decentralize power," he advised the readers of *Mariah* magazine in a 1978 interview. "Break down the big power structures, both governmental and corporate. Abolish General Motors and Exxon, restore free enterprise, encourage small business, break up the nation-state into independent, regional, more or less self-sufficient little democracies. Don't homogenize, Balkanize. I'm in favor of anything that promotes liberty, diversity, and peaceful confusion." He told a New Mexico audience that "in order to extricate ourselves . . . , we must carefully & gradually bring this machine under human control, turn its power toward human ends, and when that has been done, reduce the machine, part by part, under local social control, to a size and scale where it no longer presents a threat to health, stability, community and human freedom." Sometimes there was a menacing edge in such prescriptions. Humankind would never be free, he informed another audience, in a twist on Diderot's famous phrase, "until the last corporation executive is strangled w/ [sic] the entrails of the last bureaucrat." It was hard to say just how serious Abbey was here. Did he seriously urge violence against the Combine? He took pains to advocate explicitly nonviolent resistance to environmental destruction, but his fascination with anarchism, his belief in an armed citizenry, and the debates around books like *The Monkeywrench Gang* and *Hayduke Lives!* made the question rather thorny.[53]

Violence or no, decentralizing the technocratic state would be a task to make Sisyphus shudder. And even if the Power Combine was brought to heel, what then? What would be society's ideal new structure? Abbey was far better at criticism than reform, but he was not entirely without a plan. Here his commitment to agrarian life, environmentalism, and wilderness preservation intersected most profoundly with his political ideals. The key to maintaining decentralized power, local control, individual freedom, and community integrity could be found in a life of agrarian self-sufficiency amid a vast sea of wilderness. Recall the pastoral communities of *Good News* and the self-sufficient mountaineers of Abbey's ancestral region. His idealized vision of the future involved a return to the ways of the past, a recreation of backcountry Appalachia set within vast stretches of Western-style undeveloped wildlands. It was a vision he never laid out in much detail— gut-level anarchism again—but its general outlines were clear: human freedom needed roots in the ground.

"I envision an American society," Abbey declared in the early 1980s, "growing beyond our slavish industrialism, beyond our slavish dependence on technology, a barefoot and green anarchism of largely independent states, independent towns and cities, independent men and women, economies localized and so far as possible, self-sufficient." Sometimes such visions, already impressionistic, edged into impracticality and utopian silliness, as when Abbey told the graduating class of Aspen High School in 1971 that what was needed was "a return to regional autonomy, free cities & communes, [and] independent tribes roaming the wilderness," and allowing "a great part of the earth's surface [to] revert to a wild state—to the paradise & green Utopia which our earth, I think, was really meant to be from the beginning." Elsewhere he suggested that even agrarian life might be too organized, centralized, and environmentally destructive to be truly democratic. "I think humankind probably made a big mistake when we gave up the hunting and gathering way of life for agriculture," Abbey told his friend Jack Loeffler. "I look forward to the time when the industrial system collapses and we all go back to chasing wild cattle and buffalo on horseback." He told an interviewer that "my notion of an ideal city would be a place of splendid monuments, theaters, stadia, museums, and marketplaces inhabited by a permanent population of only caretakers. The rest of us would assemble there once a month, or once a year, for festivals, conventions, and perhaps open-air democratic decision-making assemblies in which *all* citizens, even children, would participate and cast a vote."[54]

But he was not always the unrealistic agro-wilderness utopian. Immediately after his musing on a "green and barefoot anarchism," for example, he urged the development of "a truly sophisticated technology, one so sophisticated that we're scarcely aware of its presence. And with it a small-scale industrial-agrarian economy that functions so smoothly, regularly, like a healthy body, that we need seldom give it direct attention or concern." Fantasies of hunting on horseback notwithstanding, Abbey was too sophisticated to believe that industrialism and high technology could or should be done away with, or that life in the wilderness was a truly viable option. The more immediate and realistic objective was to contain the spread of industrialism and centralization and keep other, more democratic social and technological options open. In *Mother Earth News* he argued that technology could be a good thing when it was "decentralized . . . appropriate technology . . . [that serves] people, instead of the other way around." "What is needed," he told *Utah Holiday* magazine in 1977, "is not the abolition of industrialism but the moderation of it, a sensible and wholesome balance between industrialism and agrarianism . . . , a farming and ranching sort of society . . . . It's a question, as the politicians like to say, of balance. And I agree." If Utah must have industry, he concluded wryly, let it be "light manufacturing; let's say, a nice clean well-lighted condom factory."[55]

This placed him in a paradox, however. Wouldn't "light manufacturing" simply produce light slavery, or moderate tyranny? Furthermore, a "truly sophisticated" and "appropriate" technology was precisely the sort of thing that Stewart Brand and Buckminster Fuller advocated, and Abbey had already dismissed them. If he noticed the contradictions, he made no mention of them and continued his plea for the middle ground. In 1978 he argued that "it is too late to return to the lost Eden of a hunting and gathering society—there are far too many of us—but not too late to work out a reasonable compromise among various possibilities of scence [sic], technology, democratic culture and agriculture." In the 1977 essay "Freedom and Wilderness, Wilderness and Freedom," he likewise offered hope that "it is possible to find and live a balanced way of life somewhere halfway between all-out industrialism on the one hand and a make-believe pastoral idyll on the other." But the paradox remained.[56]

Whether or not he was guilty of loose thinking when it came to the big picture, most of Abbey's concerns were of the more immediate variety, and he preferred to "protest, oppose, resist, [and] subvert" the Combine in the present. One of the best ways to do that, he argued, was environmentalism. Beginning in the late 1960s, Abbey was an enthusiastic supporter of most environmental groups and the environmental movement as a whole (although he drew the line at free-market environmentalism—John Baden was a "hired retainer" for "the same 200-year-old *laissez-faire* capitalism . . . which has made American what it is today—a polluted, strip-mined, clear-cut, over-grazed, damned-up, over-populated, socially-unjust, urbanized, industrialized, Europeanized mess"). Some of this grew out of his maturing biocentric views—he had come to believe, à la the Deep Ecology movement, in nature's intrinsic right to exist unmolested—but his primary motivation was political. He embraced environmentalism because it struck at the Combine's heart: its dependence on the exploitation of nature.[57]

As early as 1969, Abbey bemoaned the fact that *Desert Solitaire* had not made a bigger impact outside conservation circles. It had been pigeonholed by critics as mere nature writing, he felt, and the connections the book made between defending nature and human freedom had been missed. "I had hoped to reach a different group," he wrote, mainly "the college-age militants with whose aims and activities I am in deep sympathy, in an effort to close the gap that now exists between conservationists on the one hand and political activists on the other. It seems to me that the two groups should be allies, since our basic goals and our basic enemies are the same, e.g. the people now busily engaged in poisoning forests and farmlands in Vietnam are the same or closely connected with the people whose business it is to complete the pollution of our environment here in the States." Two years later, Abbey told graduating students at Aspen High School that those who "foul up our skies, poison our land & water are criminals.... Fight them in every way possible: politically, publicly, and if necessary privately." One of the best ways was to "join a conservation [organization]. It's necessary. It's the most [effective] way." Years later it was still effective—in 1988, Abbey argued: "I do my bit by giving a tithe of my income to conservation groups and conservationist politicians . . . and to neighborhood protection committees." Once again, however, a paradox emerged. How he could square his fear of organized reform groups with his support for environmental versions of them was not entirely clear, although he seemed to recognize the problem. He noted in 1976 that he felt "obliged to join or work for or at least contribute money" to environmental organizations despite his anarchism, and his later support for the anarchic grassroots group Earth First! suggested an effort to reconcile the tension.[58]

At any rate, the Combine seemed quite threatened by environmental organizations, and that was good enough for Abbey. He interpreted the Reagan administration's antienvironmental crusade, for example, as strong evidence of its fear; environmentalists and environmentalism "are under attack," he told friend and environmental activist Doug Peacock in 1982, precisely "because they present obstacles. . . . The Empire Strikes Back."

Industry too had begun "to recognize conservationists and environmentalists—not labor leaders, not government, not Marxists—as [its] chief antagonists in shaping the character of the American future." But until the Combine's power weakened sufficiently, he concluded, "we are obliged to promote what is good and resist what is evil thru more or less regular political processes—organization, publicity, public office, marches, demonstrations," and the like. Voting in the "rigged [electoral] scheme" was a sham and close "to tacit consent" to the system, but using what little ballot-box power remained to the citizenry was still important. "When in doubt, when there is little [real] choice," he told the editors of the Arizona *Republic* in 1982, "always vote against the incumbent. Keep the rascals rotating."[59]

Meanwhile, there were three other ways to fight the Combine. The first was a vigorous pursuit of Jeffersonian-style agrarianism. Like the 1960s counterculture, Abbey saw the personal as political and encouraged active avoidance of the system whenever possible. "Start your own private, personal revolution," he counseled a crowd in 1982, and "help to subvert, bankrupt, & eventually destroy" the Combine. Establishing self-reliance was the key; anything that promoted independence from high-technology and industrialism was a good thing. Build a network of friends, family, and community upon whom you can count for mutual aid and support, he advised audiences. "If possible," buy "a piece of land & build yr [sic] own house" on it, then take steps to separate yourself from reliance on the larger technoindustrial system and to protect yourself from your "always potential enemy: The State." Find seasonal work, learn a trade, hunt and fish for subsistence, use solar energy, brew your own beer, bake your own bread, and grow your own food, he further suggested, "and retreat from the cash nexus [and] develop a barter system." Cultivate "both a garden and an attitude of voluntary simplicity." And above all, "arm yrselves [sic] of course; an armed citizenry is still the best defense against authoritarian rule. Learn to shoot, and shoot straight. Load yr [sic] own ammo." Such a life was more realistic than it might first appear, because both history and contemporary society offered examples for emulation. "I believe we can find models for a better way in both the past and the present," Abbey wrote in "Freedom and Wilderness, Wilderness and Freedom." "I allude to the independent city-states of classical Greece; to the free cities of medieval Europe; to the small towns of eighteenth- and nineteenth-century America; to the tribal life of the American Plains Indians, to the ancient Chinese villages recalled by Lao-tse in his book, *The Way*." Here again, backcountry Appalachia colored

Abbey's views, as did intellectual inconsistency; he never actually practiced this sort of self-sufficiency, and he neglected to mention the antidemocratic tendencies of his historical examples.[60]

Population reduction was a second vital tactic in the fight against technocratic dictatorship. Recall Abbey's argument that large populations necessitated increased central-state control and that reducing their numbers was a necessary first step toward protecting individual freedom and establishing democracy. Similar sentiments were in the air at the time. Both Paul Ehrlich's *The Population Bomb* (1968) and Garrett Hardin's "Living on a Lifeboat" (1974), for example, placed excessive population at the center of the world's environmental ills, predicted massive social and political as well as ecological disaster if population growth persisted, and proposed controversial population-reduction policies to avert tragedy. Abbey was clearly sympathetic to their arguments, but here too he could contradict himself. Though he often took pains to encourage population reduction through "humane social policies" like tax credits and contraception, he suggested more than once that the militarization of U.S. borders might be necessary to prevent ecological and political degradation. Meanwhile, he spoke darkly about the "alien mode of life" in "the Caribbean-Latin version of civilization." Considering his mistrust of the state and the military, it was odd that Abbey put such faith in them here and even his staunchest allies cringed. "Do you have any idea," environmental journalist Bill McKibben asked him in 1988, "how difficult you are making it for those of us who have been trying . . . to maintain the population question as a legitimate issue on the antiauthoritarian agenda by making comments like that?"[61]

The third category of resistance to the Power Combine was wilderness preservation. Abbey often claimed that his support for wilderness preservation was primarily a result of his belief that nonhuman life had at least some right to exist unmolested by humans. This was perhaps an outgrowth of his anarchism; a man so steeped in ideas about human egalitarianism and individualism could easily extend those values beyond humans to the larger living world. But following closely on his biocentric defense of wilderness was an anthropocentric one. Wilderness helped keep people free, offering them refuge from the technoindustrial state and starving it of necessary resources. Wilderness provided, if nothing else, a place of mental and spiritual renewal and elementary physical adventure. Humans were wild animals, Abbey said, and a life bound by the Combine's techno/urban methods of social discipline was tantamount to living in a cage. Wilderness was outside the cage, "beyond the cities, where boys and girls, men and women, can live at least part of their lives under no control but their own . . . , free from any and all direct administration by their fellow men." Access to wild land was "a necessity of the human spirit. . . . We need danger, freedom, adventure . . . as much as we need food, air, music, dance, shelter, poetry. . . . [Without] them we become something less than men & women; we become lab subjects for Masters and Johnson, B. F. Skinner, Dr. Caligari, Prof. Caligula."[62]

Wilderness also encouraged a respect for the inherent value of the natural world, which in turn was an essential precursor to cultivating respect for humans; if domination of nature led to the domination of people, than the reverse was also true. One of the best arguments for wilderness preservation, Abbey told *Basin and Range* magazine in 1985, was that it encouraged humility. "It's immoral for us to think that we have the right to dominate the entire planet and all its diverse life forms," he declared. "Until we become tolerant enough to grant the rights of life and privacy to our fellow creatures, we aren't truly civilized," and therefore incapable of empathy with one another. In "Freedom and Wilderness, Wilderness and Freedom," Abbey argued that a nation's lack of wilderness and the attendant psychological stresses tended to foster aggression toward other nations as well as internal enemies. Japan and Germany were "bottled up" by their small geographical base and overdeveloped natural environments, and their twentieth-century histories of war and oppression offered stark examples of the dangers of life without wilderness (such an argument ignored, of course, more complex historical factors like anti-Semitism, the Depression, and the legacy of the Meiji Restoration).[63]

More important, wilderness denied the Power Combine the natural resources it needed and simultaneously provided a haven for the creation of an agrarian alternative. "Wilderness is one of several ways, maybe the best way," Abbey told an audience in Flagstaff, Arizona, in 1975, "to oppose and slow down and finally stop the degradation of our environment and the debasement of our society . . . , a small but vital front in the vast war" against the Combine. "By keeping intact our wild, primitive and natural areas," he argued a few months later,

> we can compel a halt to the crazy economic system which, by a policy
> of blind growth, threatens our health, physical & mental, and destroys
> the material basis of human existence. . . . If we in America cans save our
> parks & wilderness, and not only the wild places but also our farmlands,

rangelands, small towns, lakes, forests, rivers & seacoasts, all those places where a lucky minority can still make an honest living directly from the land, then we will set limits to the expanding economy. If we can stop the growing economy . . . then we can force the growing economy to become a rational steady-state economy—which I see as a society where all forms of power, economic as well as political, are decentralized . . . , where the emphasis is on labor-intensive production of needs [sic] rather than the capital-intensive machine-powered production of junk.

"The more wilderness we set aside," Abbey observed in *Mother Earth News* in 1984, "the less space can be devoted to industry." The ideal balance would be a mirror image of the contemporary wilderness:civilization ratio. "Instead of setting aside little patches of wilderness here and there," Abbey told the *Tucson Mountain Newsreal*, "I would like to see the whole planet declared wilderness, with little spots of civilization. Turn the whole thing around." A truly democratic society depended on "clean air, 100-mile visibility, clean drinkable water, lots of open space, wildlife habitat, wildness & wilderness & freedom." And, he declared pointedly, "I do mean lots of [wilderness], whole regions of it—not little islands of wilderness surrounded by a sea of urbanism & industrialism but the opposite—islands of civilization."[64]

Finally, wilderness was a refuge in the most literal sense, an idea Abbey had first elaborated on in *Desert Solitaire*. As the Combine closed its grip, it was in the wild mountains, forests, and deserts that the Resistance would find safety and from which they would fight back. If "this fantasy" of techno-industrial tyranny becomes a reality, Abbey warned, "then some of us may need what little wilderness remains as a place of refuge, as a base from which to carry on guerilla warfare against the totalitarianism of my nightmares." Should it come to that, he said, only half-jokingly, "I, for one, intend to light out at once for the nearest national forest, where I've been hiding cases of peanut butter, home-brew, ammunition, and C-rations for the last ten years." Levity aside, such sentiments were strongly reminiscent of The Minutemen and other right-wing militia movements, many of whom set up camp in the West's wild lands to train for their own version of the war with the powers-that-be. Like his immigration sentiments, Abbey's survivalist comments were grist for those who would link him with conservative extremism or ecofascism, but they also highlighted the degree to which his love and defense of wilderness was tied directly to his political philosophy and to his sense that the future was heading in ominous directions.[65]

During the 1970s and 1980s, Abbey finally became a household name among environmentalists. He published regularly in magazines, newspapers, and photo collections, with the best pieces republished in five essay collections: *The Journey Home* (1977), *Abbey's Road* (1979), *Down the River* (1982), *Beyond the Wall* (1984), and the posthumous *One Life at a Time, Please* (1990). Interviewers clamored for access, and he was forced to use a post office box to ward off admirers (and perhaps enemies as well). By the late 1970s, he was able to support himself and his family wholly through sales of his writings. He quit the ranger/lookout life, and by the end of his 1980s he was working at the University of Arizona as a writing instructor. His personal life remained traditionally chaotic—three more wives, three more children, and the usual assemblage of lovers, accompanied by a hearty rate of alcohol consumption, the complications of which would kill him in March 1989.[66]

Like his lectures, essays, and letters, Abbey's fiction during this period began to reflect his political critique. *Good News* (1980) may be the best example, but it was in the wickedly impertinent *The Monkeywrench Gang* (1975) that Abbey railed most fervently against the Power Combine. It was in that novel that he offered one final method to fight the Combine: to sabotage of the machinery and infrastructure it used to extract resources from the wilderness. Abbey termed it "monkeywrenching," and it would be, by far, his most controversial environmental legacy.

In large measure, *The Monkeywrench Gang* was little more than a revenge fantasy, but it revealed the seriousness of Abbey's political fears. The book chronicles the adventures of four "little humans," as he described the main characters in his journal, "against the Glittering Tower of the Power Complex, [the] Mega-machine." Three men—the rugged and bad-mannered George Washington Hayduke, former Green Beret and Vietnam veteran; the philosophical Doc Sarvis; and the salt-of-the-earth river guide and jack Mormon "Seldom Seen" Smith—and one female, the smart, outspoken, and predictably buxom Bonnie Abbzug, unite in their love of wilderness and their hatred for "Progress" and its sycophants. Together they wage an intense but ineffectual campaign of petty sabotage against the inanimate tools of the technocratic state, burning billboards, incapacitating heavy construction equipment, and blowing up a rail line that supplied coal to an Arizona power plant, all the while taking pains to avoid harming human beings. Their ultimate dream is to destroy the massive Glen Canyon dam on the Colorado River, the preeminent symbol of the Power Combine. They never get the chance; after failing to destroy a bridge, the authorities apprehend Sarvis, Smith, and Abbzug, with Hayduke presumed dead in a shootout. But their dream lives on. At the end of the novel, Hayduke resurfaces with an assumed name. He tells Sarvis that he has secured a new job: night watchman at Glen Canyon dam.[67]

It was all in good fun, Abbey liked to say of the novel, written "to amuse my friends and to aggravate our enemies." But his "disavowals" of monkeywrenching were coy and diluted with humor, and never definitive. "Would I actually blow up a dam?" Abbey asked in a letter to an environmental group in 1977. "Absolutely not. Why, such a thought has never crossed my mind. . . . I am categorically opposed to any and all forms of illegal activity, except maybe at night and then only with the written consent of your parents."[68]

At other times Abbey made no secret of his belief that monkeywrenching should be more than a fictional activity. The Combine meant business, he said, and so must the people who would resist it, and the prospect of direct physical resistance to the destruction of wilderness was one that had to be considered. The stakes were high, because the future of democracy hinged on derailing the coming technological central-state dictatorship. "We must not plan for growth but plan for war," Abbey wrote in 1976,

> a war against the strip miners, against the dam builders, against the powerplant builders, against the pipeline layers, against the freeway builders, against the model-city builders, against the forest killers, against the coal-gassifiers and shale-rock processors, a war against the whole array of arrogant and greedy swine who, if we let them, will level every mountain, dam every river, clear-cut every forest and obliterate every farm and ranch and small town. . . . Therefore I say, if political means are not sufficient to halt the advance of the iron juggernaut, if economic pressures do not serve us, if reason and loud argument and moral persuasion fail, then we are justified in resorting finally to certain forms of violence. Violence is after all the traditional way of settling serious disputes in this country, as American as pizza pie.

"Every significant development in American history," he concluded, "independence from England, the settlement of the frontier, the abolition of slavery, the enactment of civil rights, the withdrawal from . . . SE Asia [sic], has been aided, abetted, and promoted through violence." Taking down the Combine would be no different.[69]

This was not to condone violence against humans—there was a clear difference between terrorism and sabotage, Abbey declared again and again—but it certainly encouraged violence against the Combine's mechanical tools. "Be a hunter," he urged a Montana audience in 1982. "Harvest some bulldozers. Be a miner—undermine some drill rigs. Be a logger—cut down a few front-end loaders [and] skidders [and] tree clippers." In 1984 he wrote a provocative piece entitled "Forward!" for the book *Ecodefense: A Field Guide to Monkeywrenching*, a how-to manual for environmentalists who might be inspired to emulate the Monkeywrench gang. The book's primary author, Dave Foreman, was an Abbey disciple and former Wilderness Society lobbyist (as well as a former Goldwater Republican and fundamentalist Christian) who had become increasingly bitter about what he saw as the sellout mentality of his employer and the increasing power of Reagan-era antienvironmentalists. *The Monkeywrench Gang* inspired Foreman and a handful of Abbey-loving friends to form Earth First! in 1981. Passionate, obstinate, rude, crude, and unrelenting, the group soon became famous for preaching the gospel of biocentrism, performing guerilla theater, staging "tree sits," tree spiking, blocking the paths of advancing bulldozers and logging equipment, occupying corporate offices, and generally advocating an aggressive brand of environmentally-oriented civil disobedience.[70]

Abbey approved wholeheartedly of Earth First!, defending the group frequently in print and speaking regularly at its meetings and rallies. At its inaugural protest on March 21, 1981, when Foreman and a group of friends unfurled a three-hundred-foot black plastic "crack" down the face of Glen Canyon, Abbey sermonized from the bed of a nearby pickup truck: "We see now that [Glen Canyon] Dam was merely a step toward the urbanizing, industrializing and . . . militarizing of the West. . . . After ten years of modest environmental progress, the powers of industrialism & militarism have become alarmed. . . . [We must continue to] oppose, resist, subvert, delay, until the Empire begins to fall apart." With *Ecodefense's* "Forward!" he reiterated the message that "targeted" physical resistance to the Combine, as embodied in Earth First!'s no-compromise approach to environmental protection, was both necessary and proper. "Representative government in the USA represents money not people," he roared,

> and therefore has forfeited our allegiance and moral support. We owe
> it nothing but the taxation it extorts from us under threats of seizure of
> property, or prison, or in some cases already, when resisted, a sudden and

violent death by gunfire. Such is the nature of the industrial megamachine (in Lewis Mumford's term) which is now attacking the American wilderness. The wilderness is our ancestral home . . . [and] if it is threatened with invasion, pillage and destruction—as it certainly is—then we have the right to defend that home, as we would our private rooms, by whatever means necessary . . . . The majority of the American people have demonstrated on every possible occasion that they support the ideal of wilderness preservation . . . [and therefore] we are justified in defending our homes—our private home and public home—not only by common law and common morality but also by common belief.

Foreman and others in Earth First! would soon find themselves in hot water with the authorities.[71]

Reviewers from across the ideological spectrum pummeled *The Monkeywrench Gang* over the next fifteen years, from the liberal-centrist *New York Times* to the John Birch Society–affiliated *Executive Intelligence Review*. Even the academic journal *Environmental Ethics* weighed the question of "Ecological Sabotage: Pranks or Terrorism?" and determined that it was probably the latter. The sequel *Hayduke Lives!*—which involved the Gang's successful attempt to destroy a giant earth-moving machine, the "GEM"—did nothing to resolve the matter. But Abbey would not be dissuaded, staying true to his motto until his death: oppose, resist, and subvert.[72]

Abbey was fond of saying that at heart he was really an optimist. Be of good cheer, he told readers and audiences, because modern industrial society will soon collapse from its own excesses and clear the way for a more democratic alternative. But all too often, he complained, critics misinterpreted his hopes as simple misanthropy. "I am accused of being a hater," Abbey grumbled in his journal in 1983. "What those two-bit book reviewers cannot see is that every hate implies a corresponding love. I.e. I hate asphalt because I love grass. I hate militarism because I love liberty and dignity. I hate the ever-expanding industrial megamachine because I love agrarianism, wilderness and wildlife, human freedom."[73]

Abbey was right about himself. He was far more than a nature writer, concerned not only with the natural world but also with political and philosophical questions of individualism, community, state and nation, and the ideal balance among them all. Those questions, as he once said, did run like a scarlet thread through his writings. Abbey was also a product of history.

His definition of wilderness, tinged as it was by nineteenth-century Romanticism and naïve American cultural myth, were also inseparable from the
particular historical events and ideas of his day. The Vietnam War, the Cold
War, the growth of postwar conservatism, and the antiauthoritarianism of
the New Left all had their influence; and postwar economic growth, rapid
technological development, and the expansion of governmental power and
military presence, especially as they manifested themselves in the intermountain West, formed the more immediate background to the development of Abbey's thought, the source of the social disease for which he
prescribed his agrarian/wilderness cure. That prescription, in turn, had its
roots in preindustrial Appalachia and its demise, the legacy of which lin-
gered in the mountains where Abbey spent his formative years. To dismiss
him as a man simply trying to "escape history"—even when he likely would
have agreed with that description—is to miss how much he was actually
influenced by and was reacting to history.

Abbey's "political wilderness" also suggests that other criticisms of the
"wilderness cult" are sometimes wide of the mark. Such scholars as Robert
Gottlieb have argued that historically a fetish for wilderness preservation
prevented environmental groups like the Sierra Club and the Wilderness
Society from dealing squarely and honestly with issues of environmental
and social justice. While they spent time trying to preserve wild land "out
there" for much of the twentieth century, the argument goes, wilderness-
oriented groups ignored environmental problems closer to home, particularly those associated with urban environments and oppressed people like
blacks, Hispanics, poor whites, women, and the working class. Leftist critics
like Murray Bookchin have been even harsher, accusing Abbey and his ilk
of bald-faced misanthropy and inexcusable blindness to the social hierar-
chies and inequalities beneath environmental problems.[74]

There is a lot of truth in those arguments. Yet it was precisely in the
service of widespread social justice—although in a rather different form
than that intended by Gottlieb and Bookchin—that Abbey offered his
agrarian/wilderness alternative to modern technoindustrialism. Whatever
the other faults of his vision, there was never any doubt that Abbey recognized the connection between human injustice and environmental degradation, that he understood that the domination of nature and people were
closely related, and that hierarchy, inequality, powerlessness, and ecological despoliation went together. For Abbey, preserving the wilderness and
living close to the land was not only an escape from the social problems

of civilization, it was also a remedy for them. Agrarianism in the bosom of wilderness would lead to a more equitable, stable, and fulfilling life for all citizens. Naïve as that position may have been, scholars might do more to consider the social-justice angle of Abbey's agrarian/wilderness vision. He might be best understood, in fact, as an environmentally and social justice–oriented critic of high modernism. In *Seeing Like a State*, political scientist James Scott argued that one of the seminal trends of the twentieth century was the attempt by centralized states to solidify their control by "simplifying" local communities through rational organization via scientific expertise and bureaucratic management, in the process running roughshod over the traditions and rights of those communities and their members. Abbey would have recognized Scott's critiques instantly. In fact, it was precisely Scott's technologically intensive central-state management that Abbey saw as so threatening to the natural world and to human communities, and to which he offered such a radical alternative.[75]

Finally, like Barry Goldwater, antifluoridationists, and free-market environmentalists, Abbey and his ecopolitical vision serve as a sign of the resonance between American environmentalism and classic American political ideals of individualism, local sovereignty, economic and political independence, and restrained central-state power. The quest to protect nature has long proven amenable to government-centered efforts, but the example of Edward Abbey suggests that it has an equally strong antifederalist streak. Abbey himself summed up this idea: "Say what you like about my bloody murderous government, but don't insult me poor bleedin' country."[76]

— EPILOGUE —

The Fading Green Elephant;

Or, The Decline of Antistatist Environmentalism

This is all an attempt to centralize power and to give more power
to the government.

—*Republican presidential primary candidate Rick Santorum, 2012*

IN THE SUMMER OF 1984, PRESIDENT RONALD REAGAN WAS DOING A LOT
of talking about the environment. On July 12, for example, he arrived in
Bowling Green, Kentucky, after a visit to Mammoth Cave National Park to
speak to the National Campers and Hikers Association. Following routine
greetings and a lighthearted comment or two, he launched into a history of
environmental protection in the United States. Like so many of Reagan's
speeches, this one mixed vibrant patriotism with a defense of his administration's policies and some chiding of its critics, but it was unusual in the
amount of time it dedicated to environmental issues, which had seldom been
a major topic in his oratory oeuvre, and in how much credit it gave to federal
regulation. A century before, the president observed, Theodore Roosevelt
"for the first time outlined the legitimate role of the Federal Government
in protecting the environment," and thanks to the Wilderness Act of 1964,
the Endangered Species Act, and the Environmental Protection Agency,
American nature was now healthier than it had been in decades. Under his
continued guidance, Reagan promised, that progress would continue.[1]

Two days later, in a radio address from Camp David, Reagan spoke again
on government's role in environmental protection. This time he was a bit
more defensive. Despite what critics were saying about him and his administration, he sniffed, "our progress on protecting the environment is one
of the best-kept secrets in Washington." In fact, he said, he had been an

advocate of government's role in protecting nature since he had been governor of California more than a decade earlier, when "we took the lead" in controlling automobile emissions. The state served as a model for the Clean Air Act of 1970, and Reagan was "proud of having been one of the first to recognize that States and the Federal Government have a duty to protect our natural resources from the damaging effects of pollution." A month before, he had even claimed that "no task facing us is more important than preserving the American land" from ecological destruction—and there was no ideological reason to deny it. "What is a conservative after all," he mused, "but one who conserves . . . the land on which we live—our countryside, our rivers and mountains, our plains and meadows and forests." He had sounded a similar theme in January, in his third State of the Union address. "Preservation of our environment is not a liberal or a conservative challenge," he had argued. "It's common sense."[2]

Audience members might have been forgiven for reaching for the salt. Comments like these made Reagan sound like a born-again Green, but there was a strong flavor of damage control underneath them, for the president had recently endured a beating on environmental issues. Amid howls of protest from environmentalists, Reagan had gone all-out against federal environmental management from the day of his inauguration. He had gutted the Council on Environmental Quality, a presidential advisory board created by President Nixon in 1969 as part of the National Environmental Policy Act of 1969; moved to loosen restrictions on offshore oil production and mining as well as logging and grazing on public lands; slashed budgets and personnel at the Environmental Protection Agency and reduced funding for many other federal environmental management programs; used the Office of Management and Budget to apply cost-benefit analyses to "streamline" environmental regulations; placed a moratorium on acquisition of national park land; and resisted calls to address acid rain and toxic wastes and to update the Clean Air Act. And these were only *some* of his efforts. Reagan also chose ideologically friendly (and sometimes less than qualified) appointees to staff environmental bureaucracies, hoping to restrain them from within. The most famous were Interior secretary James Watt and EPA administrator Anne Gorsuch Burford, whose zealousness in pruning back their respective bureaucracies had earned the president a tongue-lashing from environmental groups. Chastened, Reagan now took a more diplomatic approach, although his commitment to eliminating large chunks of regulatory structure remained undiminished.[3]

What had happened? Only a decade before, Republican support for a governmental role in environmental protection was common. As governor, Reagan himself, under the influence of advisers Norman Livermore and William Clark, had joined with environmentalists to oppose a major Army Corps of Engineers dam project at Dos Rios. The president was certainly no nature hater; as a boy, biographer Lou Cannon writes, Reagan had loved the woods and river near his hometown of Dixon, Illinois. He was never a hardcore hiker and river-runner like Barry Goldwater, but he loved nothing more than spending time outside on his beloved Rancho del Cielo, clearing brush and riding horses around what he called his "haven." Once he even hand-collected snakes from the ranch and made his Secret Service escort wait while he released them into the surrounding wild rather than kill them. Meanwhile, references to Reagan's love and respect for nature punctuated his speeches and writings on environmental issues, and although much of it smacked of political lip service, his outdoorsy side also suggested that it was not wholly so. To put it simply, Reagan liked nature and was not opposed, at least in principle, to protecting it. But he disliked the federal government more, and that overwhelmed any propensity he may have had for protective regulation. His antistatism trumped his environmentalism.[4]

Many, if not most, Republicans since Reagan's administration have been deeply resistant to both environmentalism as a broad concept and environmental regulation in particular, even in its most market-friendly forms; witness, for example, their recent rejection of the science of climate change and cap-and-trade proposals for carbon emissions. According to coauthors Byron Daynes and Glen Sussman, the George W. Bush administration rivaled Reagan's as the most virulently antienvironmental in the nation's modern history.[5] Republicans might respond that they have not rejected environmentalism so much as it has rejected them by insisting on "radical" big-government solutions. More likely, the explanation for this position lies in the ascendancy of the party's conservative elements. In the GOP of 1970, conservatives were still a minority, but a decade later things had changed. The 1970s saw a perfect storm of events and developments—backlash against the excesses of 1960s protest movements, debates over busing, the Oil Crisis, Watergate, inflation and stagflation, growing unemployment, rising crime, and the Iran hostage crisis—that cleared the party's political decks and made possible not only the ascension of the conservative wing of the Republican Party but also its dominance. Accompanying and reinforcing this were increasing disparities of wealth and a flood of poor immigrants that pushed Republican voters, already uneasy about the redistributive and regulatory tendencies of liberalism, toward an even more conservative political position, which in turn pushed the party to the right. Thus by the 1990s, "extreme" conservative positions from a decade before came to be the default setting within the GOP.[6]

Because he entered politics in a more moderate, consensus-oriented political era, Barry Goldwater could embrace federal environmentalism despite his conservatism. That embrace became untenable as the GOP slid rightward after 1980, and traditional Republican support for federal environmentalism dropped away because the movement now became just another example of liberal statism in action, like welfare or civil rights legislation or Keynesian economics (Goldwater, in his late-career criticisms of the EPA, clearly felt the influence of that rightward slide). The deeper irony is that in rejecting the federal role in environmental protection, the Republican Party turned its back on its own legacy, much as it did when it dropped the mantle of civil rights in favor of the Southern Strategy. Reagan was right, to a point; to be conservative did once mean "to conserve." But few conservatives saw it that way by the last decade of the twentieth century.

Antistatist environmentalists outside the GOP remain a clear minority as well. To the extent that both environmentalists and politicians have embraced the market a la Paul Hawken and Amory Lovins, one might argue that antistatist environmentalism is still alive and well, if not always in the pure form that some of its advocates have hoped for. Further evidence comes from the popularity of the "crunchy con" movement of journalist Rod Dreher and in the increasing concerns about global climate change among politically conservative evangelical Christians in the "creation care" movement. But with few champions on either the right or the left, movements like free-market environmentalism seemed doomed to remain on the environmental fringe.[7]

It did not have to be this way, of course. Not often do the likes of Edward Abbey, Barry Goldwater, John Baden, Rachel Carson, General Jack D. Ripper, and Emmanuel Bronner come together in one place, but they met on the middle ground between postwar environmentalism and antistatism. Looking at them together offers us food for thought about the nature of environmentalism, conservatism and libertarianism, liberalism, antistatism, and the relationships among them. Postwar environmentalism was a movement broad enough in its ideas and values that it literally had something for almost everyone across the ideological spectrum and could be molded and remolded to accommodate a wide variety of political philosophies. That concern for the environment and a desire for its protection meshed well with the concerns of postwar liberals, leftists, and others who were comfortable with the idea of state regulation and management is well known. That it could also appeal to and be embraced by government-wary Americans on or near the political right is a less familiar idea. Environmentalism found its way into some of the deepest crevices of antistatist America, where we might least expect to find its influence, let alone acceptance.

Understanding the rise of postwar environmentalism in the United States requires more consideration of political ideology, particularly debates about the proper role of government, individual rights, private property, laissez-faire economics, and so on. Most explanations have been economic and technological ones: the desire for amenities among the postwar middle classes, the psychological impacts of nuclear weapons, the daily ecological indignities of suburban living, and so on. But big ideas matter as well, and American environmentalism's development has been deeply interwoven with classic American arguments about individual rights and centralized power.

"Conservative" and "liberal" are of limited usefulness in describing complex postwar political and cultural movements like the environmental movement. Historian Samuel Hays was onto something when he noted postwar environmentalism's tendency to "cut across" ideological boundaries. Barry Goldwater, antifluoridationists, free-market environmentalists, and Edward Abbey drive home the point that when it comes to "environmentalism," the standard ideological divisions that we use to categorize postwar American politics are not always equal to the task. Postwar environmentalism's ideological complexity needs an explicit airing, though it often floats beneath the analytical surface. The divide between Right and Left by no means disappears when the environment enters the picture, but it can become surprisingly porous.

In one of Thoreau's later essays, the antimaterialist "Life without Principle," he briefly directed his barbed wit toward the American two-party system. "Politics is, as it were, the gizzard of society," he wrote, "full of grit and gravel, and the two political parties are its two opposite halves—sometimes split into quarters, it may be, which grind on each other. Not only individuals, but States, have thus a confirmed dyspepsia, which expresses itself, you can imagine by what sort of eloquence." The Bard of Concord was never a straight-ticket man, and he resisted anything that would paint him into a political corner. In our historical explorations of the ideological nuances of postwar American environmentalism, we might do well to follow his lead.[8]

Notes

INTRODUCTION

Epigraph: Richard N. L. Andrews, *Managing the Environment, Managing Ourselves: A History of American Environmental Policy*, 2nd edition (New Haven, Conn.: Yale University Press, 2006), 4.

1. Henry David Thoreau, "Walking," in *Walden, Civil Disobedience, and Other Writings*, 3rd edition, edited by William Rossi (New York: W.W. Norton, 2008), 260–87; Henry David Thoreau, "Walden," in Rossi, *Walden, Civil Disobedience, and Other Writings*, 5–224; Henry David Thoreau, *The Maine Woods* (Boston: Houghton Mifflin, 1893), 1–111; and Henry David Thoreau, *A Week on the Concord and Merrimack Rivers* (Boston: Houghton Mifflin, 1893), 44–45.

2. Henry David Thoreau, "Civil Disobedience," in Rossi, *Walden, Civil Disobedience, and Other Writings*, 227, 242. On Thoreau's evolving abolitionist views, see Sandra Habert Petrulionis, *To Set This World Right: The Antislavery Movement in Thoreau's Concord* (Ithaca, N.Y.: Cornell University Press, 2006).

3. Thoreau, "Civil Disobedience," 227, 228; Henry David Thoreau, "Slavery in Massachusetts," in Rossi, *Walden, Civil Disobedience, and Other Writings*, 258–59. On Thoreau's antistatist individualism, see Robert A. Gross, "Quiet War with the State: Henry David Thoreau and Civil Disobedience," *Yale Review* 93 (October 2005): 1–17.

4. Edward Abbey, *Confessions of a Barbarian: Selections from the Journals of Edward Abbey, 1951–1989*, edited by David Peterson (New York: Little, Brown, 1994), 156; and Edward Abbey, "Down the River with Henry Thoreau," in Abbey, *Down the River* (New York: Penguin Books, 1982), 45.

5. Edward Abbey, *A Voice Crying in the Wilderness: Notes from a Secret Journal* (New York: St. Martin's Press, 1989), 26.

6. Edward Abbey, "A Writer's Credo," in Abbey, *One Life at a Time, Please* (New York: Henry Holt and Co., 1988), 180.

7. The best biography of Goldwater is Robert A. Goldberg, *Barry Goldwater* (New Haven, Conn.: Yale University Press, 1995).

8. Edward Abbey, *The Monkeywrench Gang* (New York: Avon Books, 1975); and Edward Abbey, "Insolent Remarks, Ariz. Sierra Club, Phoenix, Sat. 3-11-72," Folder 1, Box 8, Edward P. Abbey Papers 1947–1990 MS-271, Special Collections, University of Arizona Library, Tucson (hereafter EAP).

9. Samuel P. Hays, "From Conservation to Environment: Environmental Politics in the United States since World War II," in *Out of the Woods: Essays in Environmental*

History, edited by Char Miller and Hal Rothman (Pittsburgh: University of Pittsburgh Press, 1997), 124.

10. Adam Rome, "'Give Earth a Chance': The Environmental Movement and the Sixties," *Journal of American History* 90 (September 2003): 525–54.

11. Rebecca Klatch, *A Generation Divided: The New Left, the New Right, and the 1960s* (Berkeley: University of California Press, 1999). Klatch's book is an excellent sociological study of the members of both the left-leaning Students for a Democratic Society (SDS) and the conservative/libertarian Young Americans for Freedom (YAF), and reveals how similar their antistatist sentiments could be, especially those of SDS and YAF's libertarian wing.

12. The definitive history of federal environmental policy is Andrews, *Managing the Environment, Managing Ourselves*; on early state management of the environment, see pp. 28–93 of Andrews's book. On antebellum New England, see John T. Cumbler, *Reasonable Use: The People, the Environment, and the State, New England, 1790–1930*; Richard W. Judd, *Common Lands, Common People: The Origins of Conservation in Northern New England* (Cambridge: Harvard University Press, 1997); Theodore Steinberg, *Nature Incorporated: Industrialization and the Waters of New England* (Amherst: University of Massachusetts Press, 1991); William Cronon, *Changes in the Land: Indians, Colonists, and the Ecology of New England* (New York: Hill and Wang, 1983); and Brian Donahue, "'Dammed at Both Ends and Cursed in the Middle': The 'Flowage' of the Concord River Meadows, 1798–1862," in Miller and Rothman, *Out of the Woods*, 227–42. On the colonial South, see Timothy Silver, *A New Face on the Countryside: Indians, Colonists, and Slaves in South Atlantic Forests* (New York: Cambridge University Press, 1991). On the role of sportsmen in the development of conservation, see John F. Reiger, *American Sportsmen and the Origins of Conservation,* 3rd edition (Corvallis: Oregon State University Press, 2001). On conservationists and their conflicts with hunters, see Steven Hahn, "Hunting, Fishing, and Foraging: Common Rights and Class Relations in the Postbellum South," *Radical History Review* 26 (1982): 37–64; Adam Rome, "Nature Wars, Culture Wars: Immigration and Environmental Reform in the Progressive Era," *Environmental History* 13 (July 2008): 432–53; and Louis Warren, *The Hunter's Game: Poachers and Conservationists in Twentieth-Century America* (New Haven: Yale University Press, 1997). On urban environmental problems, see Martin Melosi, *The Sanitary City: Environmental Services in Urban America from Colonial Times to the Present* (Pittsburgh: University of Pittsburgh Press, 2000); and Andrews, *Managing the Environment*, 109–35.

13. On Progressivism and "rationalization," see Robert Wiebe's classic *The Search for Order, 1870–1920* (New York: Harper and Row, 1967).

14. The classic source on the technocratic nature of Progressive conservation remains Samuel P. Hays, *Conservation and the Gospel of Efficiency: The Progressive Conservation Movement, 1890–1920* (Cambridge: Harvard University Press, 1959). See also Andrews, *Managing the Environment*, 136–53; Char Miller, *Gifford Pinchot and the Making of Modern Environmentalism* (Washington, D.C.: Island Press, 2001); Elmo R. Richardson, *The Politics of Conservation: Crusades and Controversies, 1897–1913* (Berkeley: University of California Press, 1962); Clayton R. Koppes, "Efficiency, Equity, Esthetics: Shifting Themes in American Conservation," in *The Ends of the Earth: Perspectives on Modern*

Environmental History, edited by Donald Worster (New York: Cambridge University Press, 1989), 230–51; and Donald Worster, *Rivers of Empire: Growth, Aridity, and the Growth of the American West* (New York: Oxford University Press, 1985). Donald J. Pisani offers a counterargument to the idea of reclamation as an effective expression of federal power in *Water and American Government: The Reclamation Bureau, National Water Policy, and the West, 1902–1935* (Berkeley: University of California Press, 2002).

15. On preservation, Yellowstone, Glacier, Yosemite, and the National Park Service, see Alfred Runte, *National Parks: The American Experience* (Lincoln: University of Nebraska Press, 1979). On the Lacey Act, see Theodore Whaley Cart, "The Lacey Act: America's First Nationwide Wildlife Statute," *Forest History* 17 (October 1973): 4–13; and Jennifer Price, *Flight Maps: Adventures with Nature in Modern America* (New York: Basic Books, 1999), 57–110). On Roosevelt's copious preservationist urges and actions, see Douglas Brinkley, *The Wilderness Warrior: Theodore Roosevelt and the Crusade for America* (New York: Harper, 2009). On the Antiquities Act, see Hal K. Rothman, *America's National Monuments: The Politics of Preservation* (Lawrence: University Press of Kansas, 2007); and Robert W. Righter, "National Monuments to National Parks: The Use of the Antiquities Act of 1906," *Western Historical Quarterly* 20 (August 1989): 281–301. On preservation's social impacts, see Karl Jacoby, *Crimes against Nature: Squatters, Poachers, Thieves, and the Hidden History of American Conservation* (Berkeley: University of California Press, 2001); and Mark Spence, *Dispossessing the Wilderness: Indian Removal and the Making of the National Parks* (New York: Oxford University Press, 1999).

16. On the Hetch Hetchy dam controversy, see Robert W. Righter, *The Battle over Hetch Hetchy: America's Most Controversial Dam and the Birth of Modern Environmentalism* (New York: Oxford University Press, 2005); and Roderick Frazier Nash, *Wilderness and the American Mind,* 4th edition (New Haven, Conn.: Yale University Press, 2001), 161–81. On predator control, see Ted Steinberg, *Down to Earth: Nature's Role in American History,* 2nd edition (New York: Oxford University Press, 2009), 142–45. On conservationists' forest mismanagement of forests, see Nancy Langston, *Forest Dreams, Forest Nightmares: The Paradox of Old Growth in the Inland West* (Seattle: University of Washington Press, 1995).

17. Adam Rome, "What Really Matters in History? Environmental Perspectives on Modern America," *Environmental History* 7 (April 2002): 304. On the New Deal, see Neil Maher, *Nature's New Deal: The Civilian Conservation Corps and the Roots of American Environmentalism* (New York: Oxford University Press, 2007); and Andrews, *Managing the Environment,* 154–78.

18. Samuel P. Hays, *Beauty, Health, and Permanence: Environmental Politics in the United States, 1955–1985* (Cambridge: Cambridge University Press, 1987). See also Hays's more recent *A History of Environmental Politics since 1945* (Pittsburgh: University of Pittsburgh Press, 2000).

19. Andrews, *Managing the Environment,* 201–54. On Nixon and federal environmental legislation of the early 1970s, see J. Brooks Flippen, *Nixon and the Environment* (Albuquerque: University of New Mexico Press, 2000), and *Conservative Conservationist: Russell E. Train and the Emergence of American Environmentalism* (Baton Rouge: Louisiana State University Press, 2006). On the Clean Water Act, see Paul Charles Milazzo, *Unlikely Environmentalists: Congress and Clean Water, 1945–1972* (Lawrence: University

Press of Kansas, 2006). The full text of the Wilderness Act may be found at online at http://www.law.cornell.edu/uscode/html/uscode16/usc_sec_16_00001131----000-.html (accessed December 21, 2011).

20. On the Dinosaur and Grand Canyons dams, see Mark W. T. Harvey, *A Symbol of Wilderness: Echo Park and the American Conservation Movement* (Seattle: University of Washington Press, 2000); and Byron Pearson, *Still the Wild River Runs: Congress, the Sierra Club, and the Fight to Save Grand Canyon* (Tucson: University of Arizona Press, 2002).

21. For general histories of the New Left and counterculture, see Terry Anderson, *The Movement and the Sixties* (New York: Oxford University Press, 1995); and Mark Hamilton Lytle, *America's Uncivil Wars: The Sixties Era from Elvis to the Fall of Richard Nixon* (New York: Oxford University Press, 2006).

22. Sociologist Rebecca Klatch uses the "traditionalist" versus "libertarian" distinction extensively in *A Generation Divided*. The first major piece of scholarship in what we might call "postwar conservative studies" was George H. Nash, *The Conservative Intellectual Movement in America since 1945* (New York: Basic Books, 1976). From the beginning, Nash was vexed by conservatism's diversity. It was a creature of "intriguing complexity" and he admitted there was no "compact definition" of it; thus he defined conservatives as simply people who "called themselves conservatives or because others (who called themselves conservatives) regarded them as part of their conservative intellectual movement" (xii–xiii). On Young Americans for Freedom, see John A. Andrew, *The Other Side of the Sixties: Young Americans for Freedom and the Rise of Conservative Politics* (New Brunswick, N.J.: Rutgers University Press, 1997).

23. Lisa McGirr, *Suburban Warriors: The Origins of the New American Right* (Princeton, N.J.: Princeton University Press, 2001), 10.

24. Allen J. Matusow, *The Unraveling of America: A History of Liberalism in the 1960s* (New York: Harper and Row, 1984).

25. Thomas G. Smith, *Green Republican: John Saylor and the Preservation of the American Wilderness* (Pittsburgh: University of Pittsburgh Press, 2006); Flippen, *Nixon and the Environment*; and Andrew Kirk, *Counterculture Green: The Whole Earth Catalog and American Environmentalism* (Lawrence: University of Kansas Press, 2007). Flippen has also written a book on Nixon's first EPA administrator, Russell Train, in *Conservative Conservationist*.

1. ARIZONA PORTRAITS

Epigraph: From the Introduction to Barry Goldwater, *Delightful Journey down the Green and Colorado Rivers* (Tempe: Arizona Historical Foundation, 1970).

1. See Rick Perlman, *Before the Storm: Barry Goldwater and the Unmaking of the American Consensus* (New York: Hill and Wang, 2001).

2. See Mary C. Brennan, *Turning Right in the Sixties: The Conservative Capture of the GOP* (Chapel Hill: University of North Carolina Press, 1995); and McGirr, *Suburban Warriors*, 54–110.

3. "A craven fear of death" is from the chapter "The Soviet Menace" in Barry Goldwater, *The Conscience of a Conservative* (Shepherdsville, Ky.: Victor Publishing Company,

Inc., 1960), 90. Although Goldwater did not write it directly (it was ghostwritten by aide I. Brent Bozell), the book is a concise statement of his political philosophies at the time.

4. See Goldberg, *Barry Goldwater*, xi, 328–33; and Barry Goldwater and Jack Casserly, *Goldwater* (New York: Doubleday, 1988), 385.

5. William Cronon, "When the GOP Was Green," *New York Times*, January 8, 2001.

6. "Josephine Goldwater biography 1959–66, 1985," Box 2, Folder 10, Goldwater Family Papers MSS-117, Arizona Historical Foundation, Arizona State University, Tempe (hereafter GFP-AHF); and Goldberg, *Barry Goldwater*, 27.

7. "Josephine Goldwater biography," GFP-AHF; Bert Fireman, "Unforgettable Jo Goldwater," Box 2, Folder 13, GFP-AHF; Goldberg, *Barry Goldwater*, 17; and Peter Iverson, *Barry Goldwater: Native Arizonan* (Norman: University of Oklahoma Press, 1997), 7. See also Golderg, *Barry Goldwater*, 25–26, 32.

8. Fireman, "Unforgettable Jo Goldwater," 5; and "Josephine Goldwater biography, 1959–66, 1985."

9. Barry Goldwater to Dean Smith, February 20, 1985, "Correspondence-clippings-genealogical information," Box 2, Folder 9, GFP-AHF; Goldwater and Casserly, *Goldwater*, 35; "Josephine Goldwater Biography," GFP-AHF; and "Personal Journals (mother, childhood, AZ) 1976–1980," Personal and Political Papers of Senator Barry M. Goldwater, Arizona Historical Foundation, Arizona State University, Tempe (hereafter BMG-AHF). A note on sources from the Barry M. Goldwater papers: at the time I conducted research for this book, the Goldwater papers were essentially unprocessed and were undergoing a massive reorganization. Thus citations for sources from the Goldwater papers reflect the organizational systems in use at the times of my various research trips; many citations have since changed considerably.

10. Iverson, *Native Arizonan*, 9; "Josephine Goldwater Biography," GFP-AHF; and Goldberg, *Barry Goldwater*, 27. As Mark Stoll has shown in *Protestantism, Capitalism, and Nature in America* (Albuquerque: University of New Mexico Press, 1997), the modern American environmental movement drew deeply on liberal Protestant traditions of seeing nature as a manifestation of God's goodness and human contact with it as spiritually enlightening.

11. "Josephine Goldwater Biography," GFP-AHF; Goldwater to Smith, February 20, 1985; Barry Goldwater, "Arizona the Beautiful" in "Alpha Files—Personal, Journals (AZ, outdoors), n.d.," BMG-AHF; and Barry Goldwater, *With No Apologies: The Personal and Political Memoirs of United States Senator Barry M. Goldwater* (New York: William Morrow and Company, 1979), 23.

12. Fireman, "Unforgettable Jo Goldwater," 8; Goldwater to Smith, February 20, 1985; and Goldwater, *With No Apologies*, 23.

13. See Paul Sutter, *Driven Wild: How the Fight against Automobiles Launched the Modern Wilderness Movement* (Seattle: University of Washington Press, 2002), 19–53.

14. Mary Austin, *Land of Little Rain* (New York: Penguin Books, 1988), 6.

15. Fireman, "Unforgettable Jo Goldwater," 9–10.

16. Iverson, *Native Arizonan*, 47–65.

17. Ibid., 25–26; and Barry Goldwater in Troy and Marlin Murray, eds., *Barry Goldwater and the Southwest* (Phoenix: Troy's Publications, 1976), 2.

18. Benjamin C. Bradlee to Barry Goldwater, May, 24, 1984, "Photography (unprocessed folder)," BMG-AHF; Barry Goldwater, *Arizona Portraits*, 1st edition (Phoenix: Privately printed, October 7, 1940); and Patricia Nelson Limerick, *Desert Passages: Encounters with the American Deserts* (Albuquerque: University of New Mexico Press, 1985), 115, 126. On controversies over the definition and meaning of "wild" and "wilderness," see William Cronon, ed., *Uncommon Ground: Rethinking the Human Place in Nature* (New York: W.W. Norton and Co., 1996); and Michael E. Soule and Gary Lease, eds., *Reinventing Nature? Responses to Postmodern Deconstruction* (Washington, D.C.: Island Press, 1994).

19. Harvey L. Mott, "An Arizona Bookshelf" (n.d. n.p., c. Fall 1940), Box 24OV, GFP-AHF; Goldberg, *Barry Goldwater*, 53; and Iverson, *Native Arizonan*, 20–27, 40–46. At the time of his death, Goldwater had published nearly three hundred photos in the pages of *Arizona Highways*.

20. Barry Goldwater, *The Face of Arizona* (Phoenix: Privately printed, 1964). On *The Face of Arizona*, see Nan Robertson, "Goldwater Photo Book Brings in $1,500 a Copy to Aid Campaign," *New York Times*, February 24, 1964. Goldwater's library included the Exhibit Format Series books *This Is the American Earth* (1960), *The Place No One Knew: Glen Canyon on the Colorado* (1963), *Time and River Flowing: Grand Canyon* (1964), and *Baja California and the Geography of Hope* (1967).

21. Barry Goldwater, *Delightful Journey down the Green and Colorado Rivers* (Tempe: Arizona Historical Foundation, 1970), 1–2. A summary of Goldwater's trip may be found in Iverson, *Native Arizonan*, 27–39.

22. Goldwater, *Delightful Journey*, 14, 16.

23. Ibid., 104.

24. Ibid., 118, 112.

25. Ibid., 51, 65, 67, 81.

26. Ibid., 180, 182.

27. "Barry and Peggy Goldwater—scrapbook 1939–41," Box 24OV, GFP-AHF; and Goldberg, *Barry Goldwater*, 57.

28. Quoted in Goldberg, *Barry Goldwater*, 57. See also Iverson, *Native Arizonan*, 40.

29. On the government's role in the postwar development of the West, see Gerald D. Nash, *The American West Transformed: The Impact of the Second World War* (Bloomington: Indiana University Press, 1985), and *World War II and the West: Transforming the Economy* (Lincoln: University of Nebraska Press, 1990). On the influence of postwar growth on conservatism, see McGirr, *Suburban Warriors*, 20–53; and for Arizona, both prewar and postwar, see Goldberg, *Barry Goldwater*, 35–36, 44–53, and 67–69.

30. For an overview of this period, see chapters 5, 6, and 7 in Goldberg, *Barry Goldwater*, 92–181. Elizabeth Tandy Shermer has argued that antiunion and right-to-work philosophies were key to both Goldwater's political ascension and the development of the early postwar right more broadly. See "Origins of the Conservative Ascendancy: Barry Goldwater's Early Senate Career and the De-Legitimization of Organized Labor," *Journal of American History* 95 (December 2008): 678–709.

31. Worster, *Rivers of Empire*. See also Marc Reisner, *Cadillac Desert: The American West and Its Disappearing Water* (New York: Penguin Books, 1986).

32. U.S. Bureau of Reclamation, *The Colorado River: A Natural Menace Becomes a*

National Resource: A Comprehensive Report on the Development of the Water Resources of the Colorado River Basin for Irrigation, Power Production, and Other Beneficial Uses in Arizona, Colorado, Nevada, New Mexico, Utah and Wyoming (Washington, D.C.: U.S. Department of the Interior, 1946), 107.

33. On the Colorado River Compact, the standard account is Norris C. Hundley Jr., *Water and the West: The Colorado River Compact and the Politics of Water in the American West*, 2nd edition (Berkeley: University of California Press, 2009).

34. The best account of the Echo Park battle is Harvey, *Symbol of Wilderness*. On Hetch Hetchy, see Fox, *John Muir and His Legacy: The American Conservation Movement* (Boston: Little, Brown, 1981), 139–47; Nash, *Wilderness and the American Mind*, 161–81; and Righter, *Battle over Hetch Hetchy*. On John Muir's broken heart, see Michael P. Cohen, *The History of the Sierra Club, 1892–1970* (San Francisco: Sierra Club Books, 1988), 31.

35. Harvey, *Symbol of Wilderness*, 143–72, 181–205.

36. *Congressional Record*, 83rd Cong., 1st sess., Vol. 99, pt. 13, Index, p. 703; and *Congressional Record*, 84th Cong., 1st sess., Vol. 101, pt. 3 (March 28, 1955), p. 3819.

37. The most complete account of the Hell's Canyon dam controversy is Karl Boyd Brooks, *Public Power, Private Dams: The Hells Canyon High Dam Controversy* (Seattle: University of Washington Press, 2009). See also Roy F. Bessey, "The Political Issues of the Hells Canyon Controversy," *Western Political Quarterly* 9 (September 1956): 676–90.

38. *Congressional Record*, 84th Cong., 1st sess., Vol. 101, pt. 2 (March 8, 1955), p. 2505; *Congressional Record*, 84th Cong., 2nd sess., Vol. 102, pt. 7 (May 29, 1956), pp. 9152–53, and (May 31, 1965), pp. 9296–97; *Congressional Record*, 84th Cong., 2nd sess., Vol. 102, pt. 8 (June 26, 1956), pp. 10949–50; *Congressional Record*, 84th Cong., 2nd sess., Vol. 102, pt. 9 (July 11, 1956), p. 12298; *Congressional Record*, 84th Cong., 2nd sess., Vol. 102, pt. 9 (July 16, 1956), p. 12777; *Congressional Record*, 84th Cong., 2nd sess., Vol. 102, pt. 10 (July 17, 1956), p. 13013–15; *Congressional Record*, 85th Cong., 1st sess., Vol. 103, pt. 6 (June 5, 1957), pp. 8378–79; *Congressional Record*, 85th Cong., 1st sess., Vol. 103, pt. 8 (June 21, 9916), pp. 9916–35; and *Congressional Record*, 85th Cong., 1st sess., Vol. 103, pt. 8 (June 24, 1957), p. 10088.

39. *Congressional Record*, 83rd Cong., 2nd sess., Vol. 100, pt. 8 (July 13, 1954), p. 10371; and *Congressional Record*, 85th Cong., 1st sess., Vol. 103, pt. 11 (August 9, 1957), p. 14187.

. *Congressional Record*, 87th Cong., 1st sess., Vol. 107, pt. 11 (August 8, 1961), p. 15070; and *Congressional Record*, 83rd Cong., 2nd sess., Vol. 100, pt. 8 (July 13, 1954), p. 10374.

. *Congressional Record*, 85th Cong., 1st sess., Vol. 103, pt. 11 (August 9, 1957), p. 14186; *Congressional Record*, 87th Cong., 1st sess., Vol. 107, pt. 16 (September 23, 1961), p. 20994; and *Congressional Record*, 83rd Cong., 2nd sess., Vol. 100, pt. 8 (July 13, 1954), p. 10370.

42. Barry Goldwater to Robert R. Neyland, October 29, 1963, Box 18, Folder 2, 84–88th Congs. files., BMG-AHF; Barry Goldwater to E. J. McMillian, November 1, 1963, Box 18, Folder 2, 84–88th Congs. files, BMG-AHF; *Congressional Record*, 88th Cong., 1st sess., Vol. 109, pt. 16 (November 4, 1963), pp. 21035–36; *Congressional Record*, 88th Cong., 1st sess., Vol. 109, Appendix (September 11, 1963), p. A5747; *Congressional Record*, 88th Cong., 2nd sess., Vol. 110, Appendix (October 2, 1964), p. A5068; *Congressional Record*, 88th Cong., 2nd sess., Vol. 110, pt. 17 (September 14, 1964), pp. 22030–33; and Richard Fulton to Barry Goldwater, November 6, 1963, Box 18, Folder 2, 84–88th Congs. files, BMG-AHF. On Goldwater and the TVA, see also Goldberg, *Barry Goldwater*, 177, 222.

Goldwater was not always consistent on the issue of TVA's privatization. In 1957 and again in 1961, for example, he denied ever advocating privatization. It was already too late for that, he said, as the TVA was "an accomplished fact." See *Congressional Record*, 85th Cong., 1st sess., Vol. 103, pt. 11 (August 9, 1957), pp. 14187, 14190; and *Congressional Record*, 87th Cong., 1st sess., Vol. 107, pt. 11 (August 8, 1961), p. 15070.

43. Reisner, *Cadillac Desert*, passim; on the Rampart Dam, see pp. 207–13.

44. *Congressional Record*, 84th Cong., 1st sess., Vol. 101, pt. 1 (February 4, 1955), pp. 1179–82, 1185; and *Congressional Record*, 86th Cong., 1st sess., Vol. 105, pt. 11 (July 24, 1959), p. 14244. On the Salt River Project, see Worster, *Rivers of Empire*, 172–74.

45. Goldberg, *Barry Goldwater*, 72–74; and *Congressional Record*, 87th Cong., 1st sess., Vol. 107, pt. 2 (February 24, 1961), p. 2720.

46. *Congressional Record*, 85th Cong., 1st sess., Vol. 103, pt. 1 (January 17, 1957), pp. 671–72, 678–79; *Congressional Record*, 85th Cong., 1st sess., Vol. 103, pt. 8 (June 26, 1957), pp. 10318–19; *Congressional Record*, 86th Cong., 1st sess., Vol. 105, pt. 6 (May 5, 1959), p. 7412; *Congressional Record*, 86th Cong., 2nd sess., Vol. 106, pt. 1 (January 21, 1960), p. 956; *Congressional Record*, 87th Cong., 1st sess., Vol. 107, pt. 1 (January 5, 1961), p. 138–39; Barry Goldwater to Wilbur Dexheimer, March 15, 1956, Box 10, Folder 1, 84–88th Congs. Files, BMG-AHF; Barry Goldwater to Fred Seaton, September 26, 1956, Box 10, Folder 2, 84–88th Congs. Files, BMG-AHF; and Barry Goldwater to Leo C. Smith, April 27, 1960, Box 10, folder 4, 84–88th Congs. Files, BMG-AHF.

47. A concise summary of the CAP, especially its legislative history, is Jack L. August Jr., "Water, Politics, and the Arizona Dream: Carl Hayden and the Modern Origins of the Central Arizona Project, 1922–63," *Journal of Arizona History* 40 (Winter 1999): 391–414. See also Robert Dean, "'Dam Building Still Had Some Magic Then': Stewart Udall, the Central Arizona Project, and the Evolution of the Pacific Southwest Water Plan, 1963–1968," *Pacific Historical Review* 66 (February 1997): 81–98.

48. *Congressional Record*, 88th Cong., 1st sess., Vol. 109, pt. 4 (April 1, 1964), p. 5267; and *Congressional Record*, 85th Cong., 1st sess., Vol. 103, pt. 9 (July 22, 1957), p. 12280. See also Barry Goldwater to Paul Sexson et al., Box 10, Folder 4, 84–88 Congs. Files, BMG-AHF; and *Congressional Record*, 88th Cong., 1st sess., Vol. 109, pt. 4 (April 1, 1964), p. 5267.

49. The most thorough treatment of the Grand Canyon dam controversy is Pearson, *Still the Wild River Runs*. See also Dean, "'Dam Building Still Had Some Magic Then,'" 83–84, 92–98; and Nash, *Wilderness and the American Mind*, 227–37.

50. Pearson, *Still the Wild River Runs*, 116–18, 123, 144–48; and Nash, *Wilderness and the American Mind*, 227–37.

51. Barry Goldwater to Robert Michael, January 7, 1964, Box 5, Folder 12, 84–88th Congs. Files, BMG-AHF.

52. Pearson, *Still the Wild River Runs*, xiii–xvi and passim; Dean, "'Dam Building Still Had Some Magic Then,'" 81–83; Reisner, *Cadillac Desert*, 289–305; and Worster, *Rivers of Empire*, 275–76. An overview of the current state of the CAP may be found on BuRec's website at http://www.usbr.gov/projects/Project.jsp?proj_Name=Central+Arizona+Project (accessed December 7, 2012). Goldwater appears to have been aware as early as 1959 that the CAP would supply drinking water to urban Phoenix and Tucson despite his public ideological opposition to any federal project that took over "local duties." In a memo

marked "PLEASE KEEP THIS CONFIDENTIAL," he discussed the merits of the CAP for Arizona's domestic and industrial water needs with Central Arizona Project Association president Lawrence Mehren, noting that "wherever that water goes in Arizona, it means money in the pockets of all Arizonans." See Barry Goldwater to Lawrence Mehren, July 1, 1959, Legislative Series, 86th Congress, Box 11, BMG-AHF.

53. On Douglas McKay, see Elmo Richardson. "The Interior Secretary As Conservation Villain: The Notorious Case of Douglas 'Giveaway' McKay," *Pacific Historical Review* 41 (August 1972): 333–45; *Congressional Record*, 84th Cong., 2nd sess., Vol. 102, pt. 4 (March 9, 1956), p. 4410; *Congressional Record*, 84th Cong., 2nd sess., Vol. 102, pt. 9 (July 11, 1956), p. 12297; *Congressional Record*, 84th Cong., 2nd sess., Vol. 102, pt. 11 (July 26, 1956), pp. 14612–13; *Congressional Record*, 86th Cong., 1st sess., Vol. 105, pt. 11 (July 27, 1959), p. 14277; *Congressional Record*, 86th Cong., 2nd sess., Vol. 106, pt. 3 (February 24, 1960), p. 3370; *Congressional Record*, 87th Cong., 1st sess., Vol. 107, pt. 2 (February 24, 1961), p. 2669; and *Congressional Record*, 88th Cong., 1st sess., Vol. 109, pt. 5 (April 10, 1963), p. 6263.

54. On the Wilderness Act's passage, see Nash, *Wilderness and the American Mind*, 220–27. The text of the Wilderness Act may be found online at http://www.law.cornell.edu/uscode/html/uscode16/usc_sec_16_00001131——000-.html (accessed December 21, 2011).

55. *Congressional Record*, 88th Cong., 1st sess., Vol. 109, pt. 5 (April 8, 1963), p. 5895; Barry Goldwater to K.W. Macdonald, 16 May 1963, Box 15, Folder 1, 84–88th Congs. Files, BMG-AHF; and *Congressional Record*, 87th Cong., 1st sess., Vol. 107, pt. 13 (September 5, 1961), p. 18087–88.

56. *Congressional Record*, 87th Cong., 1st sess., Vol. 107, pt. 13 (September 5, 1961), p. 18087.

. *Congressional Record*, 88th Cong., 1st sess., Vol. 109, pt. 5 (April 8, 1963), p. 5895–96.

58. "The Irony of Victory" is the title of chapter 15 in Nash, *Wilderness and the American Mind*, 316–41.

59. The best treatment of Goldwater's involvement with Camelback Mountain is Peter Iverson, "'This Old Mountain Is Worth the Fight: Barry Goldwater and the Campaign to Save Camelback Mountain," *Journal of Arizona History* 38 (Spring 1997): 41–56. See also Iverson, *Native Arizonan*, 201–11.

60. Quoted in Dan Dedera, "Goldwater Fights for a Mountain," (San Diego) *Union*, May 22, 1965; and Iverson, "'This Old Mountain Is Worth the Fight,'" 47–50. The "shame of the state" quotation is on p. 47. The Barry Goldwater Papers at the Arizona Historical Foundation have extensive files on Goldwater's involvement with the Camelback campaign.

61. Iverson, "'This Old Mountain Is Worth the Fight,'" 50–51.

2. PRECIOUS BODILY FLUIDS

Epigraph: John Stuart Mill, "On Liberty," in John Gray, ed., *On Liberty and Other Essays* (Oxford: Oxford University Press, 1998), 17.

1. Rachel Carson, *Under the Sea-Wind* (New York: Simon and Schuster, 1941); Rachel

Carson, *The Sea around Us* (New York: Oxford University Press, 1951); Rachel Carson, *The Edge of the Sea* (New York: Houghton Mifflin, 1955); and Rachel Carson, *Silent Spring* (New York: Houghton Mifflin, 1962). The seminal treatment of Carson's life and writings is Linda Lear, *Rachel Carson: Witness for Nature* (New York: Henry Holt, 1997), and a good concise one is Mark Hamilton Lytle, *The Gentle Subversive: Rachel Carson, Silent Spring, and the Rise of the Environmental Movement* (New York: Oxford University Press, 2007). See also Carol B. Gartner, *Rachel Carson* (New York: Frederick Ungar Publishing, 1983); and Linda Lear, "Rachel Carson's *Silent Spring*," *Environmental History Review* 17 (Summer 1993): 23–48.

2. Gail Gideon to Rachel Carson, May 23, 1963, box 90, folder 1588, Rachel Carson Papers, Yale Collection of American Literature, Beinecke Rare Book and Manuscript Library, Yale University, New Haven, Conn. (hereafter RCP).

3. Henry C. Jackson to Rachel Carson, October 22, 1963, box 90, folder 1588, RCP; Evelyn E. Melvin to Rachel Carson, May 22, 1963, box 90, folder 1588, RCP; George Waldbott to Rachel Carson, December 11, 1962, June 15, 1963, and July 23, 1963, box 90, folder 1588, RCP; George L. Waldbott, *A Struggle with Titans: Forces behind Fluoridation* (New York: Carlton Press, 1965). Waldbott, a Michigan allergist, would go on to be one of the most famous antifluoridation activists in the United States, and *A Struggle with Titans*, one of its premier polemics. Waldbott's wife, meanwhile, would publish the antifluoridationist periodical *National Fluoridation News*.

4. The best introduction to the American antifluoridation movement is R. Allan Freeze and Jay H. Lehr's breezily written but well-researched and detailed *The Fluoride Wars: How a Modest Public Health Measure Became America's Longest-Running Political Melodrama* (Hoboken, N.J.: John Wiley and Sons, 2008).

5. Brian Martin, "The Sociology of the Fluoridation Controversy: A Reexamination," *Sociological Quarterly* 30 (March 1989): 63.

6. Christopher Sellers and Gretchen Ann Reilly, two of the only historians who have treated antifluoridationists in detail, have argued for historicizing them in the context of postwar concerns about bodily health and integrity. This chapter builds on that argument. See Gretchen Ann Reilly, "'This Poisoning of Our Drinking Water': The American Fluoridation Controversy in Historical Context," Ph.D. diss., George Washington University, 2001; and Christopher Sellers, "The Artificial Nature of Fluoridated Water: Between Nations, Knowledge, and Material Flows," *Osiris* 19 (2005): 182–202.

7. See, for example, Barry Goldwater to E. G. Darbo, November 18, 1971, "Fluoridation (Anti) correspondence," 92nd Cong., Box 13, Folder 7, BMG-AHF.

8. A good summary of fluoridation's discovery and early history is Freeze and Lehr, *Fluoride Wars*, 92–126. See also Reilly, "'This Poisoning of Our Drinking Water,'" 3–11; Donald R. McNeil, *The Fight for Fluoridation* (New York: Oxford University Press, 1957), and McNeil, "America's Longest War: The Fight over Fluoridation, 1950–," *Wilson's Quarterly* 9 (Summer 1985): 140–53; Betul Kargul, Esber Caglar, and Ilknur Tanboga, "History of Water Fluoridation," *Journal of Clinical Pediatric Dentistry* 27 (Spring 2003): 213–17; David B. Scott, "The Dawn of a New Era," *Journal of Public Health Dentistry* 5 (1996): 235–38; and Jill Peterson, "Solving the Mystery of the Colorado Brown Stain," *Journal of the History of Dentistry* 45 (July 1997): 57–61.

9. Freeze and Lehr, *Fluoride Wars*, 102–5; and Reilly, "'This Poisoning of Our Drinking Water,'" 5–8.

10. Freeze and Lehr, *Fluoride Wars*, 105–16; and Reilly, "'This Poisoning of Our Drinking Water,'" 8–11.

11. Reilly, "'This Poisoning of Our Drinking Water,'" 12–13. For period summaries of fluoridation's safety, see Kenneth R. Elwell and Kenneth A. Easlick, "Classification and Appraisal of Objections to Fluoridation," School of Public Health, University of Michigan, 1960, in "Fluoridation Opposition Claims, 1961," American Dental Association archives, Chicago, Illinois (hereafter ADA); James M. Dunning, "Medical Progress: Current Status of Fluoridation," *New England Journal of Medicine* 272, in "Fluoridation, History Prior to 1969," ADA; "Summary of Studies and Evaluations since 1976 Refuting Allegations of an Association between Cancer and Water Fluoridation," Center for Disease Control, U.S. Department of Health and Human Services, October 1981, in "Fluoridation Opposition Claims, 1975–77," ADA; and "Analyzing Selected Criticisms of Water Fluoridation," *Canadian Dental Association Journal* 47 (March 1981), in "Fluoridation Opposition Claims, 1980–84," ADA. For a period example of profluoridationist complaints about antis, see Donald R. McNeil, "Time to Walk Boldly," in "Fluoridation Opposition Claims, 1960–69," ADA.

12. For a summary of sociological studies of antifluoridationists, see Freeze and Lehr, *Fluoride Wars*, 61–67. On the antis' demographics, see A. Stafford Metz, "An Analysis of Some Determinants of Attitude toward Fluoridation," *Social Forces* 44 (June 1966): 477–84; John E. Mueller, "The Politics of Fluoridation in Seven California Cities," *Western Political Quarterly* 19 (March 1966): 54–67; and Rochele Arcus-Ting, Richard Tessler, and James Wright, "Misinformation and Opposition to Fluoridation," *Polity* 10 (Winter 1977): 281–89.

13. J. I. Rodale, "The Organic Creed," *Organic Farming and Gardening* 3 (March 1956): 72–75; J. I. Rodale, "What Does Organic Mean?" *Organic Farming and Gardening* 5 (November 1958): 13–15; and Robert Rodale, "The Organic Way of Life," *Organic Farming and Gardening* 9 (April 1962): 22. On the Rodale Press's support for Carson, see Thomas Powell, "The Battle to Halt Mass Poisoning Is On," *Organic Farming and Gardening* 4 (December 1957): 49–54; and Robert Rodale, "Rachel Carson's Masterpiece," *Organic Farming and Gardening* 9 (September 1962): 17–19. For examples of *Organic Gardening and Farming's* antifluoride sentiments, see M. C. Goldman, "Poison on Tap," *Organic Farming and Gardening* 1 (January 1954): 42–50; J. I. Rodale, "Medical Men versus Pure Water," *Organic Farming and Gardening* 7 (April 1960): 19–26; and J. I. Rodale, "Chemicals in Water," *Organic Farming and Gardening* 7 (February 1960): 21–22. On *The Anti-Fluoridationist*, see J. I. Rodale, "How It All Started," *The Anti-Fluoridationist* 1, vol. 2 (c. 1961), Box 69, Folder 11, Greb Collection, Laird Wilcox Collection of Contemporary Political Movements, Kenneth Spencer Research Library, University of Kansas, Lawrence (hereafter GC-LWC). For "Enemies of the People" see J. I. Rodale, "Fluoridation: A Series," *Organic Farming and Gardening* 8 (January 1961): 45–8; and J. I. Rodale, "Fluoridation: A Dramatic Series," *Organic Farming and Gardening* 8 (February 1961): 72, 73–74, 76.

14. Reilly, "'This Poisoning of Our Drinking Water,'" 43–66. "A Monstrous Commie Plot," *Dr. Strangelove, or, How I Learned to Stop Worrying and Love the Bomb*, directed by Stanley Kubrick (Columbia Pictures, 1964).

15. Mrs. Allan Sapora to Rachel Carson, March 24, 1963, box 90, folder 1588, RCP.

16. H. Patricia Hynes, "Ellen Swallow, Lois Gibbs, and Rachel Carson: Catalysts of the American Environmental Movement," *Women's Studies International Forum* 8 (1985): 291–98; McGirr, *Suburban Warriors*, 6, 4; Joseph McCarthy, *McCarthyism—The Fight for America: Documented Answers to Questions Asked by Friend and Foe* (New York: Devin-Adair, 1952); Joseph McCarthy, *America's Retreat from Freedom: The Story of George Catlett Marshall* (New York: Devin-Adair, 1954); and Leonard Wickenden, *Our Daily Poison: The Effects of DDT, Fluoride, Hormones, and Other Chemicals on Modern Man* (New York: Devin-Adair, 1956). On conservative women, see also Michele M. Nickerson, *Mothers of Conservatism: Women and the Postwar Right* (Princeton, N.J.: Princeton University Press, 2012); and for "municipal housekeeping," see Suellen Hoy, *Chasing Dirt: The American Pursuit of Cleanliness* (New York: Oxford University Press, 1995), 59–122.

17. On Hamilton's concerns, see Robert Gottlieb, "Reconstructing Environmentalism: Complex Movements, Diverse Roots," *Environmental History Review* 17 (Winter 1993): 7–10. A broader treatment of the industrial health hazards is Christopher Sellers, *Hazards of the Job: From Industrial Disease to Environmental Health Science* (Chapel Hill: University of North Carolina Pres, 1997); and James Whorton, *Before Silent Spring: Pesticides and Public Health in Pre-DDT America* (Princeton, N.J.: Princeton University Press, 1974), 3–35, 68–92.

18. Whorton, *Before Silent Spring*, 175, 176–94, 205; Arthur Kallet and F. J. Schlink, *100,000,000 Guinea Pigs: Dangers in Everyday Foods, Drugs, and Cosmetics* (New York: Vanguard Press, 1933), 47–60; and Ruth deForest Lamb, *American Chamber of Horrors: The Truth about Food and Drugs* (New York: Farrar and Rinehart, 1936), 196–251.

19. Edmund P. Russell, *War and Nature: Fighting Humans and Insects with Chemicals from World War I to Silent Spring* (New York: Cambridge University Press, 2001), 124–30, 165–75. See also Russell's articles "The Strange Career of DDT: Experts, Federal Capacity, and Environmentalism in World War II," *Technology and Culture* 40 (Fall 1999): 788–93, and "'Speaking of Annihilation': Mobilizing for War against Human and Insect Enemies," *Journal of American History* 82 (March 1996): 1505–29. For the history of DDT's development, see also Thomas R. Dunlap, *DDT: Scientists, Citizens, and Public Policy* (Princeton, N.J.: Princeton University Press, 1981), 59–75.

20. Russell, "Strange Career of DDT," 780–93; the "startling toxicity" quotation is from p. 780. See also Russell, *War and Nature*, 156–64; and Dunlap, *DDT*, 63–68, 76–97.

21. Valerie J. Gunter and Craig K. Harris, "Noisy Winter: The DDT Controversy in the Years before *Silent Spring*," *Rural Sociology* 63 (June 1998): 179–98; and Russell, *War and Nature*, 196–98, 208–11, 216–21. On concerns about the U.S. Department of Agriculture's fire ant eradication program, see Joshua Blu Buhs, *The Fire Ant Wars: Nature, Science, and Public Policy in Twentieth-Century America* (Chicago: University of Chicago Press, 2004), 81–169. Similar concerns about both public and private pesticide use may be found in Pete Daniel, *Toxic Drift: Pesticides and Health in the Post–World War II South* (Baton Rouge: Louisiana State University Press, 2005). "The pertinent point in terms of the subsequent controversy development," Gunter and Harris ("Noisy Winter," 182) write, "is that, prior to the publication of *Silent Spring*, the public had over a decade and a half of at least some exposure to claims about DDT that *could be read as negative*, regardless of whether this was the reading intended by the original claimant." Emphasis in the original.

22. Ralph Lutts, "Chemical Fallout: Rachel Carson's *Silent Spring*, Radioactive Fallout, and the Environmental Movement," *Environmental Review* 9 (Fall 1985): 211–23; the quotation is on p. 222.

23. Arthur Daemmrich, "A Tale of Two Experts: Thalidomide and Political Engagement in the United States and West Germany," *Social History of Medicine* 15 (April 2002): 137–58; and Lytle, *Gentle Subversive*, 145.

24. Lear, *Rachel Carson*, 358–60; and Lytle, *Gentle Subversive*, 144–45.

25. "Elixirs of Death" is the title of chapter 3 of Carson's *Silent Spring*, 15–37.

26. Ibid., 188, 21–23, 16, 182.

27. Ibid., 16–17, 188–243, 192, 198.

28. Ibid., 13, 297. On Carson's politics, see Lear, *Witness for Nature*, 256–57, 375–76.

29. Carson, *Silent Spring*, 86, 13, 178.

30. Ibid., 127, 12–13.

31. Ibid., 12, 277–97, 13.

32. Mehr to Carson, February 1, 1963; Reilly, "'This Poisoning of Our Drinking Water,'" 153; Fanchon Battelle, "Fluoridation Unmasked" (Long Beach, California, 1953), 5, 22, Box 70, Folder 5, GC-LWC; Charles B. Hudson, "Fluoridation Folly," *Common Sense* 1, March 1961, Box 69, Folder 11, GC-LWC; and Goldman, "Poison on Tap," 42.

33. Lyle F. Sheen, "More about Fluoridation: An Offense against All Civilization," *The Cross and the Flag* (October 1961): 22, Box 69, Folder 11, GC-LWC.

34. Robert H. Poritzky, DDS, to the Peekskill, New York, *Evening Star*, October 27, 1954, reproduced in an undated flyer from the National Defense Committee of the National Society of the Daughters of the American Revolution, Box 69, Folder 11, GC-LWC; "Say 'NO' to Poison-Fluorine In Your Drinking Water," undated flyer from the Citizens Committee Against Fluoridation, c. 1960, Ephemera folder 1652, Laird Wilcox Collection on Contemporary Political Movements, Kenneth Spencer Research Library, University of Kansas, Lawrence (hereafter LWC-EPH, plus the folder number); and Carson, *Silent Spring*, 7, 16.

35. Fanchon Battelle, "Fluoridation Unmasked," 10–11; Dr. Robert C. Olney, MD, "Effects of Fluorine," undated flyer, c. 1965–67, Box 69, Folder 10, GC-LWC; Goldman, "Poison on Tap," 42–50; David O. Woodbury, "Fluoridation: Look Ma, No Cavities!" *American Opinion* (March 1968): 6; and H. C. Moolenburgh, "Of More Than Passing Interest: Mass Control," *The Covenant Message* (October 1978): 20, LWC-EPH 3372.

36. Patriotic Network of Letter Writers, "What They Haven't Told You about . . . Fluoridation," Box 69, Folder 12, GC-LWC.

37. "Say 'NO' to Poison-Fluorine In Your Drinking Water," LWC-EPH 1652; "Figures Do Not Lie," undated flyer published by the Citizens Action Program for Safe Wisconsin Water Inc., c. 1977, Box 69, Folder 3, GC-LWC; Battelle, "Fluoridation Unmasked," 12–13; George C. McGrath, "Is Fluoridated Water *Really* a Killer?" *Police Gazette* (October 1963), Box 69, Folder 12, GC-LWC; Ray L. Elliott, "Water Fluoridation Opposed," *Arizona Republic*, March 18, 1962, Box 69, Folder 13, GC-LWC; "Fluoridation: Questions and Answers," *The Cross and the Flag* (June 1967): 31; "Does Jewish Fluoride Really Fight Cavities in Childrens [sic] Teeth," undated booklet published by the Aryan Nations c. 1977, LWC-EPH 2097.8; Robert Olney, "Fluoride Poisoning," undated flyer published

by the Health Protection Association, c. 1968, Box 69, Folder 10, GC-LWC; and Robert C. Olney, "Open Letter to All Doctors: Stop Fluoride Diseases," *The Cross and the Flag* (December 1968), p. 23, Box 69, Folder 12, GC-LWC.

38. "Fluoridation Opposed," flyer published by the National Defense Committee of the National Society of the Daughters of the American Revolution, 1957, Box 69, Folder 11, GC-LWC; "How Does Fluoridation Affect You and Your Family?" flyer published by an unknown anti group, c. 1962–63, Box 70, Folder 2, GC-LWC; "Keep Your Water Supply Safe," undated flyer published by the Network of Patriotic Letter Writers, c. early to mid-1960s, Box 69, Folder 12, GC-LWC; and Anonymous, "Brubaker Health Hints," *Christian Vanguard* (December 1972): 9, Box 69, Folder 15, GC-LWC.

39. McGrath, "Is Fluoridated Water *Really* a Killer?" GC-LWC.

40. Carson, *Silent Spring*, 154–84; "Don't Wash Dollars down the Drain!" undated flyer published by Citizens Opposed to Compulsory Fluoridation, Kansas City, Missouri, c. early 1960s , Box 69, Folder 11, GC-LWC.

41. Dan Smoot, *The Dan Smoot Report* 10 (December 7, 1964): 338, Box 69, Folder 11, GC-LWC.

42. David O. Woodbury, "Fluoridation, Champion of Uncertainty," from the *York Weekly*, March 4, 1971, reprinted in a flyer by the Network of Patriotic Letter Writers, c. early 1970s, Box 69, Folder 12, GC-LWC.

43. "Facts about Fluoridation," flyer published by the Ohio Pure Water Association, April 1959, Box 70, Folder 1, GC-LWC; "What Do You Know about Fluoridation?" undated flyer from the California Committee of the Pure Water Association of America, Inc., c. late 1950s, Box 70, Folder 2, GC-LWC.

44. Battelle, "Fluoridation Unmasked," 6; Reilly, "'This Poisoning of Our Drinking Water," 32–38; H. S. Riecke Jr. to members of the Paul Revere Associated Yeoman, Inc., May 1968, Box 69, Folder 12, GC-LWC.

45. Carson, *Silent Spring*, 13; and Gerald Markowitz and David Rosner, *Deceit and Denial: The Deadly Politics of Industrial Pollution* (Berkeley: University of California Press, 2002).

46. "Uncle Sam Shoves It Down Your Throat Despite Experts and Evidence," *The Spotlight*, December 13, 1976.

47. "Fluoridation," undated flyer published by the National Defense Committee of the Daughters of the American Revolution, c. 1958, LWC-EPH 3589; "A Look at Fluoridation," undated newsletter from the National Defense Committee of the Daughters of the American Revolution, c. 1958, Box 69, Folder 10, GC-LWC; undated flyer from the "Freedom Center" of Kansas City, Missouri, c. 1957, Box 69, Folder 11, GC-LWC; Vera E. Adams, "Dear Members and Friends," untitled newsletter published by the National Committee Against Fluoridation, Inc., November 2, 1962, Box 69, Folder 12, GC-LWC; "Application for Membership," California Committee of the Pure Water Association of America, Inc., no date, c. mid-late 1960s, Box 69, Folder 12, GC-LWC; and Philip E. Zanfagna, "Fluoridation and Bureaucracy," LWC-EPH, 3589. For Zanafagna's correspondence with Carson, see Philip E. Zanfagna to Rachel Carson, November 3, 1962, RCP, Box 90, Folder 1588.

48. F. B. Exner, "The Real Issue Behind Fluoridation," *American Opinion* 5 (May

1962): 11; and "Communism or Freedom?" undated flyer from an unknown anti group, c. early 1960s, Box 69, Folder 10, GC-LWC.

49. Clive M. McKay to unknown, February 14, 1958, Box 69, Folder 10, GC-LWC; "WHO and Fluoridation," *American Opinion* 1 (May 1958); 33; and Ethel B. Dinning, "A Plea From Inundation," c. 1975, LWC-EPH 3589.

50. Gottlieb, *Forcing the Spring*, 3–10.

51. Reilly, "'This Poisoning of Our Drinking Water,'" 37–38, 50–51. For details on Bronner's life and career, see Charles Leroux, "Soap Opera," *Chicago Tribune*, December 7, 1999.

3. THE ENVIRONMENTAL CONSCIENCE OF A CONSERVATIVE

Epigraphs: Goldwater, *The Conscience of a Majority* (Englewood Cliffs, N.J.: Prentice Hall, 1970), 222, and Goldwater, *With No Apologies*, 296–97.

1. Barry Goldwater, *Conscience of a Majority*, 212.

2. Ibid., 224–25, 216–20, 221.

3. Ibid., 214–15, 222–23, 226–32.

4. *Dallas Morning News,* January 23, 1970; and Karl Hess, "Radical Contradictions," *Washington Post*, September 23, 1970, B8.

5. A good overview of this era is Matusow, *Unraveling of America*, 275–440.

6. On environmentalism, see Hays, *Beauty, Health, and Permanence*; Adam Rome, *The Bulldozer in the Countryside: Suburban Sprawl and the Rise of American Environmentalism* (New York: Cambridge University Press, 2001); Hal K. Rothman, *The Greening of a Nation? Environmentalism in the United States since 1945* (Fort Worth, Tex.: Harcourt Brace, 1998); and Donald Worster, *Nature's Economy: A History of Ecological Ideas,* 2nd edition (Cambridge: Cambridge University Press, 1994), 342–87. On Earth Day, see Rothman, *Greening of a Nation*, 121–25. The best source on environmentalism as a liberal initiative is Rome, "'Give Earth a Chance.'"

7. Rome, *Bulldozer in the Countryside*; Barry Goldwater to Charles H. Orme Jr., January 20, 1970, 91st Cong. Files, Box 33, Folder 5, BMG-AHF; Barry Goldwater to Charles H. Orme Jr., November 22, 1971, Constituent Service, 92nd Congress (1971–1972), Box 12, "EPA (1 of 2)," BMG-AHF.

8. Barry Goldwater to Gary H. Driggs, October 23, 1972, Box 1, Series 2, Folder 8, Special Collections and Archives, Cline Library, Northern Arizona University, Flagstaff. Goldwater wrote about the trip in detail, sans any environmental concerns, in "A Dream Come True," *McCall's* 93 (March 1966): 64, 68, 185–56, 188. He did admit in the article that Glen Canyon Dam, whatever its other effects, had rendered the Colorado's water "clear and blue and so cold that drinking it is pure pleasure" (p. 185). On the 1965 trip, see also Iverson, *Barry Goldwater: Native Arizonan*, 211–12.

9. Barry Goldwater to C. F. DeMott, March 25, 1970, 91st Cong. Files, Box 30, Folder 16, BMG-AHF; Barry Goldwater to Robert C. Capen, April 12, 1970, 91st Cong. Files, Box 30, Folder 16, BMG-AHF; and Barry Goldwater to Jean A. Hogg, January 22, 1970, 91st Cong. Files, Box 7, Folder 2, BMH-AHF.

10. Goldwater to Orme, January 20, 1970; and Barry Goldwater to Robert A. Erkins,

December 11, 1969, Legislative Series, 91st Cong., Public Works Committee, Box 15, "Air and Water Pollution (1 of 5)," BMG-AHF.

11. Flippen, *Nixon and the Environment*, 17–18, 102, 129–219, 136–38, 180, 225–31.

12. Goldwater's copy of Nixon's environmental message may be found in "SP" Series, Box 3SP, Folder 27, BMG-AHF; *Congressional Record*, 91st Cong., 2nd sess., Vol. 116, pt. 3 (February 18, 1970), p. 3731; Barry Goldwater to Barbara P. Kerr, September 25, 1970, Legislative Series, 91st Cong., Box 15, "Public Works—Air & Water Pollution (5 of 5)," BMG-AHF; Barry Goldwater to Sergeant George J. Zay Jr., October 15, 1970, 91st Cong. Files, Box 46, Folder 5, BMG-AHF; Barry Goldwater to James W. Pullaro, December 7, 1970, "BS" Series, Box 1, Folder 49, BMG-AHF; and Barry Goldwater to David Sterzing, December 12, 1969, 91st Cong. Files, Box 7, Folder 1, BMG-AHF.

13. Barry Goldwater to Danny Ellenberger, 92nd Cong. Files, Box 41, Folder 3, BMG-AHF; and Barry Goldwater to Michele Moots, February 2, 1971, "BS" Series, Box 1, Folder 49, BMG-AHF.

14. Barry Goldwater to George B. Munroe, March 31, 1971, "BS" Series, Box 1, Folder 49, BMG-AHF; Barry Goldwater to T. C. Basham, December 10, 1969, 91st Cong., Files, Box 7, Folder 2, BMG-AHF; Barry Goldwater to Lawrence Mehren, June 17, 1970, 91st Cong. Files, Box 7, Folder 4, BMG-AHF; Barry Goldwater to William P. Reilly, July 30, 1971, Constituent Service, 92nd Cong., Box 7, "Issue mail, Pollution (letters from students)," BMG-AHF; and Barry Goldwater to Keith Andersen, March 13, 1975, Constituent Service, 94th Cong., "Issue mail, Auto Emissions," BMG-AHF.

15. Mark Zajac, "Goldwater Pans Pollution," *The Delphian*, April 29, 1970.

16. *Congressional Record*, 91st Cong., 2nd sess., Vol. 116, pt. 24, p. 33120; *Congressional Roll Call* [1972]: *A Chronology and Analysis of Votes in the House and Senate, 92nd Congress, Second Session* (Washington, D.C.; Congressional Quarterly, 1973), 28–S, 65–S, 66–S, 69–S, 74–S, 81–S; and *Congressional Roll Call 1973: A Chronology and Analysis of Votes in the House and Senate, 93rd Congress, First Session* (Washington, D.C.: Congressional Quarterly, 1974), 51–S.

17. *Congressional Record*, 93rd Cong., 1st sess., Vol. 119, pt. 24 (September 24, 1973), p. 31033; *Congressional Record*, 93rd Cong., 1st sess., Vol. 119, pt. 30 (December 5, 1973), p. 39757; *Congressional Record*, 93rd Cong., 2nd sess., Vol. 120, pt. 3 (February 19, 1974), p. 3339; *Congressional Record*, 93rd Cong., 2nd sess., Vol. 120, pt. 23 (September 17, 1974), p. 31433; *Congressional Record*, 94th Cong., 1st sess., Vol. 121, pt. 7 (March 26, 1975), p. 8753; and *Congressional Record*, 94th Cong., 1st sess., Vol. 121, pt. 23, p. 9138 (April 7, 1975). See also Barry Goldwater to Edward F. Medley, July 17, 1975, 94th Cong. Files, Box 26, Folder 4, BMG-AHF.

18. Barry Goldwater to Mary Caldwell, July 24, 1969, 91st Cong. Files, Box 42, Folder 10, BMG-AHF. See also Barry Goldwater to Mrs. Samuel H. Fowler, May 25, 1970, 91st Cong. Files, Box 34, Folder 8, BMG-AHF; *Congressional Record*, 93rd Cong., 1st sess., Vol. 119, pt. 21 (July 27, 1973), p. 26359; Draft Press Release, Goldwater Senate Office, n.d. [c. July 27, 1973], "BS" series, Box 7, Folder 40, BMG-AHF; and Barry Goldwater to Jack Stone, February 10, 1975, "BS" series, Box 7, Folder 40, BMG-AHF. See also Barry Goldwater to G. D. Van Voorhis, April 1, 1974, "BS" series, Box 6, Folder 93, BMG-AHF.

19. *Congressional Record*, 92nd Cong., 1st sess., Vol. 117, pt. 9 (July 12, 1971), pp.

24526–31; and Barry Goldwater to John A. McComb, July 1, 1971, "BS" series, Box 3, Folder 17, BMG-AHF.

20. On Glen Canyon Dam and Rainbow Bridge, see Russell Martin, *A Story That Stands Like a Dam: Glen Canyon and the Struggle for the Soul of the West* (New York: Henry Holt and Co., 1989); and Jared Farmer, *Glen Canyon Dammed: Inventing Lake Powell and the Canyon Country* (Tucson: University of Arizona Press, 1999). See also Harvey, *Symbol of Wilderness*, 224–25, 280–82, 297–301. For Goldwater's varying thoughts on Rainbow Bridge, see Barry Goldwater to Stewart Udall, October 29, 1959, Legislative Series, 86th Cong., Box 12, "Rainbow Bridge," BMG-AHF, Barry Goldwater to Floyd Dominy, February 19, 1960, 84–88th Congs. Files, Box 15, Folder 1, BMG-AHF; and Barry Goldwater to Devereux Butcher, January 22, 1962, 84–88th Congs. Files, Box 15, Folder 1, BMG-AHF.

21. *Congressional Record*, 94th Cong., 2nd sess., Vol. 122, pt. 22 (August 30, 1976), pp. 28408–9; and *Congressional Quarterly Roll Call 1976: A Chronology and Analysis of Votes in the House and Senate, 94th Congress, Second Session* (Washington, D.C.: Congressional Quarterly, 1977), p. 74-S.

22. Barry Goldwater to Bruce E. Stafford, January 26, 1982, "E" Series, Box 2, Folder 4, BMG-AHF; and Barry Goldwater to John D. Leshy, September 10, 1982, "E" Series, Box 2, Folder 10, BMG-AHF.

23. Goldwater to Leshy, September 10, 1982.

24. Barry Goldwater to Emery Carl Gall, October 1, 1969, 91st Cong. Files, Box 45, Folder 5, BMG-AHF; and *Congressional Record*, 93rd Cong., 1st sess., Vol. 119, pt. 22 (September 5, 1973), pp. 28498–99.

25. *Congressional Record*, 91st Cong., 1st sess., Vol. 115, pt. 12 (June 12, 1969), pp. 15524–26.

26. *Congressional Record*, 93rd Cong., 1st sess., Vol. 119, pt. 7 (March 20, 1973), pp. 8690–94. On Goldwater's support for Native Americans, see Iverson, *Barry Goldwater: Native Arizonan*, 151–88, and on his 1973 enlargement plan, see pp. 211–15.

27. Barry Goldwater to Raymond Sherwin, May 1, 1973, Personal/Political II Files, Box 13P. Folder 16, BMG-AHF; and *Congressional Record*, 93rd Cong., 1st sess., Vol. 119, pt. 7 (March 20, 1973), pp. 8690, 8692.

28. A good summary of the Sierra Club's position is John McComb, "Southwest: Grand Canyon Giveaway," *Sierra Club Bulletin* 58 (July–August 1973): 23–24; and *Congressional Record*, 91st Cong., 1st sess., Vol. 115, pt. 22 (October 13, 1969), p. 29637. McComb and Goldwater corresponded at length about the senator's bill and its pros and cons. See Constituent Service, 91st Cong., Interior and Insular Affairs, Box 11, "Enlarge Boundaries of Grand Canyon National Park," folders 4 and 5.

29. *Congressional Record*, 93rd Cong., 1st sess., Vol. 119, pt. 21 (August 2, 1973), pp. 27538–40.

30. *Congressional Record*, 93rd Cong., 2nd sess., Vol. 120, pt. 12 (May 20, 1974), pp. 15356–57; and Barry Goldwater to Raymond Sherwin, July 12, 1973, Personal/Political II Files, Box 13P, Folder 16, BMG-AHF.

31. On the SST, see Mel Horwitch, *Clipped Wings: The American SST Conflict* (Cambridge: MIT Press, 1982); and Joshua Rosenbloom, "The Politics of the American SST Programme: Origin, Opposition, and Termination," *Social Studies of Science* 11 (November 1981): 403–23.

32. Rosenbloom, "Politics of the American SST Programme," 407–19.

33. *Congressional Record*, 91st Cong., 2nd sess., Vol. 116, pt. 15 (June 18, 1970), p. 20419.

34. *Congressional Record*, 91st Cong., 1st sess., Vol. 115, pt. 29 (December 17, 1969), p. 39600; Barry M. Goldwater, "The Big Lie and the SST," *New York Times*, December 16, 1970, p. 47; and Barry Goldwater to Mrs. Douglas Hale, September 17, 1970, 91st Cong. Files, Box 34, Folder 8, BMG-AHF.

35. *Congressional Record*, 91st Cong., 2nd sess., Vol. 116, pt. 32 (December 18, 1970), p. 42476; *Congressional Record*, 92nd Cong., 1st sess., Vol. 117, pt. 4 (March 1, 1971), p. 4433; *Congressional Record*, 92nd Cong., 1st sess., Vol. 117, pt. 5 (March 9, 1971), p. 5527; and *Congressional Record*, 92nd Cong., 1st sess., Vol. 117, pt. 6 (March 24, 1971), p. 7795. See also "SP" series, Box 1SP, Folder 42, BMG-AHF.

36. *Congressional Record*, 91st Cong., 2nd sess., Vol. 116, pt. 26 (October 2, 1970), p. 34767; Barry Goldwater to Kermit L. Smith, July 16, 1973, Personal/Political II Files, Box 13P, Folder 16, BMG-AHF; and *Congressional Record*, 94th Cong., 2nd sess., Vol. 122, pt. 6 (March 17, 1976), p. 6827.

37. *Congressional Record*, 94th Cong., 1st sess., Vol. 121, pt. 11 (May 15, 1975), p. 14716; Barry Goldwater to F. Richard Campbell, May 7, 1976, 94th Cong. Files, Box 9, Folder 7, BMG-AHF; and Barry Goldwater to Wayne Pratt, November 7, 1975, 94th Cong. Files, Box 12, Folder 2, BMG-AHF.

38. *Congressional Record*, 95th Cong., 2nd sess., Vol. 124, pt. 8 (August 8, 1978), pp. 24851, 24855, 24833; Barry Goldwater to James E. Patrick II, March 11, 1976, 94th Cong. Files, Box 9, Folder 8, BMG-AHF; and Barry Goldwater to Angelo Mercine, February 3, 1977, Constituent Service, 95th Cong., Issue Mail, "EPA," BMG-AHF.

39. Barry Goldwater to Governor Raul H. Castro, March 12, 1976, 94th Cong. Files, Box 9, Folder 8, BMG-AHF.

40. *Congressional Record*, 94th Cong., 2nd sess., Vol. 122, pt. 19, p. 23843; *Congressional Roll Call 1976*, pp. 63–S, 64–S, 66–S; and *Congressional Roll Call 1977: A Chronology and Analysis of Votes in the House and Senate, 95th Congress, First Session*, (Washington, D.C.: Congressional Quarterly, Inc., 1978), 28–S, 29–S, 30–S.

41. Rothman, *Greening of a Nation*, 132–33.

42. *Congressional Record*, 93rd Cong., 1st sess., Vol. 119, pt. 18 (July 12, 1973), p. 23547; *Congressional Record*, 93rd Cong., 1st sess., Vol. 119, pt. 28 (November 15, 1973), p. 37265; and *Congressional Record*, 96th Cong., 1st sess., Vol. 125, pt. 19 (September 19, 1979), p. 25290.

43. *Congressional Roll Call 1973*, p. 79–S; *Congressional Roll Call 1974: A Chronology and Analysis of Votes in the House and Senate, 93rd Congress, Second Session* (Washington, D.C.: Congressional Quarterly, Inc., 1975), 61–S; *Congressional Roll Call 1975: A Chronology and Analysis of Votes in the House and Senate, 94th Congress, First Session*, (Washington, D.C.: Congressional Quarterly, Inc., 1976), 11–S; *Congressional Roll Call 1976*, p. 5–S; and *Congressional Roll Call 1977*, p. 25–S, 44–S.

44. A good introduction to the two movements and similar ones, like the county supremacy and property-rights movements, is Jacqueline Vaughn Switzer, *Green Backlash: The History and Politics of Environmental Opposition in the U.S.* (Boulder: Lynne Rienner Publishers, 1997). For a provocative discussion of western antigovernment

sentiments and conservative politics, see Richard White, "The Current Weirdness in the West," *Western Historical Quarterly* 28 (Spring 1997): 5–16.

45. Switzer, *Green Backlash*, 191–225. See also Rothman, *Greening of a Nation*, 196–203.

46. Switzer, *Green Backlash*, 171–90; and Rothman, *Greening of a Nation*, 167–80. For a detailed discussion of the Sagebrush Rebellion, see R. Macgregor Cawley, *Federal Land, Western Anger: The Sagebrush Rebellion and Environmental Politics* (Lawrence: University Press of Kansas, 1993). On the Rebellion's relationship to conservative politics, see James Morton Turner, "'The Specter of Environmentalism': Wilderness, Environmental Politics, and the Evolution of the New Right," *Journal of American History* 96 (June 2009): 123–48.

47. Switzer, *Green Backlash*, 176; Cawley, *Federal Land, Western Anger*, 92; Barry Goldwater, "Interview of Senator Barry Goldwater," interview by Joe Fields, "SP" series, Box 25P, Folder 64, BMG-AHF; *Congressional Record*, 96th Cong., 2nd sess., Vol. 126, pt. 8 (May 6, 1980), p. 10089; *Congressional Record*, 97th Cong., 1st sess., Vol. 127, pt. 8 (May 20, 1981), p. 10477; *Congressional Record*, 96th Cong., 1st sess., Vol. 125, pt. 17 (August 3, 1979), p. 22362; *Congressional Record*, 96th Cong., 1st sess., Vol. 125, pt. 12 (June 18, 1979), p. 15239; *Congressional Record*, 96th Cong., 1st sess., Vol. 125, pt 18 (September 12, 1979), p. 24135; and *Congressional Roll Call 1979: A Chronology and Analysis of Votes in the House and Senate, 96th Congress, First Session* (Washington, D.C.: Congressional Quarterly, 1980), 70–S. See also "BS" series, Box 13, Folder 26, BMG-AHF.

48. Barry Goldwater to Samuel R. Lammie, September 1, 1982, "E" series, Box 2, Folder 10, BMG-AHF; Barry Goldwater to Dollie Teshe, March 18, 1982, "E" Series, Box 2, Folder 5, BMG-AHF; and Barry Goldwater to William H. Long, February 26, 1982, "E" Series, Box 2, Folder 4, BMG-AHF.

49. Nash, *Wilderness and the American Mind*, 272. On the whole Alaska wilderness controversy, see pp. 272–315.

50. Ibid., 292–315; *Congressional Quarterly*, 96th Cong., 2nd sess., Vol. 126, pt. 6 (April 15, 1980), p. 7872; Barry Goldwater to Stan Turley, August 14, 1980, Constituent Service, 96th Cong., Issue Mail, no box, no folder; and *Congressional Roll Call 1980: A Chronology and Analysis of Votes in the House and Senate, 96th Congress, Second Session* (Washington, D.C.: Congressional Quarterly, 1981), 48–S, 49–S, 50–S, 51–S.

51. Watt's controversial comments are quoted in Rothman, *Greening of a Nation*, 187. His comments on the Grand Canyon are quoted in Nash, *Wilderness and the American Mind*, 355. On Watt in general, see C. Brant Short, *Ronald Reagan and the Public Lands: America's Conservation Debate* (College Station: Texas A&M Press, 1989), 51–80; and also Rotham, *Greening of a Nation*, 169–74, Stoll, *Protestantism, Capitalism, and Nature in America*, 188–92; and Switzer, *Green Backlash*, 8, 164, 185–87, 252. For the Sierra Club's "Dump Watt" campaign, see *Sierra* 66 (May–June 1981): 82–83; Nathaniel Pryor Reed, "On the Matter of Mr. Watt," *Sierra* 66 (July–August 1981): 6–8, 11–15; and Doug Scott, "Reagan's First Year: We Know Watt's Wrong," *Sierra* 67 (January–February 1982): 30, 128–29.

52. *Congressional Record*, 97th Cong., 1st sess., Vol. 127, pt. 18 (October 20, 1981), p. 24533; *Congressional Record*, 97th Cong., 2nd sess., Vol. 128, pt. 15 (August 11, 1982), p. 20471; *Congressional Record*, 98th Cong., 1st sess., Vol. 129, pt. 19 (September 29, 1983), p.

26398; and *Congressional Record*, 978h Cong., 1st sess., Vol. 129, pt. 20 (October 17, 1983), p. 26398. See also "E" series, Box 2, Folder 9, BMG-AHF; Barry Goldwater to Joseph Zashin, January 28, 1982, "E" Series, Box 2, Folder 4, BMG-AHF; Barry Goldwater to Mike Quinn, March 15, 1982, "E" Series, Box 2, Folder 5, BMG-AHF; and James G. Watt to Barry Goldwater, October 28 1983, "unprocessed," BMG-AHF.

53. *Congressional Record*, 95th Cong., 2nd sess., Vol. 124, pt 12 (June 5, 1978), p. 16235; *Congressional Record*, 96th Cong., 1st sess., Vol. 125, pt. 12 (June 18, 1979), pp. 15208–9; *Congressional Record*, 96th Cong., 1st sess., Vol. 125, pt 17 (August 1, 1979), pp. 21844–45; *Congressional Record*, 96th Cong., 2nd sess., Vol. 126, pt 12 (June 16, 1980), p. 14879; *Congressional Record*, 97th Cong., 1st sess., Vol. 127, pt 6 (April 28, 1981), pp. 7579–81; *Congressional Record*, 97th Cong., 2nd sess., Vol. 128, pt 1 (February 4, 1982), pp. 913–14; *Congressional Record*, 98th Cong., 1st sess., Vol. 129, pt 8 (April 27, 1983), p. 10099; *Congressional Record*, 98th Cong., 1st sess., Vol. 129, pt 16 (July 29, 1983), p. 21642; and *Congressional Record*, 98th Cong., 2nd sess., Vol. 130, pt 15 (July 25, 1984), p. 20923. See also "Statement of Senator Barry Goldwater," April 26, 1983, "E" Series, Box 1, Folder 18, BMG-AHF, Barry Goldwater to Senator Quentin Burdick, August 18 1982, "E" Series, Box 1, Folder 18, BMG-AHF; *Congressional Record*, 96th Cong., 2nd sess., Vol. 126, pt. 10 (May 22, 1980), p. 12065; *Congressional Record*, 95th Cong., 1st sess., Vol. 123, pt. 6 (March 9, 1977), pp. 6946–47; *Congressional Record*, 95th Cong., 1st sess., Vol. 123, pt. 19 (July 15, 1977), p. 23356; *Congressional Record*, 95th Cong., 2nd sess., Vol. 124, pt. 8 (April 10, 1978), pp. 9466–67; *Congressional Record*, 95th Cong., 2nd sess., Vol. 124, pt. 8 (April 13, 1978), pp. 10066–67; *Congressional Record*, 95th Cong., 2nd sess., Vol. 124, pt. 10 (May 9, 1978), pp. 13005–6; *Congressional Record*, 95th Cong., 2nd sess., Vol. 124, pt. 18 (August 8, 1978), p. 24901; *Congressional Record*, 96th Cong., 1st sess., Vol. 125, pt. 4 (March 14, 1979), p. 5018; *Congressional Record*, 96th Cong., 1st sess., Vol. 125, pt. 19 (September 14, 1979), pp. 24596–98; *Congressional Record*, 96th Cong., 2nd sess., Vol. 126, pt. 25 (December 11, 1980), pp. 33556–57; *Congressional Record*, 97th Cong., 1st sess., Vol. 127, pt. 15 (September 9, 1981), pp. 19783–85; *Congressional Record*, 97th Cong., 1st sess., Vol. 127, pt. 20 (October 29, 1981), pp. 26032–33; *Congressional Record*, 97th Cong., 1st sess., Vol. 127, pt. 21 (November 18, 1981), p. 27950; *Congressional Record*, 97th Cong., 2nd sess., Vol. 128, pt. 12 (July 15, 1982), p. 16418; *Congressional Record*, 97th Cong., 2nd sess., Vol. 128, pt. 18 (September 24, 1982), pp. 25118–19; *Congressional Record*, 97th Cong., 2nd sess., Vol. 128, pt. 21 (December 6, 1982), pp. 28857; *Congressional Record*, 97th Cong., 2nd sess., Vol. 128, pt. 21 (December 8, 1982), pp. 29402–3; *Congressional Record*, 98th Cong., 1st sess., Vol. 129, pt. 3 (March 3, 1983), p. 3788; *Congressional Record*, 98th Cong., 1st sess., Vol. 129, pt. 4 (March 9, 1983), p. 4440; *Congressional Record*, 98th Cong., 2nd sess., Vol. 130, pt. 1 (January 26, 1984), p. 622; and *Congressional Record*, 98th Cong., 2nd sess., Vol. 130, pt. 5 (March 21, 1984), pp. 6129–30. On Goldwater's Tellico Dam votes, see *Congressional Roll Call 1979*, pp. 23–S and 24–S. On Hualapai Dam, see *Congressional Record*, 96th Cong., 2nd sess., Vol. 126, pt. 6 (April 15, 1980), p. 7873.

54. "From the Office of Barry Goldwater (R-AZ), 14 November 1980," "SP" Series, Box 25P, Folder 15, BMG-AHF; and Barry Goldwater to Larry Fester, January 25, 1982, "E" Series, Box 2, Folder 4, BMG-AHF. For the motor versus oars controversy, see Nash, *Wilderness and the American Mind*, 329–41. On Goldwater's stance on motorized Grand

Canyon river trips, see also Barry Goldwater to Interior Secretary Cecil Andrus, June 6, 1980, Box 1, Series 2, Folder 9, Special Collections, Cline Library, Northern Arizona University, Flagstaff; "Office of Barry Goldwater (R-AZ)," June 6, 1980, "SP" Series, Box 25P, Folder 37, BMG-AHF; "Office of Barry Goldwater (R-Ariz)," August 26, 1980, "SP" Series, Box 25P, Folder 139, BMG-AHF; and *Congressional Record*, 96th Cong., 2nd sess., Vol. 126, pt. 22 (November 14, 1980), pp. 29648–50.

55. *Congressional Roll Call 1976*, p. 51–S; *Congressional Roll Call 1977*, p. 55–S; *Congressional Roll Call 1978*, pp. 35–S and 36–S; *Congressional Roll Call 1980*, p. 68–S; *Congressional Record*, 97th Cong., 2nd sess., Vol. 128, pt. 5 (March 31, 1982), p. 6200; Barry Goldwater to Jeffrey Hill, January 31, 1984, "E" Series, Box 6, Folder 31, BMG-AHF; *Congressional Roll Call 1985: A Chronology and Analysis of Votes in the House and Senate, 99th Congress, First Session* (Washington, D.C.: Congressional Quarterly, 1986), 25–S; and *Congressional Roll Call 1986: A Chronology and Analysis of Votes in the House and Senate, 99th Congress, Second Session* (Washington, D.C.: Congressional Quarterly, 1987), 56–S. On Goldwater's support for renewable energy in the 1980s, see also "E" Series, Box 2, Folders 4 and 5, BMG-AHF.

56. *Congressional Record*, 97th Cong., 2nd sess., Vol. 128, pt. 6 (April 29, 1982), pp. 8302, 8306.

57. Ibid., 8306.

58. *Congressional Record*, 98th Cong., 2nd sess., Vol. 130, pt. 1 (February 1, 1984), pp. 1316, 1318–21; and *Congressional Record*, 98th Cong., 2nd sess., Vol. 130, pt. 17 (August 9, 1984), p. 23438.

59. *Congressional Record*, 98th Cong., 2nd sess., Vol. 130, pt. 1 (February 1, 1984), p. 1318. On RARE II, see Rothman, *Greening of a Nation*, 130–32.

60. *Congressional Record*, 99th Cong., 2nd sess., Vol. 132, pt. 14, p. 20206.

61. See, for example, Lloyd Grove, "Barry Goldwater's Left Turn," *Washington Post*, July 28, 1994.

62. Goldberg, *Barry Goldwater,* 333, 338; and Bill Rentschler, *Goldwater: A Tribute to a Twentieth-Century Political Icon* (Chicago: Contemporary Books, 2000), 186.

63. Rothman, *Greening of a Nation*, 4–5, 209–10.

4. TENDING NATURE WITH THE INVISIBLE HAND

Epigraph: Terry Anderson and Donald R. Leal. *Free Market Environmentalism* (Boulder: Westview Press, 1991), 185.

1. Kirk, *Counterculture Green,* see in particular chapter 6, "Free Minds, Free Markets," 82–209.

2. Ted Steinberg, "Can Capitalism Save the Planet? On the Origins of Green Liberalism," *Radical History Review* 107 (Spring 2010): 7–24; Maureen A. Flanagan, "Gender and Urban Political Reform: The City Club and the Women's City Club of Chicago in the Progressive Era," *American Historical Review* 95 (October 1990): 1032–50; and Maureen A. Flanagan, "The City Profitable, The City Livable: Environmental Policy, Gender, and Power in Chicago in the 1910s," *Journal of Urban History* 22 (January 1996): 163–90. On Resources For the Future, see David Pearce, "An Intellectual History of Environmental

Economics," *Annual Review of Energy and the Environment* 27 (2002): 58–81.

3. This synopsis of free-market environmentalism is a result of wide reading in the literature; there are only a few comprehensive introductions to the movement and its ideas. The best is Anderson and Leal's *Free Market Environmentalism*. Other general sources include Terry L. Anderson, "The New Resource Economics: Old Ideas and New Applications," *American Journal of Agricultural Economics* 64 (December 1982): 928–34; Terry L. Anderson and Donald R. Leal, "Free Market versus Political Environmentalism," *Harvard Journal of Law and Public Policy* 15 (Spring 1992): 297–310; Richard L. Stroup and John A. Baden, *Natural Resources: Bureaucratic Myths and Environmental Management* (San Francisco: Pacific Institute for Public Policy Research, 1983); and John A. Baden and Robert Ethier, "Linking Liberty, Economy, and Ecology," *The Freeman* 43 (September 1993): 340–42.

4. The standard source on Progressive conservation and scientific management is Hays, *Conservation and the Gospel of Efficiency.*

5. John A. Baden, "The Failure of America's Sylvan Socialism," *Seattle Times,* February 5, 1997; and Gary D. Libecap and Ronald N. Johnson, "Property Rights, Nineteenth-Century Federal Timber Policy, and the Conservation Movement," *Journal of Economic History* 39 (March 1979): 129–42.

6. There is a great deal of "free-market" analysis on the Forest Service. This section draws mostly from Randal O'Toole, *Reforming the Forest Service* (Washington, D.C.: Island Press, 1988). See also Robert T. Deacon and M. Bruce Johnson, *Forestlands: Public and Private* (Cambridge, Mass.: Ballinger Publishing Company, 1985); William F. Hyde, "Compounding Clear Cuts: The Social Failures of Public Timber-Management in the Rockies," in John Baden and Richard L. Stroup, eds., *Bureaucracy vs. Environment: The Environmental Costs of Bureaucratic Governance* (Ann Arbor: University of Michigan Press, 1981), 186–202; Stroup and Baden, "Timber Beasts, Tree Huggers, and the Old Folks at Home," in Stroup and Baden, *Natural Resources,* 111–27; and chapter 5, "Bureaucracy versus Environment: The Beat Goes On," in Anderson and Leal, *Free Market Environmentalism,* revised edition, 47–58; Randal O'Toole, *The Best-Laid Plans: How Government Planning Harms Your Quality of Life, Your Pocketbook, and Your Future* (Washington, D.C.: Cato Institute, 2007).

7. On the Knutson-Vandenberg Act of 1930, see http://www.law.cornell.edu/uscode/html/uscode16/usc_sec_16_00000500——-000-notes.html, (accessed March 15, 2011).

8. On marketizing the Forest Service, see O'Toole, *Reforming the Forest Service,* 196–237. John Baden has been an especially vocal supporter of the private-trust idea. See Baden, "The Forest Service Is Long Overdue for an Overhaul," *Seattle Times,* February 9, 1993; Baden, "Forest Trusts: A Better Way to Conserve Western Lands," *Seattle Times,* February 26, 2002; and John A. Baden and Tim O'Brien, "A Radical Proposal To Bail Out Smokey: Privatization," *Seattle Times,* May 25, 1993.

9. On BLM mismanagement, see Stroup and Baden, *Natural Resources,* 46–49; Sabine Kremp, "A Perspective on BLM Grazing," and Robert M. Lanner, "Chained to the Bottom," in Baden and Stroup, *Bureaucracy vs. Environment,* 124–69; and John A. Baden and Richard Ethier, "New Range Wars and the Grazing-fee Dilemma," *Seattle Times,* December 22, 1992. On the Bureau of Reclamation, see Bernard Shanks, "Dams and Disasters:

The Social Problems of Water Development Policies," in Baden and Stroup, *Bureaucracy vs. Environment*; John A. Baden, "What Price Must the Salmon Pay To Keep Power Rates Low?" *Seattle Times*, November 23, 1994; John A. Baden and Douglas S. Noonan, "Conquest of the Columbia Carried Tremendous Costs," *Seattle Times*, August 21, 1996; and Zach Willey, "Behind Schedule and Over Budget: The Case of Markets, Water, and Environment," *Harvard Journal of Law and Public Policy* 15 (Spring 1992): 396–402. On national parks, see John Baden, "Park Problems? Try Trusts," (Bozeman) *Daily Chronicle*, September 10, 2003.

10. Anderson and Leal, *Free Market Environmentalism*, 71–79, 159–63, 167–74; John A. Baden, "How To Cope with the Runaway Endangered Species Act," *Seattle Times*, June 13, 1991; John A. Baden and Tim O'Brien, "Creating Positive Rewards for Species Preservation," *Seattle Times*, October 20, 1993; and John A. Baden and Douglas S. Noonan, "The Adverse Consequences of the ESA," *Seattle Times*, October 25, 1993.

11. Anderson and Leal, *Free Market Environmentalism*, 154.

12. For a general history of economic thinking about environmental issues, see Ehrun Kula, *History of Environmental Economic Thought* (New York: Routledge, 1998). See also Igne Røpke, "The Early History of Modern Ecological Economics," *Ecological Economics* 50 (2004): 293–314; and Pearce "Intellectual History of Environmental Economics," 57–81.

13. K. William Kapp, *The Social Costs of Private Enterprise* (Cambridge: Harvard University Press, 1950), 231, 233.

14. Kula, *History of Environmental Economic Thought*, 82–101.

15. Switzer is careful to note that most Wise Use adherents do not fit the stereotype of simplistic right-wing extremists, blindly opposed to big government, federal power, and environmental protection alike. Indeed, it is even questionable to what extent the "movement" as a national phenomenon even exists. It is true, however, that Wise Use leaders like Ron Arnold made it their mission to "delegitimize" the environmental movement, equating it with communism, for example, or accusing it of intentionally destroying the resource industry, charges that play well among some member on the grassroots far right. See Switzer, *Green Backlash*, 209–11.

16. H. Scott Gordon, "The Economic Theory of a Common-Property Resource: The Fishery," *Journal of Political Economy* 62 (April 1954): 124–42. See also Gordon, "Economics and the Conservation Question," *Journal of Law and Economics* 1 (October 1958): 110–21. Arthur F. McEvoy discusses Gordon's "Fishery" article in depth in *The Fisherman's Problem: Ecology and Law in the California Fisheries* (New York: Cambridge University Press, 1986), 10–12; and John H. Dales, *Pollution, Property, and Prices* (Toronto: University of Toronto Press, 1968). On Crocker, see Thomas H. Tietenberg, *Emissions Trading: Principles and Practice*, 2nd edition (Washington, D.C.: Resources for the Future, 2006), 40–45.

17. Ronald Coase, "The Problem of Social Cost," *Journal of Law and Economics* 3 (October 1960): 1–44. On Coase's influence, see Richard A. Posner, "Nobel Laureate: Ronald Coase and Methodology," *Journal of Economic Perspectives* 7 (Autumn 1993): 195–210; David Warsh, "When the Revolution Was a Party: How Privatization Was Invented in the 1960s," *Boston Globe*, October 20, 1991; and Harold Demsetz, "Toward a Theory of

Property Rights," *American Economic Review* 57 (May 1967): 347–59.

18. Frederick A. Hayek, "The Use of Knowledge in Society," *American Economic Review* 35 (September 1945): 519–30; and Milton Friedman, *Capitalism and Freedom* (Chicago: University of Chicago Press, 1962).

19. Garrett Hardin, "The Tragedy of the Commons," *Science* 62 (December 13, 1968): 1243–48; the quotation is on p. 1244.

20. Ibid., 1247.

21. See "VITA—January 1982—John A. Baden" in "A Report on the Center for Political Economy & Natural Resources 1978–1982—March 11,1982," Print Archives-Subject (organization) files: Political Economy and Natural Resources (Center For), Merrill G. Burlingame Special Collections, Montana State University Libraries, Bozeman. For Baden's comments on Friedman, see "Happy Birthday, Uncle Milty," (Bozeman) *Daily Chronicle*, July 24, 2002.

22. Garrett Hardin and John A. Baden, eds., *Managing the Commons* (San Francisco: W. H. Freeman and Co., 1977). For Baden's contributions, see John Baden, "A Primer for the Management of Common Pool Resources," 137–46; Kari Bullock and John Baden, "Communes and the Logic of the Commons," 182–99; John Baden and Richard Stroup, "Property Rights, Environmental Quality, and the Management of National Forests," 229–40; "Neospartan Hedonists, Adult Toy Aficionados, and the Rationing of Public Lands," 241–51; and "Population, Ethnicity, and Public Goods: The Logic of Interest-Group Strategy," 252–60; and M. Bruce Johnson, "Report on the Site Visitation Committee—Center For Political Economy and Natural Resources," available online at http://www.free-eco.org/pdfs/report.pdf (accessed October 16, 2004).

23. For *Bureaucracy vs. Environment*, see note 6 in this chapter, and for the center's funding, see "Financial Report" in "A Report on the Center for Political Economy & Natural Resources, 1978–1982—March 11,1982," p. 15, Print Archives-Subject (organization) files: Political Economy and Natural Resources (Center For), Merrill G. Burlingame Special Collections, Montana State University Libraries, Bozeman.

24. See *Cato Journal* 2 (Spring 1982). On the rise of conservative and libertarian think tanks, see James G. McGann, "Academics to Ideologues: A Brief History of the Public Policy Research Industry," *PS: Political Science and Politics* 25 (December 1992): 733–40; Donald E. Abelson, "From Policy Research to Political Advocacy: The Changing Role of Think Tanks in American Politics," *Canadian Review of American Studies* 25 (Winter 1995): 93–126; and Niels Bjerre-Poulsen, "The Heritage Foundation: A Second-Generation Think Tank," *Journal of Policy History* 3 (1991): 152–72.

25. Julian L. Simon, *The Ultimate Resource* (Princeton, N.J.: Princeton University Press, 1981). On Simon, see Julian L. Simon, *A Life against the Grain: The Autobiography of an Unconventional Economist* (New Brunswick, N.J.: Transaction Publishers, 2003).

26. O'Toole, *Reforming the Forest Service*, 183.

27. Ibid., 173–234.

28. For *Free Market Environmentalism*, see note 3 in this chapter.

29. William Funk, "Free Market Environmentalism: Wonder Drug or Snake Oil?" *Harvard Journal of Law and Public Policy* 15 (Spring 1992): 511–16. On the history of tradable permits, see Tietenberg, *Emissions Trading*, 1–17.

30. Edward Brunet, "Debunking Wholesale Private Enforcement of Environmental Rights," *Harvard Journal of Law and Public Policy* 15 (Spring 1992): 312, 315; Peter S. Menell, "Institutional Fantasylands: From Scientific Management to Free Market Environmentalism," *Harvard Journal of Law and Public Policy* 15 (Spring 1992): 503–5; and James E. Krier, "The Tragedy of the Commons, Part Two," *Harvard Journal of Law and Public Policy* 15 (Spring 1992): 339–46. On industry's influence on the regulatory process, see also Hays, *History of Environmental Politics since 1945*, 122–36; and Switzer, *Green Backlash*, 103–68.

31. On tradable permits, see Herman E. Daly, "Free Market Environmentalism: Turning a Good Servant into a Bad Master," in his *Ecological Economics and the Ecology of Economics: Essays in Criticism* (Cheltenham, UK: Edward Elgar Publishing, 1999); Daniel H. Cole, "Clearing the Air: Four Propositions about Property Rights and Environmental Protection," *Duke Environmental Law and Policy Forum* 10 (1999): 109–17; and Thomas Michael Power, "The Price of Everything: Free Market Environmentalism," *Sierra* (November–December 1993): 86–96.

32. See, for example, Eric Freyfogle, *The Land We Share: Private Property and the Common Good* (Washington, D.C.: Island Press, 2003), 165–66, 177–78. Herman Daly makes a similar argument—see his *Ecological Economics*, 37. See also Reuben C. Plantico, "A Property Rights Strategy for Protecting the Environment: A Comment on Stroup and Goodman," *Harvard Journal of Law and Public Policy* 15 (Spring 1992): 458; and Menell, "Institutional Fantasylands," 596, 500–1. On the "anecdote" criticism, see Cole, "Clearing the Air," 104, 119–22. On the Dust Bowl, see Donald Worster, *Dust Bowl: The Southern Plains in the 1930s* (New York: Oxford University Press, 1979). Worster argues that capitalism was the fundamental cause of the ecological degradation behind the dust storms. The capitalist system, he maintains, encourages ecological destruction because it views nature as mere resources to be turned into profit. Such a view makes "stewardship" of private property an immensely difficult thing to achieve—it ignores ecological limits to exploitation and makes all land use subject only to short-term goals of profit.

33. See Freyfogle, *Land We Share*, 65–134; Daly, *Ecological Economics*, 35; and David Roodman, "Another Take on Free Market Environmentalism: A Friendly Critique," available online at http://www.perc.org/articles/article146.php (accessed March 15, 2011). The classic treatment of the evolution of "industrial-friendly law" is Morton J. Horwitz, *The Transformation of American Law, 1780–1860* (Cambridge: Harvard University Press, 1977). On the New England textile industry and the legal battles over dams, see also Steinberg, *Nature Incorporated*.

34. On communal management, see Elinor Ostrom, *Governing the Commons: The Evolution of Institutions for Collective Action* (Cambridge: Cambridge University Press, 1990).

35. Terry Anderson and Peter J. Hill, "The Evolution of Property Rights: A Study of the American West," *Journal of Law and Economics* 18 (April 1975): 163–79; and Richard Stroup, "Environmentalism, Free-Market," available online at http://www.econlib.org/library/Enc1/EnvironmentalismFreeMarket.html (accessed March 10, 2010).

36. Daly, *Ecological Economics*, 35–37.

37. "Bush Administration's Environmental Policies: Environmental Report Card 2001–2," available online at http://www.perc.org/articles/article469.php (accessed March 11, 2010); J. R. Pegg, "Bush Supporters Unhappy with Environmental Policy,"

available online at http://www.ens-newswire.com/ens/jan2003/2003-01-22-10.html (accessed December 13, 2012); and Eric Painin, "Free-market Environmentalists Gaining Stature," *Washington Post*, June 4, 2001. On Baden's troubles, see Ruth Marcus, "Issues Groups Fund Seminars for Judges," *Washington Post*, April 9, 1998; Dustin Solberg, "Judges Get FREE Lessons on Property Rights," *High Country News*, July 6, 1998; Joe Stephens, "Judges' Free Trips Go Unreported," *Washington Post*, June 30, 2000; George Lardner Jr., "Report Links Environmental Rulings, Judges' Free Trips," *Washington Post*, July 25, 2000; and Anne Gearan, "3 Federal Judges Are Sued Over Ethics," *Seattle Post-Intelligencer*, March 22, 2004. On criticisms of corporate funding, see Curtis Moore, "Rethinking the Think Tanks: How Industry-Funded 'Experts' Twist the Environmental Debate," *Sierra* 87 (July–August 2002): 56–59, 73.

38. See, for example, Stroup and Baden, "The Demise of the Sagebrush Rebellion and Other Vanquished Dreams," in Stroup and Baden, *Natural Resources*, 99–110; and John Baden, "Political Economy Perspectives on the Sagebrush Rebellion," Box 3, Folder 8, Roy E. Huffman Papers, Merrill G. Burlingame Special Collections, Montana State University Libraries, Bozeman.

39. Cronon, *Changes in the Land.* "That Wilderness Should Turn a Mart" is Cronon's title for chapter 8, pp. 159–70. "A World of Fields and Fences" is the title for chapter 7, pp. 127–58.

40. James C. Scott, *Seeing Like a State: How Certain Schemes To Improve the Human Condition Have Failed* (New Haven, Conn.: Yale University Press, 1998).

41. Ibid., 13.

42. Ibid., 412.

5. LIKE A SCARLET THREAD

Epigraph: Edward Abbey, *Confessions of a Barbarian*, 276.

1. Edward Bellamy, *Looking Backward, 2000–1887*, edited by Robert C. Elliott (Boston: Houghton Mifflin, 1966). On *Looking Backward*'s influence, see James J. Kopp, "Looking Backward at Edward Bellamy's Influence in Oregon, 1888–1936," *Oregon Historical Quarterly* 104 (Spring 2003): 62–95.

2. Bellamy, *Looking Backward*, 96; Aldous Huxley, *Brave New World* (New York: HarperCollins, 1998); and George Orwell, *1984* (London: Secker and Warburg, 1949). *Brave New World* was first published in 1932.

3. Edward Abbey, *Good News* (New York: Penguin Books, 1980), 1, 2.

4. Edward Abbey to Charmaine Balian, November 13, 1981, Box 2, Folder 4, Edward Abbey Papers 1947–1990 MS-271, Special Collections, University of Arizona Libraries, Tucson (EAP): Edward Abbey, "Insolent Remarks, Ariz. Sierra Club, Phoenix, Sat. 3-11-72," Box 8, Folder 1, EAP; and Edward Abbey, "Introductory Remarks, Wilderness Society Medicine Show, Santa Fe, NM, April 22, 1975," Box 8, Folder 2, EAP.

5. Edward Abbey, "The Conscience of the Conqueror," in Abbey, *Abbey's Road* (New York: Penguin Books, 1979), 137; and Edward Abbey, "Freedom and Wilderness, Wilderness and Freedom," in Abbey, *The Journey Home: Some Words in Defense of the American West* (New York: Penguin Books, 1977), 235–36.

6. Abbey, *Journey Home*, xi, xiii; Edward Abbey, *Earth Apples: The Poetry of Edward Abbey*, edited by David Petersen (New York: St. Martin's Griffin, 1995), 82–84; and Edward Abbey, *Desert Solitaire: A Season on the Wilderness* (New York: Ballantine Books, 1968).

7. Edward Abbey, "The Author's Preface to His Own Book," in Abbey, *Slumgullion Stew: An Edward Abbey Reader* (New York: E.P. Dutton, 1984), ix; and Edward Abbey, "A Writer's Credo," in Abbey, *One Life at a Time*, 177–78.

8. William Cronon, "The Trouble with Wilderness; or, Getting Back to the Wrong Nature," in Cronon, *Uncommon Ground*, 79; Limerick, *Desert Passages*, 153, 162; and Elliott West, *The Way to the West: Essays on the Central Plains* (Albuquerque: University of New Mexico Press, 1995), 146.

9. Sutter, *Driven Wild*, 3–18. For a provocative criticism of the "wilderness critique," see Donald Worster, "The Wilderness of History," *Wild Earth* 7 (Fall 1997): 9–13

10. James C. Calahan, *Edward Abbey: A Life* (Tucson: University of Arizona Press, 2001), 3–26. See also James C. Calahan, "Edward Abbey, Appalachian Easterner," *Western American Literature* 31 (November 1996): 233–53; and James C. Calahan, "'My People': Edward Abbey's Appalachian Roots in Indiana County, Pennsylvania (Part One)," *Pittsburgh History* 79 (Fall 1996): 92–107, and "'My People': Edward Abbey's Appalachian Roots in Indiana County, Pennsylvania (Part Two)," *Pittsburgh History* 79 (Winter 1996–97): 160–79. For a less useful treatment of Abbey's life, see James Bishop Jr., *Epitaph for a Desert Anarchist: The Life and Legacy of Edward Abbey* (New York: Antheneum, 1994).

11. Edward Abbey and Eliot Porter, *Appalachian Wilderness: The Great Smoky Mountains* (New York: Arrowood Press, 1988), 13–16, 74–87; Edward Abbey, "Blood Sport," in Abbey, *One Life at a Time, Please*, 33–40; and Edward Abbey, "Shadows from the Big Woods," in Abbey, *Journey Home*, 223–26. See also Edward Abbey, "Thus I Reply to Rene Dubos," in Abbey, *Down the River* (New York: Penguin Books, 1982), 111. On Abbey's birth and early life, see Calahan, *Edward Abbey*, 4–26.

12. Edward Abbey, *The Fool's Progress: An Honest Novel* (New York: Avon Books, 1988).

13. Ronald Eller, *Miners, Millhands, and Mountaineers: Industrialization of the Appalachian South, 1880–1930* (Knoxville: University of Tennessee Press, 1982), 3, 6. On preindustrial Appalachian social structure, see also Paul Salstrom, *Appalachia's Path to Dependency: Rethinking a Region's Economic History, 1730–1940* (Lexington: University Press of Kentucky, 1994), especially chapter 3, "Rural Appalachia's Subsistence-Barter-and-Borrow Systems," 41–59; Ronald Lewis, *Transforming the Appalachian Countryside: Railroads, Deforestation, and Social Change in West Virginia, 1880–1920* (Chapel Hill: University of North Carolina Press, 1998), explores preindustrial Appalachian culture while avoiding agrarian, antimarket stereotypes of its people.

14. Eller, *Miners, Millhands, and Mountaineers*, 16–22.

15. Ibid., 10.

16. Ibid., 39–160.

17. Ibid., 55–57, 64, 228.

18. Ibid., 161–98.

19. Ibid., 199–224; the quotation is on p. 212.

20. Lewis, *Transforming the Appalachian Countryside*, 9; and Eller, *Miners, Millhands, and Mountaineers*, 160.

21. Abbey, *Voice Crying in the Wilderness*, 19. Howard Abbey is quoted in Calahan, *Edward Abbey*, 7.

22. Calahan, *Edward Abbey*, 7–8; Paul Abbey to Edward Abbey, April 1, 1970, Box 2, Folder 2, EAP; Paul Abbey to Edward and Clarke Abbey, September 10, 1984, Box 2, Folder 2, EAP; and Paul Abbey to Edward Abbey, July 20, 1987, Box 2, Folder 2, EAP.

23. Edward Abbey to the Editors of *New York Review of Books*, March 30, 1973, Box 3, Folder 7, EAP.

24. Edward Abbey, "My Life as a P.I.G., or, the True Adventures of Smoky the Cop," in Abbey, *Abbey's Road*, 150, 149.

25. Quoted in Calahan, *Edward Abbey*, 35; and Edward Abbey, "Freedom and Wilderness, Wilderness and Freedom," in Abbey, *Journey Home*, 231–32. A redacted copy of Abbey's FBI file may be found in Box 1, Folder 6, EAP.

26. Edward Abbey, "Hallelujah on the Bum," in Abbey, *Journey Home*, 1–2; and Edward Abbey, "How It Was," in Abbey and Philip Hyde, *Slickrock* (San Francisco: Sierra Club Books, 1971), 18. On Abbey's first trip west, see Calahan, *Edward Abbey*, 37–45.

27. Calahan, *Edward Abbey*, 27–96.

28. Abbey, *Confessions of a Barbarian*, 6; Edward Abbey, "Anarchism and the Morality of Violence" (master's thesis, University of New Mexico, 1959), Box 9, Folder 2, EAP; Edward Abbey, transcript of interview with Jack Loeffler (1983), p. 19, Box 1, Folder 5, EAP]; Harold Alderman, "Abbey as Anarchist," in Peter Quigley, ed., *Coyote in the Maze: Tracking Edward Abbey in a World of Words* (Salt Lake City: University of Utah Press, 1998), 137–49, the quotation is on p. 143.

29. On postwar development and the role of the federal government in the West, see Nash, *American West Transformed* and *World War II and the West*.

30. Edward Abbey, *Fire on the Mountain* (New York: Avon Books, 1962).

31. Edward Abbey, *The Brave Cowboy: An Old Tale in a New Time* (New York: Avon Books, 1956).

32. Twelve Southerners, *I'll Take My Stand: The South and the Agrarian Tradition* (New York: Harper, 1930). On the Agrarians, see Paul V. Murphy, *The Rebuke of History: The Southern Agrarians and American Conservative Thought* (Chapel Hill: University of North Carolina Press, 2001); and Paul K. Conklin, *The Southern Agrarians* (Knoxville: University of Tennessee Press, 1988); and Wendell Berry to Edward Abbey, March 4, 1972, Box 2, Folder 4, EAP.

33. Calahan, *Edward Abbey*, 79–124. Abbey garnered some much-needed cash in 1962 when *The Brave Cowboy* was made into a movie starring Kirk Douglas and adapted by famous Hollywood Ten member Dalton Trumbo.

34. Calahan, *Edward Abbey*, 98–106, 123–25.

35. Abbey, *Desert Solitaire*, 25–26, 45–92.

36. Ibid., 149.

37. Ibid., 149–51, emphasis in the original.

38. Edward Abbey, "Boulder, 11-16-78, University of Colorado, 'Nuclear Weapons & the Attack on the Human Condition,'" Box 8, Folder 4, EAP; and Edward Abbey to

Editors, *New York Review of Books*, February 1976 (n.d.), Box 3, Folder 10, EAP.

39. Abbey, "'Nuclear Weapons & the Attack on the Human Condition"; Edward Abbey to Karen Evans, June 18, 1984, Box 3, Folder 16, EAP; and Edward Abbey, "Theory of Anarchy," in Abbey, *One Life at a Time, Please*, 27.

40. Edward Abbey, "Joy Shipmates Joy!" Box 7, Folder 7, EAP; Edward Abbey to *Playboy* magazine, January 23, 1988, Box 3, Folder 19, EAP; Abbey, *Confessions of a Barbarian*, 308; Edward Abbey to "Miss Hawkins," December 29, 1980, Box 3, Folder 13, EAP; Edward Abbey to Editors, *American West*, October 27, 1984, Box 3, Folder 16, EAP; Edward Abbey to John Macrae III, February 5, 1988, Box 3, Folder 19, EAP; Edward Abbey to Harold Gilliam, August 2, 1988, Box 3, Folder 19, EAP; and Edward Abbey to "Ms. Wulf," August 28, 1983, Box 3, Folder 16, EAP.

41. Edward Abbey, "The Right to Arms," in his *Abbey's Road*, 132; Edward Abbey to Editor, (Arizona) *Daily Star*, December 5, 1985, Box 3, Folder 16, EAP; Edward Abbey, "Women's Liberation—Some Second Thoughts," Box 24, Folder 1, EAP; Edward Abbey, "Violent Crime and Violent Criminals: A Modest but Serious Proposal," Box 25, Folder 3, EAP; and Abbey, "Nuclear Weapons & the Attack on the Human Condition," EAP.

42. On Bookchin's comments, see Jay Walljasper, "Social Ecology vs. Deep Ecology," *Utne Reader* 30 (November–December 1988): 134–35; Philip L. Goodwin to Editor, *Audubon* magazine, September 7, 1970, Box 3, Folder 3, EAP; Robert J. Matuszak to *Playboy* magazine, n.d. (c. 1975), Box 3, Folder 3, EAP; Abbey, interview with Loeffler, p. 18; Edward Abbey, "The Plowboy Interview: Edward Abbey: Slowing the Industrialization of Planet Earth," *Mother Earth News* 87 (May–June 1984): 17; and Edward Abbey, "Edward Abbey: 'The Thoreau of the American West,'" interview by Wilfred Blevins, *Mariah* (October–November 1978), Box 1 Folder 4, EAP. For an especially good example of Abbey's complex politics, see "Remarks, Utah Wilderness Assoc., SLC, Oct. 1, 1982," Box 8, Folder 7, EAP.

43. Edward Abbey, "Remarks to the NAU Forum, Oct. 22, 1975: 'The Plundered SW," Box 7, Folder 6, EAP. See also Edward Abbey, "Some Remarks on the Environmental Situation in America Today," Box 7, Folder 5, EAP; and C. Wright Mills, *The Power Elite* (Oxford University Press, 1956).

44. Edward Abbey, "Advise and Dissent," Box 24, Folder 10, EAP.

45. Edward Abbey, "Remarks, Watt Party, Tucson, 9–15–81," Box 7, Folder 7, EAP; Abbey, "Nuclear Weapons & the Attack on the Human Condition, " EAP; Abbey, "Introductory Remarks, Wilderness Society Medicine Show," Box 8, Folder 2, EAP; Edward Abbey, "Arizona: How Big Is Big Enough?" in Abbey, *One Life at a Time, Please*, 23.

46. Abbey, "Plowboy Interview," 20; Edward Abbey to "Mr. Woodworth," April 24, 1984, Box 3, Folder 16, EAP; Edward Abbey, "Free Speech, Scottsdale Arizona, Feb. 7, 1980," Box 8, Folder 6, EAP; and Edward Abbey to Editors, *Mother Jones*, January 20, 1983, Box 3, Folder 16.

47. Abbey, "Plowboy Interview," 24; Abbey, "NAU Forum," EAP; and Abbey, "Nuclear Weapons & the Attack on the Human Condition," EAP.

48. On Buckminster Fuller, see Hsiao-Yun Chu and Robert G. Trujillo, eds., *New Views on R. Buckminster Fuller* (Stanford: Stanford University Press, 2009).

49. The best treatment of Brand and *Whole Earth Catalog* is Kirk, *Counterculture Green*; Ernest Callenbach, *Ecotopia: The Notebooks and Reports of William Weston* (New York: Bantam, 1975); and Edward Abbey to the *Daily Wildcat*, April 14, 1973, Box 3, Folder 7, EAP.

50. Abbey, "Writer's Credo," 169; Abbey, "Advise and Dissent," EAP, emphasis in the original; Abbey, "NAU forum," EAP; Edward Abbey to Senator Frank E. Moss, November 8, 1970, Box 3, Folder 6, EAP; Edward Abbey to Editor, (Tucson) *Daily Citizen*, September 20, 1972, Box 3, Folder 7, EAP; Edward Abbey to Gilbert Neiman, July 17, 1976, Box 3, Folder 10, EAP; Abbey, "Introductory Remarks, Wilderness Society Medicine Show," 11–12, EAP; Edward Abbey, "Answers to questions for *Time* interview on Water & the SW [n.d.]," Box 1, Folder 4, EAP; and Abbey, "Interview with Jack Loeffler," 2, EAP.

51. Abbey, "Thus I Reply to Rene Dubos," 117–18; Abbey to Balian, November 13, 1981, EAP; and Abbey, "Nuclear Weapons & the Attack on the Human Condition," EAP.

52. Abbey, "Introductory Remarks, Wilderness Society Medicine Show," EAP; and Edward Abbey, "To the graduating class, Aspen [Colorado] High School, 6–4–71, Box 7, Folder 6, EAP.

53. Abbey, "Edward Abbey: Thoreau of the American West," 91; Abbey, "Introductory Remarks, Wilderness Society Medicine Show," EAP; and Edward Abbey, "Remarks, Missoula Film Conference, April 17, 1982," Box 7, Folder 7, EAP.

54. Abbey, "Some Remarks on the Environmental Situation," EAP; Abbey, "To the graduation class . . . ," EAP; Abbey, interview with Loeffler, EAP; and Edward Abbey to "Miss Hawkins," December 29, 1980, Box 3, Folder 13, EAP.

55. Abbey, "Some Remarks on the Environmental Situation," EAP; Abbey "Plowboy Interview," 24; and Edward Abbey to "Mr. Williams," *Utah Holiday* magazine, November 26, 1977, Box 3 Folder 11, EAP.

56. Edward Abbey to "Editor the [Tucson, Arizona] *Daily Citizen*," March 1, 1973, Box 3, Folder 7, EAP; Edward Abbey, book review of Warren Johnson, *Muddling toward Frugality* (San Francisco: Sierra Club Books, 1978), Box 25, Folder 5, EAP; and Edward Abbey, "Freedom and Wilderness, Wilderness and Freedom," 234, 235.

57. Edward Abbey, "Western Winds Feature Interview: Edward Abbey," interview by Paul Bousquet, *Western Winds* (Winter 1987–88), Box 1, Folder 4, EAP; and Edward Abbey to editor, *High Country News*, March 31, 1981, Box 3, Folder 13, EAP. Deep Ecology, championed by philosophers such as Arne Naess, George Sessions, and others, is a "biocentric" system of environmental ethics stressing the inherent right of nonhuman life to its own existence, the value of ecological diversity, the moral equivalency of all life forms, and the obligation of human beings to respect the rights of the nonhuman world through population reduction, the rejection of ideologies of endless economic growth and utilitarian "stewardship" ideas, and the cultivation of a larger sense of kinship with nature. See Bill Devall and George Sessions, *Deep Ecology: Living As If Nature Mattered* (Layton, Utah: Gibbs-Smith, 1985).

58. Edward Abbey to John Macrae III, June 23, 1969, Box 3, Folder 6, EAP; Abbey, "To the graduating class . . . ," EAP; Edward Abbey to "Ms. Pringle," August 3, 1988, Box 3, Folder 19, EAP; and Edward Abbey to Professor Florence Krall, University of Utah, September 26, 1976, Box 3, Folder 10, EAP.

59. Edward Abbey to Doug Peacock, March 29, 1982, Box 3, Folder 14, EAP; Abbey,

"The Conscience of the Conqueror," in his *Abbey's Road*, 135; Abbey, "UNH, Nov. 6, '79," Box 7, Folder 7, EAP; and Edward Abbey to the Editors, (Arizona) *Republic*, October 22, 1982, Box 3, Folder 14, EAP.

60. Edward Abbey, "Remarks, Missoula Film Conference, April 17, 1982," EAP; Abbey, "To the graduating class . . . ," EAP; and Abbey, "Freedom and Wilderness, Wilderness and Freedom," 234. See various letters in Abbey's "hate mail" file for readers' charges of hypocrisy.

61. Paul R. Ehrlich, *The Population Bomb* (New York: Ballantine Books, 1968); Garret Hardin, "Commentary: Living on a Lifeboat," *Bioscience* 24 (October 1974): 561–68; Edward Abbey, "Immigration and Liberal Taboos," in Abbey, *One Life at a Time, Please*, 43; and Bill McKibben to Edward Abbey, January 1, 1988, Box 3, Folder 4, EAP. On militarizing the borders see, for example, the "Western Winds Feature Interview," EAP, and Edward Abbey to Editors, *Industrial Worker*, October 1, 1988, Box 3, Folder 19, EAP.

62. Abbey, "Freedom and Wilderness, Wilderness and Freedom," 235; and Abbey, "Insolent Remarks, Ariz. Sierra Club," EAP.

63. Abbey, *Basin and Range* interview, Box 1, Folder 4, EAP; and Abbey, "Freedom and Wilderness, Wilderness and Freedom," 232–33.

64. Abbey, "NAU forum," EAP; Abbey, "Plowboy Interview," EAP; Edward Abbey, interview by Doug Biggers, "From Abbey's Tower," *Tucson Mountain Newsreal* (September 1979): 6, Box 1, Folder 4, EAP; and Edward Abbey, comments at the Peery Hotel, Salt Lake City, Utah , January 15, 1988, Box 7, Folder 5, EAP.

65. Abbey, "Wilderness and Freedom, Freedom and Wilderness," 231.

66. Edward Abbey, *Beyond the Wall: Essays from the Outside* (New York: Holt, Rinehart and Winston, 1984). See previous notes in this chapter for the others. On Abbey's life in the 1970s and 1980s, see Calahan, *Edward Abbey*, 125–261

67. Abbey, *Monkeywrench Gang*.

68. Edward Abbey to Eugene C. Hargrove, November 3, 1982, Box 3, Folder 14, EAP; and Edward Abbey to "Friends of the River," February 15, 1977, Box 3, Folder 11, EAP.

69. Abbey, "Joy Shipmates Joy! Survival with honor . . . ," EAP.

70. Abbey, "Remarks, Missoula Film Conference . . . ," EAP. On Dave Foreman and Earth First! see Foreman's *Confessions of an Eco-Warrior* (New York: Harmony Books, 1991); Stewart McBride, "The Real Monkey Wrench Gang," *Outside* (December 1982–January 1983): 34–38, 69–73; Rik Scarce, *Eco-Warriors: Understanding the Radical Environmental Movement* (Chicago: Noble Press, Inc., 1990); and Susan Zakin, *Coyotes and Town Dogs: Earth First! and the Environmental Movement* (New York: Viking, 1996).

71. Edward Abbey, "Remarks, GC Dam, Spring Equinox, 1981," Box 7, Folder 7, EAP; and Edward Abbey, "Forward!" in David Foreman and Bill Haywood, *Ecodefense: A Field Guide to Monkeywrenching*, 2nd edition (Tucson, Ariz.: Ned Ludd Books, 1987), 7–9. On the "cracking" of Glen Canyon Dam, see Christopher Manes, *Green Rage: Radical Environmentalism and the Unmaking of Civilization* (Boston: Little, Brown, and Co., 1990), 6.

72. Jim Harrison, review of *The Monkeywrench Gang*, in the *New York Times Book Review*, November 14, 1976; Margaret Sexton, "Mother Earth's Little Eco-terrorist Helpers," *Executive Intelligence Review* (April 20, 1990): 67–68, Box 26, Folder 8, EAP; Eugene C. Hargrove, "Ecological Sabotage: Pranks of Terrorism?" *Environmental Ethics*

4 (November 1982): 291–92; and Edward Abbey, *Hayduke Lives!* (New York: Little, Brown, and Co, 1990).

73. Abbey, *Confessions of a Barbarian*, 310.

74. See Robert Gottlieb, *Forcing the Spring: The Transformation of the American Environmental Movement* (Washington, D.C.: Island Press, 1993), 3–10, and passim, for a primary example. An interesting exploration of Bookchin's criticisms of Abbey as well as Dave Foreman may be found in Mark Stoll, "Green versus Green: Religion, Ethics, and the Bookman-Foreman Dispute," *Environmental History* 6 (July 2001): 412–27.

75. Sutter, *Driven Wild*, 194–238. On Scott, see note 40 in chapter 4.

76. Abbey, *Voice Crying in the Wilderness*, 33.

EPILOGUE

Epigraph: Rick Santorum's comments were found at http://foxnewsinsider. com/2012/02/20/was-rick-santorum-questioning-president-obama%E2%80%99s-christian-faith-gop-candidate%E2%80%99s-comments-invoke-outrage-from-the-left/ (accessed December 7, 2012).

1. Ronald Reagan, "Remarks to the National Campers and Hikers Association in Bowling Green, Kentucky," July 12, 1984, available online from Gerhard Peters and John T. Woolley, *The American Presidency Project*, http://www.presidency.ucsb.edu/ ws/?pid=40151 (accessed April 16, 2012). On Reagan's presidency in general, see Gil Troy, *Morning in America: How Ronald Reagan Invented the 1980s* (Princeton, N.J.: Princeton University Press, 2005).

2. Ronald Reagan, "Radio Address to the Nation on Environmental Issues," July 14, 1984, available online from Gerhard Peters and John T. Woolley, *The American Presidency Project*, http://www.presidency.ucsb.edu/ws/?pid=40157 (accessed April 16, 2012); Ronald Reagan, "Remarks on Signing Four Bills Designating Wilderness Areas," June 19, 1984, available online from Gerhard Peters and John T. Woolley, *The American Presidency Project*, http://www.presidency.ucsb.edu/ws/?pid=40069 (accessed April 16, 2012); Ronald Reagan, "Remarks at Dedication Ceremonies for the New Building of the National Geographic Society," June 19, 1984, available online from Gerhard Peters and John T. Woolley, *The American Presidency Project*, http://www.presidency.ucsb.edu/ ws/?pid=400063 (accessed April 16, 2012); and Ronald Reagan, "Address before a Joint Session of the Congress on the State of the Union," January 25, 1984, available online from Gerhard Peters and John T. Woolley, *The American Presidency Project*, http://www. presidency.ucsb.edu/ws/?pid=40205 (accessed April 16, 2012).

3. Hays, *Beauty, Health, and Permanence*, 491–526; Jeffrey K. Stine, "Natural Resources and Environmental Policy," in W. Elliot Browlee and Hugh Davis Graham, *The Reagan Presidency: Pragmatic Conservatism and Its Legacy* (Lawrence: University Press of Kansas, 2003), 233–58; and Byron W. Danes and Glen Sussman, *White House Politics and the Environment: Franklin D. Roosevelt to George W. Bush* (College Station: Texas A&M Press, 2010), 173–88. Spirited contemporary criticisms of Reagan include Jonathan Lash, *A Season of Spoils* (New York: Pantheon Books, 1984); and Friends of the Earth et al., *Ronald Reagan and the American Environment* (San Francisco: Brick House Publishing Company,

1982). Working with the National Resources Defense Council, the Wilderness Society, the Sierra Club, the National Audubon Society, the Environmental Defense Fund Environmental Policy Center, Environmental Action, Defenders of Wildlife, and the Solar Lobby, Friends of the Earth subtitled *Ronald Reagan and the American Environment* "An Indictment"—a phrase bluntly indicative of the emotions Reagan generated among many environmentalists.

4. Lou Cannon, *Reagan* (New York: G.P. Putnam and Sons, 1982), 28; and Lou Cannon, *President Reagan: The Role of a Lifetime* (New York: Simon and Schuster), 525–29.

5. Daynes and Sussman, *White House Politics and the Environment*, 189–209.

6. Nolan McCarty, Keith T. Poole, and Howard Rosenthal, *Polarized America: The Dance of Ideology and Unequal Riches* (Cambridge: MIT Press, 2006).

7. Paul Hawken, Amory Lovins, and L. Hunter Lovins, *Natural Capitalism: Creating the Next Industrial Revolution* (New York: Little, Brown, 1999); and Rod Dreher, *Crunchy Cons: How Birkenstocked Burkeans, Gun-Loving Organic Gardeners, Evangelical Free-Range Farmers, Hip Homeschooling Mamas, Right-Wing Nature Lovers, and Their Diverse Tribe of Countercultural Conservatives Plan to Save America (or At Least the Republican Party)* (New York: Crown Forum, 2006).

8. The text of "Life without Principle" is available online at http://www.vcu.edu/engweb/transcendentalism/authors/thoreau/lifewithoutprinciple.html (accessed April 16, 2012).

Selected Bibliography

ARCHIVAL SOURCES

Edward P. Abbey Papers, Special Collections, University of Arizona Library (EAP)
Goldwater Family Papers, Arizona Historical Foundation, Tempe, Arizona (GFP-AHF)
Laird Wilcox Collection on Contemporary Political Movements, Kenneth Spencer Research Library, University of Kansas (GC-LWC)
Personal and Political Papers of Senator Barry M. Goldwater Papers, Arizona Historical Foundation, Tempe, Arizona (BMG-AHF)
Print Archives, Merrill G. Burlingame Special Collections, Montana State University Libraries
Rachel Carson Papers, Yale Collection of American Literature, Beinecke Rare Book and Manuscript Library, Yale University (RCP)
Roy E. Huffman Papers, Merrill G. Burlingame Special Collections, Montana State University Libraries
Special Collections, Cline Library, Northern Arizona University

BOOKS AND ARTICLES

Abbey, Edward. *Abbey's Road.* New York: Penguin Books, 1979.
———. *Beyond the Wall: Essays from the Outside.* New York: Holt, Rinehart, and Winston, 1984.
———. *Black Sun.* New York: Avon Books, 1971.
———. *The Brave Cowboy: An Old Tale in a New Time.* New York: Avon Books, 1956.
———. *Cactus Country.* New York: Time-Life Books, Inc., 1973.
———. *Confessions of a Barbarian: Selections from the Journals of Edward Abbey, 1951–1989.* Edited by David Peterson. New York: Little, Brown, 1994.
———. *Desert Solitaire: A Season in the Wilderness.* New York: Ballantine Books, 1968.
———. *Down the River.* New York: Penguin Books, 1982.
———. *Earth Apples: The Poetry of Edward Abbey.* Edited by David Petersen. New York: St. Martin's Griffin, 1995.
———. *Fire on the Mountain.* New York: Avon Books, 1962.
———. *The Fool's Progress: An Honest Novel.* New York: Avon Books, 1988.
———. *Good News.* New York: Penguin Books, 1980.

———. *The Journey Home: Some Words in Defense of the American West.* New York: Penguin Books, 1977.

———. *The Monkeywrench Gang.* New York: Avon Books, 1975.

———. *One Life at a Time, Please.* New York: Henry Holt and Co., 1988.

———. *The Serpents of Paradise.* Edited by John Macrae. New York: Henry Holt and Company, 1994.

———. *Slumgullion Stew: An Edward Abbey Reader.* New York: E.P. Dutton, 1984.

———. *A Voice Crying in the Wilderness: Notes from a Secret Journal.* New York: St. Martin's Press, 1989.

———, and Eliot Porter. *Appalachian Wilderness: The Great Smoky Mountains.* New York: Arrowood Press, 1988.

———, and Philip Hyde. *Slickrock.* San Francisco: Sierra Club Books, 1971.

Abelson, Donald E. "From Policy Research to Political Advocacy: The Changing Role of Think Tanks in American Politics." *Canadian Review of American Studies* 25 (Winter 1995): 93–126.

Agnello, Richard, and Lawrence P. Donnelley. "Property Rights and Efficiency in the Oyster Industry." *Journal of Law and Economics* 18 (October 1975): 521–33.

Anderson, Terry H. *The Movement and the Sixties.* New York: Oxford University Press, 1995.

Anderson, Terry L. "The New Resource Economics: Old Ideas and New Applications." *American Journal of Agricultural Economics* 64 (December 1982): 882–934.

———. *Water Crisis: Ending the Policy Drought.* Washington, D.C.: Cato Institute and Johns Hopkins University Press, 1983.

———, and Peter J. Hill. "The Evolution of Property Rights: A Study of the American West." *Journal of Law and Economics* 18 (April 1975): 163–79.

———, and P. J. Hill. "Privatizing the Commons: An Improvement?" *Southern Economic Journal* 50 (October 1983): 438–50.

———, and Donald R. Leal. *Free Market Environmentalism.* Boulder: Westview Press, 1991.

———. *Free Market Environmentalism.* Revised edition. New York: Palgrave, 2001.

———. "Free Market versus Political Environmentalism." *Harvard Journal of Law and Public Policy* 15 (Spring 1992): 297–310.

Andrew, John A. *The Other Side of the Sixties: Young Americans for Freedom and the Rise of Conservative Politics.* New Brunswick, N.J.: Rutgers University Press, 1997.

Andrews, Richard N. L. *Managing Nature, Managing Ourselves: A History of American Environmental Policy.* 2nd edition. New Haven, Connecticut: Yale University Press, 2006.

Arcus-Ting, Rochele, Richard Tessler, and James Wright. "Misinformation and Opposition to Fluoridation." *Polity* 10 (Winter 1977): 281–89.

August Jr., Jack. "Water, Politics, and the Arizona Dream: Carl Hayden and the Modern Origins of the Central Arizona Project." *Journal of Arizona History* (Winter 1999): 391–414.

Austin, Mary. *Land of Little Rain.* New York: Penguin Books, 1988.

Baden, John A., and Robert Ethier. "Linking Liberty, Economy, and Ecology." *The Freeman* 43 (September 1993): 340–42.

Baden, John, and Richard Stroup. "The Environmental Costs of Government Action." *Policy Review* 4 (Summer 1978): 23–26.

————. "Saving the Wilderness: A Radical Proposal." *Reason* 13 (July 1981): 28–36.

Baden, John, and Richard L. Stroup. *Natural Resources: Bureaucratic Myths and Environmental Management.* San Francisco: Pacific Institute for Public Policy Research, 1983.

————, eds. *Bureaucracy vs. Environment: The Environmental Costs of Bureaucratic Governance.* Ann Arbor: University of Michigan Press, 1981.

Bell, Frederick W. "Technological Externalities and Common-Property Resources: An Empirical Study of the U.S. Northern Lobster Fishery." *Journal of Political Economy* 80 (January–February 1972): 148–58.

Bellamy, Edward. *Looking Backward, 2000–1887.* Edited by Robert C. Elliott. Boston: Houghton Mifflin, 1966.

Bess, Michael. *The Light-Green Society: Ecology and Technological Modernity in France, 1960–2000.* Chicago: University of Chicago Press, 2003.

Bessey, Roy F. "The Political Issues of the Hells Canyon Controversy." *Western Political Quarterly* 9 (September 1956): 676–90.

Bishop Jr., James. *Epitaph for a Desert Anarchist: The Life and Legacy of Edward Abbey.* New York: Atheneum, 1994.

Bjerre-Poulsen, Niels. "The Heritage Foundation: A Second-Generation Think Tank." *Journal of Policy History* 3 (1991): 152–72.

————. *Right Face: Organizing the American Conservative Movement.* Copenhagen: Museum Tusculanum Press, 2002.

Bliese, John R. E. *The Greening of Conservative America.* Boulder: Westview Press, 2001.

Blum, Elizabeth D. *Love Canal Revisited: Race, Class, and Gender in Environmental Activism.* Lawrence: University Press of Kansas, 2008.

Blumm, Michael C. "The Fallacies of Free Market Environmentalism." *Harvard Journal of Law and Public Policy* 15 (Spring 1992): 371–89.

Boyer, Paul. *When Time Shall Be No More: Prophecy Belief in Modern American Culture.* Cambridge: Harvard University Press, 1992.

Brennan, Mary C. *Turning Right in the Sixties: The Conservative Capture of the GOP.* Chapel Hill: University of North Carolina Press, 1995.

Brinkley, Alan. "The Problem of American Conservatism." *American Historical Review* 99 (April 1994): 409–29

————. "Response to the Comments of Leo Ribuffo and Susan Yohn." *American Historical Review* 99 (April 1994): 450–52.

————. "Richard Hofstadter's the Age of Reform: A Reconsideration: A Review of The Age of Reform: From Bryan to F.D.R." *Reviews in American History* 13 (September 1985): 462–80.

Brinkley, Douglas. *The Wilderness Warrior: Theodore Roosevelt and the Crusade for America.* New York: Harper, 2009.

Brooks, Karl Boyd. *Public Power, Private Dams: The Hells Canyon High Dam Controversy.* Seattle: University of Washington Press, 2006.

Brunet, Edward. "Debunking Wholesale Private Enforcement of Environmental Rights." *Harvard Journal of Law and Public Policy* 15 (Spring 1992): 311–24.

Buell, Frederick. *From Apocalypse to Way of Life: Environmental Crisis in the American Century.* New York: Routledge, 2003.

Buhs, Joshua Blu. *The Fire Ant Wars: Nature, Science, and Public Policy in Twentieth-Century America*. Chicago: University of Chicago Press, 2004.

Calahan, James C. *Edward Abbey: A Life*. Tucson: University of Arizona Press, 2001.

———. "Edward Abbey, Appalachian Easterner." *Western American Literature* 31 (November 1996): 233–53.

———. "'My People': Edward Abbey's Appalachian Roots in Indiana County, Pennsylvania (Part One)." *Pittsburgh History* 79 (Fall 1996): 92–107.

———. "'My People': Edward Abbey's Appalachian Roots in Indiana County, Pennsylvania (Part Two)." *Pittsburgh History* 79 (Winter1996–97): 160–79.

Callenbach, Ernest. *Ecotopia: The Notebooks and Reports of William Weston*. New York: Bantam, 1975.

Cannon, Lou. *President Reagan: The Role of a Lifetime*. New York: Simon and Schuster, 1991.

———. *Reagan*. New York: G.P. Putnam and Sons, 1982.

Carson, Rachel. *The Edge of the Sea*. New York: Houghton Mifflin, 1955.

———. *The Sea around Us*. New York: Oxford University Press, 1951.

———. *Silent Spring*. New York: Houghton Mifflin, 1962.

———. *Under the Sea-Wind*. New York: Simon and Schuster, 1941.

Cart, Theodore Whaley. "The Lacey Act: America's First Nationwide Wildlife Statute." *Forest History* 17 (October 1973): 4–13.

Carter, Dan T. *The Politics of Rage: George Wallace, the Origins of the New Conservatism, and the Transformation of American Politics*. New York: Simon and Schuster, 1995.

Cawley, R. Macgregor. *Federal Land, Western Anger: The Sagebrush Rebellion and Environmental Politics*. Lawrence: University Press of Kansas, 1993.

Chu, Hsiao-Yun, and Robert G. Trujillo. *New Views on R. Buckminster Fuller*. Stanford: Stanford University Press, 2009.

Coase, Ronald. "The Problem of Social Cost." *Journal of Law and Economics* 3 (October 1960): 1–44.

Cohen, Michael P. *The History of the Sierra Club, 1892–1970*. San Francisco: Sierra Club Books, 1988.

Cole, Daniel H. "Clearing the Air: Four Propositions about Property Rights and Environmental Protection." *Duke Environmental Law and Policy Forum* 10 (1999): 109–17.

Conklin, Paul K. *The Southern Agrarians*. Knoxville: University of Tennessee Press, 1988.

Crespino, Joseph. *In Search of Another Country: Mississippi and the Conservative Counterrevolution*. Princeton, New Jersey: Princeton University Press, 2007.

Cronon, William. *Changes in the Land: Indian, Colonists, and the Ecology of New England*. New York: Hill and Wang, 1983.

———. "Modes of Prophecy and Production: Placing Nature in History." *Journal of American History* 76 (March 1990): 1122–31.

———. "When the GOP Was Green." *New York Times*. January 8, 2001.

———, ed. *Uncommon Ground: Rethinking the Human Place in Nature*. New York: W.W. Norton and Co., 1996.

Cumbler, John T. *Reasonable Use: The People, the Environment, and the State, New England 1790–1930*. New York: Oxford University Press, 2001.

Cuzán, Alfred. "A Critique of Collectivist Water Resources Planning." *Western Political Quarterly* 32 (September 1979): 320–26.

Daemmrich, Arthur. "A Tale of Two Experts: Thalidomide and Political Engagement in the United States and West Germany." *Social History of Medicine* 15 (April 2002): 137–58.

Dales, John F. *Pollution, Property, and Prices.* Toronto: University of Toronto Press, 1968.

Daly, Herman E. *Ecological Economics and the Ecology of Economics: Essays in Criticism.* Northampton, Massachusetts: Edward Elgar Press, 1999.

Danes, Byron W., and Glen Sussman. *White House Politics and the Environment: Franklin D. Roosevelt to George W. Bush.* College Station: Texas A&M Press, 2010.

Deacon, Robert T., and M. Bruce Johnson, eds. *Forestlands: Public and Private.* San Francisco: Pacific Institute for Policy Research, 1985.

Davis, Morris. "Community Attitudes toward Fluoridation." *Public Opinion Quarterly* 23 (Winter 1959–60): 478.

Dean, Robert. "'Dam Building Still Had Some Magic Then': Steward Udall, the Central Arizona Project, and the Evolution of the Pacific Southwest Water Plan, 1963–1968." *Pacific Historical Review* 66 (February 1997): 81–98.

Demetsz, Harold. "Toward a Theory of Property Rights." *American Economic Review* 57 (May 1967): 347–59.

Devall, Bill, and George Sessions, *Deep Ecology: Living As If Nature Mattered.* Layton, Utah: Gibbs-Smith, 1985.

Donahue, Brian. "'Dammed at Both Ends and Cursed in the Middle': The 'Flowage' of the Concord River Meadows, 1798–1862." In *Out of the Woods: Essays in Environmental History,* edited by Char Miller and Hal Rothman. Pittsburgh: University of Pittsburgh Press, 1997.

Dreher, Rod. *Crunchy Cons: How Birkenstocked Burkeans, Gun-Loving Organic Gardeners, Evangelical Free-Range Farmers, Hip Homeschooling Mamas, Right-Wing Nature Lovers, and Their Diverse Tribe of Countercultural Conservatives Plan to Save America (or At Least the Republican Party).* New York: Crown Forum, 2006.

Dublin, Louis I. "Water Fluoridation: Facts, Not Myths." *Public Affairs Pamphlet* 251 (1957): 1–28.

Dunlap, Thomas R. *DDT: Scientists, Citizens, and Public Policy.* Princeton, New Jersey: Princeton University Press, 1981.

———. *Faith in Nature: Environmentalism As Religious Quest.* Seattle: University of Washington Press, 2005.

Eller, Ronald D. *Miners, Millhands, and Mountaineers: Industrialization of the Appalachian South, 1880–1930.* Knoxville: University of Tennessee Press, 1982.

Epstein, Richard. "The Principles of Environmental Protection: The Case of Superfund." *Cato Journal* 2 (Spring 1982): 1–34.

Ehrlich, Paul R. *The Population Bomb.* New York: Ballantine Books, 1968.

Farber, David. *The Rise and Fall of Modern American Conservatism: A Short History.* Princeton, New Jersey: Princeton University Press, 2010.

———. *Taken Hostage: The Iran Hostage Crisis and America's First Encounter with Radical Islam.* Princeton, New Jersey: Princeton University Press, 2005.

Farber, David, and Jeff Roche, eds. *The Conservative Sixties*. New York: Peter Lang, 2003.

Farmer, Jared. *Glen Canyon Dammed: Inventing Lake Powell and the Canyon Country*. Tucson: University of Arizona Press, 1999.

Flanagan, Maureen A. "The City Profitable, the City Livable: Environmental Policy, Gender, and Power in Chicago in the 1910s." *Journal of Urban History* 22 (January 1996): 163–90.

———. "Gender and Urban Political Reform: The City Club and the Women's City Club of Chicago in the Progressive Era." *American Historical Review* 95 (October 1990): 1032–50

Flippen, J. Brooks. *Conservative Conservationist: Russell E. Train and the Emergence of American Environmentalism*. Baton Rouge: Louisiana State University Press, 2006.

———. *Nixon and the Environment*. Albuquerque: University of New Mexico Press, 2000.

Foreman, Dave. *Confessions of an Eco-Warrior*. New York: Harmony Books, 1991.

———, and Bill Haywood. *Ecodefense: A Field Guide to Monkeywrenching*. 2nd edition. Tucson, Arizona: Ned Ludd Books, 1987.

Fox, Stephen. *John Muir and His Legacy: The American Conservation Movement*. Boston: Little, Brown, and Co., 1981.

Freeze, R. Allan, and Jay H. Lehr. *The Fluoride Wars: How a Modest Public Health Measure Became America's Longest-Running Political Melodrama*. Hoboken, New Jersey: John Wiley and Sons, 2008.

Freyfogle, Eric T. *The Land We Share: Private Property and the Common Good*. Washington, D.C.: Island Press, 2003.

Friedman, Milton. *Capitalism and Freedom*. Chicago: University of Chicago Press, 1962.

Friends of the Earth et al. *Ronald Reagan and the American Environment*. San Francisco: Brick House Publishing, 1982.

Funk, William. "Free Market Environmentalism: Wonder Drug or Snake Oil?" *Harvard Journal of Law and Public Policy* 15 (Spring 1992): 511–16.

Gamson, William A. "The Fluoridation Dialogue: Is It an Ideological Conflict?" *Public Opinion Quarterly* 25 (Winter 1961): 526–37.

Gartner, Carol B. *Rachel Carson*. New York: Frederick Ungar Publishing, 1983.

Goldberg, Robert A. *Barry Goldwater*. New Haven: Yale University Press, 1995.

Goldman, M. C. "Poison on Tap." *Organic Farming and Gardening* 1 (January 1954): 42–50.

Goldwater, Barry. *Arizona Portraits*. 1st edition. Phoenix: Privately printed, October 7, 1940.

———. *The Conscience of a Conservative*. Shepardsville, Kentucky: Victor Publishing Company, 1960.

———. *The Conscience of a Majority*. Englewood Cliffs, New Jersey: Prentice-Hall, 1970.

———. *Delightful Journey down the Green and Colorado Rivers*. Tempe: Arizona Historical Foundation, 1970.

———. *The Face of Arizona*. Phoenix: Privately printed, 1964.

———. *With No Apologies: The Personal and Political Memoirs of United States Senator Barry M. Goldwater*. New York: William Morrow, 1979.

———, and Jack Casserly. *Goldwater*. New York: Doubleday, 1988.

Gordon, H. Scott. "The Economic Theory of a Common Property Resource: The Fishery." *Journal of Political Economy* 62 (April 1953): 124–42.

————. "Economics and the Conservation Question." *Journal of Law and Economics* 1 (October 1958): 110–21.

Gottlieb, Robert. *Forcing the Spring: The Transformation of the American Environmental Movement.* Washington, D.C.: Island Press, 1993.

————. "Reconstructing Environmentalism: Complex Movements, Diverse Roots." *Environmental History Review* 17 (Winter 1993): 7–10.

Gross, Robert A. "Quiet War with the State: Henry David Thoreau and Civil Disobedience." *Yale Review* 93 (October 2005): 1–17.

Gunter, Valerie J., and Craig K. Harris. "Noisy Winter: The DDT Controversy in the Years before *Silent Spring.*" *Rural Sociology* 63 (June 1998): 179–98.

Hahn, Steven. "Hunting, Fishing, and Foraging: Common Rights and Class Relations in the Postbellum South." *Radical History Review* 26 (1982): 37–64.

Hardin, Garrett. "The Tragedy of the Commons." *Science* 62 (13 December 1968): 1243–48.

————. "Commentary: Living on a Lifeboat." *Bioscience* 24 (October 1974): 561–68.

————, and John Baden, eds. *Managing the Commons.* San Francisco: W.H. Freeman, 1977.

Harvey, Mark W. T. *A Symbol of Wilderness: Echo Park and the American Conservation Movement.* Albuquerque: University of New Mexico Press, 1994.

Hawken, Paul, Amory Lovins, and L. Hunter Lovins. *Natural Capitalism: Creating the Next Industrial Revolution.* New York: Little, Brown, 1999.

Hayek, Frederick A. *The Road to Serfdom.* Chicago: University of Chicago Press, 1944.

————. "The Use of Knowledge in Society." *American Economic Review* 35 (September 1945): 519–30.

Hays, Samuel P. *Beauty, Health, and Permanence: Environmental Politics in the United States, 1955–1985.* Cambridge: Cambridge University Press, 1987.

————. *Conservation and the Gospel of Efficiency: The Progressive Conservation Movement, 1890–1920.* Cambridge: Harvard University Press, 1959.

————. "From Conservation to Environment: Environmental Politics in the United States since World War II." In *Out of the Woods: Essays in Environmental History,* edited by Char Miller and Hal Rothman. Pittsburgh: University of Pittsburgh Press, 1997.

————. *A History of Environmental Politics since 1945.* Pittsburgh: University of Pittsburgh Press, 2000.

Hepworth, James R., and McNamess, Gregory, eds. *Resist Much, Obey Little: Remembering Ed Abbey.* San Francisco: Sierra Club Books, 1996.

Himmelstein, Jerome L. *To the Right: The Transformation of American Conservatism.* Berkeley: University of California Press, 1989.

Hofstader, Richard. "The Paranoid Style in American Politics." *Harper's* (November 1964): 77–86.

Horwitch, Mel. *Clipped Wings: The American SST Conflict.* Cambridge: MIT Press, 1982.

Horwitz, Morton J. *The Transformation of American Law, 1780–1860.* Cambridge: Harvard University Press, 1977.

Hotelling, Harold. "The Economics of Exhaustible Resources." *Journal of Political Economy* 39 (April 1931): 137–75.

Hoy, Suellen. *Chasing Dirt: The American Pursuit of Cleanliness.* New York: Oxford University Press, 1995.

Huffman, James L. "Protecting the Environment from Orthodox Environmentalism." *Harvard Journal of Law and Public Policy* 15 (Spring 1992): 349–69.

Hundley Jr., Norris C. *Water and the West: The Colorado River Compact and the Politics of Water in the American West.* Second edition. Berkeley: University of California Press, 2006.

Huxley, Aldous. *Brave New World.* New York: HarperCollins, 1998.

Hynes, H. Patricia. "Ellen Swallow, Lois Gibbs, and Rachel Carson: Catalysts of the American Environmental Movement." *Women's Studies International Forum* 8 (1985): 291–98.

Iverson, Peter. *Barry Goldwater: Native Arizonan.* Norman: University of Oklahoma Press, 1997.

———. "'This Old Mountain Is Worth the Fight': Barry Goldwater and the Campaign to Save Camelback Mountain." *Journal of Arizona History* 38 (Spring 1997): 41–56.

Jacoby, Karl. *Crimes against Nature: Squatters, Poachers, Thieves, and the Hidden History of American Conservation.* Berkeley: University of California Press, 2001.

Johnson, Robert N., and Gary D. Libecap. "Contracting Problems and Regulation: The Case of the Fishery." *American Economic Review* 12 (December 1982): 1005–22.

Judd, Richard W. *Common Lands, Common People: The Origins of Conservation in Northern New England.* Cambridge: Harvard University Press, 1997.

Kallet, Arthur, and F. J. Schlink, *100,000,000 Guinea Pigs: Dangers in Everyday Foods, Drugs, and Cosmetics.* New York: Vanguard Press, 1933.

Kapp, K. William. *The Social Costs of Private Enterprise.* Cambridge: Harvard University Press, 1950.

Kargul, Betul, Esber Caglar, and Ilknur Tanboga. "History of Water Fluoridation." *Journal of Clinical Pediatric Dentistry* 27 (Spring 2003): 213–17.

Kazin, Michael. "The Grass-Roots Right: New Histories of U.S. Conservatism in the Twentieth Century." *American Historical Review* 97 (February 1992): 136–55.

Kirk, Andrew G. *Counterculture Green: The Whole Earth Catalog and American Environmentalism.* Lawrence: University Press of Kansas, 2007.

Klatch, Rebecca E. *A Generation Divided: The New Left, the New Right, and the 1960s.* Berkeley: University of California Press, 1999.

Knize, Perri. "The Mismanagement of the National Forests." *Atlantic Monthly* 268 (October 1991): 98–100, 103–4, 107–8, 111–12.

Kopp, James J. "Looking Backward at Edward Bellamy's Influence in Oregon, 1888–1936." *Oregon Historical Quarterly* 104 (Spring 2003): 62–95.

Koppes, Clayton R. "Efficiency, Equity, Esthetics: Shifting Themes in American Conservation." In *The Ends of the Earth: Perspectives on Modern Environmental History,* edited by Donald Worster. New York: Cambridge University Press, 1989.

Krier, James E. "The Tragedy of the Commons, Part Two." *Harvard Journal of Law and Public Policy* 15 (Spring 1992): 325–47.

Kruse, Kevin. *White Flight: Atlanta and the Making of Modern Conservatism.* Princeton, New Jersey: Princeton University Press, 2006.

Kula, Ehrun. *History of Environmental Ecological Thought.* New York: Routledge, 1998.

Lamb, Ruth deForest. *American Chamber of Horrors: The Truth about Food and Drugs.* New York: Farrar and Rinehart, 1936.

Langston, Nancy. *Forest Dreams, Forest Nightmares: The Paradox of Old Growth in the Inland West*. Seattle: University of Washington Press, 1995.

Lasch, Christopher. *The True and Only Heaven: Progress and Its Critics*. New York: W.W. Norton and Co., 1991.

Lash, Jonathan. *A Season of Spoils*. New York: Pantheon Books, 1984.

Lassiter, Matthew D. *The Silent Majority: Suburban Politics in the Sunbelt South*. Princeton, New Jersey: Princeton University Press, 2007.

Lear, Linda. "Rachel Carson's *Silent Spring*." *Environmental History Review* 17 (Summer 1993): 23–48.

———. *Rachel Carson: Witness for Nature*. New York: Henry Holt, 1997.

Lewis, Ronald L. *Transforming the Appalachian Countryside: Railroads, Deforestation, and Social Change in West Virginia, 1880–1920*. Chapel Hill: University of North Carolina Press, 1998.

Libecap, Gary D. "Bureaucratic Issues and Environmental Concerns: A Review of the History of Federal Land Ownership and Management." *Harvard Journal of Law and Public Policy* 15 (Spring 1992): 467–87.

———, and Ronald N. Johnson. "Property Rights, Nineteenth-Century Federal Timber Policy, and the Conservation Movement." *Journal of Economic History* 39 (March 1979): 129–42.

Limerick, Patricia Nelson. *Desert Passages: Encounters with the American Deserts*. Albuquerque: University of New Mexico Press, 1985.

Lutts, Ralph. "Chemical Fallout: Rachel Carson's *Silent Spring*, Radioactive Fallout, and the Environmental Movement." *Environmental Review* 9 (Fall 1985): 210–25.

Lytle, Mark Hamilton. *America's Uncivil Wars: The Sixties Era from Elvis to the Fall of Richard Nixon*. New York: Oxford University Press, 2006.

———. *The Gentle Subversive: Rachel Carson, Silent Spring, and the Rise of the Environmental Movement*. New York: Oxford University Press, 2007.

Maher, Neil. *Nature's New Deal: The Civilian Conservation Corps and the Roots of American Environmentalism*. New York: Oxford University Press, 2007.

Manes, Christopher. *Green Rage: Radical Environmentalism and the Unmaking of Civilization*. Boston: Little, Brown, and Co., 1990.

Marland, Charles. "Dr. Strangelove (1964): Nightmare Comedy and the Ideology of the Liberal Consensus." *American Quarterly* 31 (Winter 1979): 697–717.

Martin, Brian. "The Sociology of the Fluoridation Controversy: A Reexamination." *Sociological Quarterly* 30 (March 1989): 59–76.

Martin, Russell. *A Story That Stands Like a Dam: Glen Canyon and the Struggle for the Soul of the West*. New York: Henry Holt and Co., 1989.

Martin, William C. *With God on Our Side: The Rise of the Religious Right in America*. New York: Broadway Books, 1996.

Matusow, Allen J. *The Unraveling of America: A History of Liberalism in the 1960s*. New York: Harper and Row, 1984.

Mausner, Bernard, and Judith Mausner. "The Anti-scientific Attitude." *Scientific American* 192 (February 1955): 35–39.

McBride, Stewart. "The Real Monkey Wrench Gang." *Outside* (December 1982–January 1983): 34–38, 69–73.

McCann, Garth. *Edward Abbey*. Boise, Idaho: Boise State University Western Writers Series, 1977.

McCarthy, Joseph. *America's Retreat from Freedom: The Story of George Catlett Marshall*. New York: Devin-Adair, 1954.

———. *McCarthyism—The Fight for America: Documented Answers to Questions Asked by Friend and Foe*. New York: Devin-Adair, 1952.

McCarty, Nolan, Keith T. Poole, and Howard Rosenthal. *Polarized America: Dance of Ideology and Unequal Riches*. Cambridge: MIT Press, 2006.

McClure, Frank J. *Water Fluoridation: The Search and the Victory*. Bethesda, Maryland: National Institute of Dental Research, 1970.

McComb, John. "Southwest: Grand Canyon Giveaway." *Sierra Club Bulletin* 58 (July–August 1973): 23–24.

McEvoy, Arthur F. *The Fisherman's Problem: Ecology and Law in the California Fisheries*. New York: Cambridge University Press, 1986.

McGann, James G. "Academics to Ideologues: A Brief History of the Public Policy Research Industry." *PS: Political Science and Politics* 25 (December 1992): 733–40.

McGirr, Lisa. *Suburban Warriors: The Origins of the New American Right*. Princeton: Princeton University Press, 2001.

McNeil, Donald R. "America's Longest War: The Fight over Fluoridation, 1950–." *Wilson's Quarterly* 9 (Summer 1985): 140–53.

———. *The Fight for Fluoridation*. New York: Oxford University Press, 1957. Melosi, Martin. *The Sanitary City: Environmental Services in Urban America from Colonial Times to the Present*. Pittsburgh: University of Pittsburgh Press, 2000.

Menell, Peter S. "Institutional Fantasylands: From Scientific Management to Free Market Environmentalism." *Harvard Journal of Law and Public Policy* 15 (Spring 1992): 489–510.

Metz, A. Stafford. "An Analysis of Some Determinants of Attitude toward Fluoridation." *Social Forces* 44 (June 1966): 477–84.

Milazzo, Paul Charles. *Unlikely Environmentalists: Congress and Clean Water, 1955–1972*. Lawrence: University Press of Kansas, 2006.

Miller, Char. *Gifford Pinchot and the Making of Modern Environmentalism*. Washington, D.C.: Island Press, 2001.

Moore, Curtis. "Rethinking the Think Tanks: How Industry-Funded 'Experts' Twist the Environmental Debate." *Sierra* 87 (July–August 2002): 56–59, 73.

Moore, Leonard Joseph. "Good Old-Fashioned New Social History and the Twentieth-Century American Right." *Reviews in American History* 24 (December 1996): 555–73.

Mueller, John E. "The Politics of Fluoridation in Seven California Cities." *Western Political Quarterly* 19 (March 1966): 54–67.

Murphy, Paul V. *The Rebuke of History: The Southern Agrarians and American Conservative Thought*. Chapel Hill: University of North Carolina Press, 2001.

Murray, Troy, and Marlin, eds. *Barry Goldwater and the Southwest*. Phoenix, Arizona: Troy's Publications, 1976.

Nash, George H. *The Conservative Intellectual Movement in America since 1945*. New York: Basic Books, 1976.

Nash, Gerald D. *The American West Transformed: The Impact of the Second World War.* Bloomington: Indiana University Press, 1985.

———. *World War II and the West: Transforming the Economy.* Lincoln: University of Nebraska Press, 1990.

Nash, Linda. *Inescapable Ecologies: A History of Environment, Disease, and Knowledge.* Berkeley: University of California Press, 2006.

Nash, Roderick Frazier. *The Rights of Nature: A History of Environmental Ethics.* Madison: University of Wisconsin Press, 1989.

———. *Wilderness and the American Mind.* 3rd edition. New Haven: Yale University Press, 1982.

Nelson, Richard, Barry Lopez, and Terry Tempest Williams. *Patriotism and the American Land.* Great Barrington, Massachusetts: The Orion Society, 2002.

Nickerson, Michele M. *Mothers of Conservatism: Women and the Postwar Right.* Princeton, New Jersey: Princeton University Press, 2012.

Olsen, Jonathan. *Nature and Nationalism: Right Wing Ecology and the Politics of Identity in Contemporary Germany.* Basingstoke: Macmillan, 2000.

Oliver, Kendrick. "'Post-Industrial Society' and the Psychology of the American Far Right, 1950–57." *Journal of Contemporary History* 34 (October 1999): 601–18.

Opie, John. *Nature's Nation: An Environmental History of the United States.* Fort Worth, Texas: Harcourt Brace College Publishers, 1998.

Orwell, George. *1984.* London: Secker and Warburg, 1949.

Ostrum, Elinor. *Governing the Commons: The Evolution of Institutions for Collective Action.* Cambridge: Cambridge University Press, 1990.

O'Toole, Randal. *The Best-Laid Plans: How Government Planning Harms Your Quality of Life, Your Pocketbook, and Your Future.* Washington, D.C.: Cato Institute, 2007.

———. *Reforming the Forest Service.* Washington, D.C.: Island Press, 1988.

Pearce, David. "An Intellectual History of Environmental Economics." *Annual Review of Energy and the Environment* 27 (2002): 57–81.

Pearson, Byron. *Still the Wild River Runs: Congress, the Sierra Club, and the Fight to Save Grand Canyon.* Tucson: University of Arizona Press, 2002.

Perlstein, Rick. *Before the Storm: Barry Goldwater and the Unmaking of the American Consensus.* New York: Hill and Wang, 2001.

Peterson, Jill. "Solving the Mystery of the Colorado Brown Stain." *Journal of the History of Dentistry* 45 (July 1997): 57–61.

Petrulionis, Sandra Habert. *To Set This World Right: The Antislavery Movement in Thoreau's Concord.* Ithaca, New York: Cornell University Press, 2006.

Phillipon, Daniel L. *Conserving Words: How American Nature Writers Shaped the Environmental Movement.* Athens: University of Georgia Press, 2004.

Phillips-Hein, Kim, et al. "Conservatism: A Roundtable." *Journal of American History* 98 (December 2011): 723–73.

Pigou, Arthur C. *The Economics of Welfare.* London: Macmillan, 1920.

Pisani, Donald J. *Water and American Government: The Reclamation Bureau, National Water Policy, and the West, 1902–1935.* Berkeley: University of California Press, 2002.

Plantico, Reuben C. "A Property Rights Strategy for Protecting the Environment: A

Comment on Stroup and Goodman." *Harvard Journal of Law and Public Policy* 15 (Spring 1992): 455–66.

Plaut, Thomas F. A. "Analysis of Voting Behavior on a Fluoridation Referendum." *Public Opinion Quarterly* 23 (Summer 1959): 213–32.

Posner, Richard A. "Nobel Laureate: Ronald Coase and Methodology." *Journal of Economic Perspectives* 7 (Autumn 1993): 195–210.

Powell, Thomas. "The Battle To Halt Mass Poisoning Is On." *Organic Farming and Gardening* 4 (December 1957): 49–54

Power, Thomas Michael. "The Price of Everything: Free Market Environmentalism." *Sierra* (November–December 1993): 86–96.

Price, Jennifer. *Flight Maps: Adventures with Nature in Modern America*. New York: Basic Books, 1999.

Pryor Reed, Nathaniel Pryor. "On the Matter of Mr. Watt." *Sierra* 66 (July–August 1981): 6–8, 11–15.

Quigley, Peter, ed. *Coyote in the Maze: Tracking Edward Abbey in a World of Words*. Salt Lake City: University of Utah Press, 1998.

Reiger, John F. *American Sportsmen and the Origins of Conservation*. 3rd edition. Corvallis: Oregon State University Press, 2001.

Reilly, Gretchen Ann. "'This Poisoning of Our Drinking Water': The American Fluoridation Controversy in Historical Context, 1950–1990." Ph.D. dissertation, George Washington University, 2001.

Reisner, Marc. *Cadillac Desert: The American West and Its Disappearing Water*. New York: Viking Penguin, 1986.

Rentschler, Bill. *Goldwater: A Tribute to a Twentieth-Century Political Icon*. Chicago: Contemporary Books, 2000.

Ribuffo, Leo P. "Why Is There So Much Conservatism in the United States and Why Do So Few Historians Know Anything about It?" *American Historical Review* 99 (April 1994): 438–49.

Richardson, Elmo. "The Interior Secretary As Conservation Villain: The Notorious Case of Douglas 'Giveaway' McKay." *Pacific Historical Review* 41 (August 1972): 333–45.

Righter, Robert W. *The Battle over Hetch Hetchy: America's Most Controversial Dam and the Birth of Modern Environmentalism*. New York: Oxford University Press, 2005.

———. "National Monuments to National Parks: The Use of the Antiquities Act of 1906." *Western Historical Quarterly* 20 (August 1989): 281–301.

Rodale, Jerome I. "Chemicals in Water." *Organic Farming and Gardening* 7 (February 1960): 21–24.

———. "Fluoridation: A Dramatic Series." *Organic Farming and Gardening* 8 (February 1961): 72, 73–74, 76.

———. "Fluoridation: A Series," *Organic Farming and Gardening* 8 (January 1961): 45–8.

———. "Medical Men versus Pure Water." *Organic Farming and Gardening* 7 (April 1960): 19–26.

———. "The Organic Creed." *Organic Farming and Gardening* 3 (March 1956): 72–75.

———. "What Does Organic Mean?" *Organic Farming and Gardening* 5 (November 1958): 13–5.

Rodale, Robert. "The Organic Way of Life." *Organic Farming and Gardening* 9 (April 1962): 21–23.

———. "Rachel Carson's Masterpiece." *Organic Farming and Gardening* 9 (September 1962): 17–19.

Rodgers, Daniel T. *Atlantic Crossings: Social Politics in a Progressive Age.* Cambridge: Harvard University Press, 1998.

Rome, Adam. *The Bulldozer in the Countryside: Suburban Sprawl and the Rise of American Environmentalism.* New York: Cambridge University Press, 2001.

———. "'Give Earth a Chance': The Environmental Movement and the Sixties." *Journal of American History* 90 (September 2003): 525–54.

———. "'Political Hermaphrodites': Gender and Environmental Reform in Progressive America." *Environmental History* 11 (July 2006): 440–63.

———. "What Really Matters in History? Environmental Perspectives on Modern America." *Environmental History* 7 (April 2002): 303–18.

Ronald, Ann. *The New West of Edward Abbey.* Reno: University of Nevada Press, 1982.

Røpke, Igne. "The Early History of Modern Ecological Economics." *Ecological Economics* 50 (2004): 293–314.

Rosenbloom, Joshua. "The Politics of the American SST Programme: Origin, Opposition, and Termination." *Social Studies of Science* 11 (November 1981): 403–23.

Rossi, William, ed. *Walden, Civil Disobedience and Other Writings.* Third edition. New York: W. W. Norton, 2008.

Rothman, Hal K. *America's National Monuments: The Politics of Preservation.* Lawrence: University Press of Kansas, 2007.

———. *The Greening of a Nation? Environmentalism in the United States since 1945.* Fort Worth, Texas: Harcourt Brace, 1998.

Runte, Alfred. *National Parks: The American Experience.* Lincoln: University of Nebraska Press, 1979.

Russell, Edmund. "'Speaking of Annihilation': Mobilizing for War against Human and Insect Enemies." *Journal of American History* 82 (March 1996): 1505–29.

———. "The Strange Career of DDT: Experts, Federal Capacity, and Environmentalism in World War II." *Technology and Culture* 40 (Fall 1999): 788–93.

———. *War and Nature: Fighting Humans and Insects with Chemicals from World War I to Silent Spring.* New York: Cambridge University Press, 2001.

Salstrom, Paul. *Appalachia's Path to Dependency: Rethinking a Region's Economic History, 1730–1940.* Lexington: University Press of Kentucky, 1994.

Sapolsky, Harvey. "The Fluoridation Controversy: An Alternative Explanation." *Public Opinion Quarterly* 33 (Summer 1969): 240–48.

Scarce, Rik. *Eco-Warriors: Understanding the Radical Environmental Movement.* Chicago: Noble Press, Inc., 1990.

Schulman, Bruce J., and Julian E. Zelizer, eds. *Rightward Bound: Making American Conservative in the 1970s.* Cambridge: Harvard University Press, 2008.

Scott, David B. "The Dawn of a New Era." *Journal of Public Health Dentistry* 5 (1996): 235–38.

Scott, Doug. "Reagan's First Year: We Know Watt's Wrong." *Sierra* 67 (January–February 1982): 30, 128–29.

Scott, James C. *Seeing Like a State: How Certain Schemes To Improve the Human Condition Have Failed.* New Haven: Yale University Press, 1998.

Sellers, Christopher. *Hazards of the Job: From Industrial Disease to Environmental Health Science.* Chapel Hill: University of North Carolina Press, 1999.

Shapiro, Judith. *Mao's War on Nature: Politics and the Environment in Revolutionary China.* New York: Cambridge University Press, 2001.

Shaw, James H., ed. *Fluoridation As a Public Health Measure.* Washington, D.C.: American Association for the Advancement of Science, 1954.

Shermer, Elizabeth Tandy. "Origins of the Conservative Ascendancy: Barry Goldwater's Early Senate Career and the De-Legitimization of Organized Labor." *Journal of American History* 95 (December 2008): 678–709.

Short, C. Brant. *Ronald Reagan and the Public Lands: America's Conservation Debate.* College Station: Texas A&M Press, 1989.

Silver, Timothy. *A New Face on the Countryside: Indians, Colonists, and Slaves in South Atlantic Forests.* New York: Cambridge University Press, 1991.

Smith Jr., Fred L. "A Free-Market Environmental Program." *Cato Journal* 11 (Winter 1992): 457–75.

Smith, Robert J. "Resolving the Tragedy of the Commons By Creating Private Property Rights in Wildlife." *Cato Journal* 1 (Fall 1981): 439–68.

Smith, Thomas G. *Green Republican: John Saylor and the Preservation of America's Wilderness.* Pittsburgh: University of Pittsburgh Press, 2006.

Soule, Michael E., and Gary Lease, eds. *Reinventing Nature? Responses to Postmodern Deconstruction.* Washington, D.C: Island Press, 1994.

Spence, Mark. *Dispossessing the Wilderness: Indian Removal and the Making of the National Parks.* New York: Oxford University Press, 1999.

Steinberg, Theodore. "Can Capitalism Save the Planet? On the Origins of Green Liberalism." *Radical History Review* 107 (Spring 2010): 7–24.

———. *Down to Earth: Nature's Role in American History.* New York: Oxford University Press, 2002.

———. *Nature Incorporated: Industrialization and the Waters of New England.* Amherst: University of Massachusetts Press, 1991.

———. *Slide Mountain, Or, the Folly of Owning Nature.* Berkeley: University of California Press, 1995.

Stoll, Mark. "Green versus Green: Religion, Ethics, and the Bookman-Foreman Dispute." *Environmental History* 6 (July 2001): 412–27.

———. *Protestantism, Capitalism, and Nature in America.* Albuquerque: University of New Mexico Press, 1997.

Stroup, Richard, and John Baden. "Endowment Areas: A Clearing in the Policy Wilderness?" *Cato Journal* 2 (Winter 1982): 91–108.

———. "Externality, Property Rights, and the Management of Our National Forests." *Journal of Law and Economics* 16 (October 1973): 303–12.

———. *Natural Resources: Bureaucratic Myths and Environmental Management.* Cambridge, Massachusetts: Ballinger Press, 1983.

———. "Privatizing the Environment." *Policy Review* 20 (Spring 1982): 11–50.

Stroup, Richard L., and Sandra L. Goodman. "Property Rights, Environmental Resources, and the Future." *Harvard Journal of Law and Public Policy* 15 (Spring 1992): 427–54.

Sugrue, Thomas J. "Crabgrass-Roots Politics: Race, Rights, and the Reaction against Liberalism in the Urban North, 1940–1964." *Journal of American History* 82 (September 1995): 551–78.

Sutter, Paul S. *Driven Wild: How the Fight against Automobiles Launched the Modern Wilderness Movement*. Seattle: University of Washington Press, 2002.

Switzer, Jacqueline Vaughn. *Green Backlash: The History and Politics of Environmental Opposition in the U.S.* Boulder: Lynne Rienner Publishers, 1997.

Thoreau, Henry David. *The Maine Woods*. Boston: Houghton Mifflin, 1893.

———. *Walden, Civil Disobedience, and Other Writings*. 3rd edition. New York: W.W. Norton, 1966.

———. *A Week on the Concord and Merrimack Rivers*. Boston: Houghton Mifflin, 1893.

Tietenberg, Thomas H. *Emissions Trading: Principles and Practice*. Second edition. Washington, D.C.: Resources for the Future, 2006.

Troy, Gil. *Morning in America: How Ronald Reagan Invented the 1980s*. Princeton, New Jersey: Princeton University Press, 2005.

Turner, James Morton. "'The Specter of Environmentalism': Wilderness, Environmental Politics, and the Evolution of the New Right." *Journal of American History* 96 (June 2009): 123–48.

Twelve Southerners. *I'll Take My Stand: The South and the Agrarian Tradition*. New York: Harper, 1930.

U.S. Bureau of Reclamation. *The Colorado River: A Natural Menace Becomes a National Resource: A Comprehensive Report on the Development of the Water Resources of the Colorado River Basin for Irrigation, Power Production, and Other Beneficial Uses in Arizona, Colorado, Nevada, New Mexico, Utah and Wyoming*. Washington, D.C.: U.S. Department of the Interior, 1946.

Waldbott, George L. *A Struggle with Titans: Forces behind Fluoridation*. New York: Carlton Press, 1965.

Walljasper, Jay. "Social Ecology vs. Deep Ecology." *Utne Reader* 30 (November–December 1988): 134–35.

Warren, Louis. *The Hunter's Game: Poachers and Conservationists in Twentieth-Century America*. New Haven: Yale University Press, 1997.

Warsh, David. "When the Revolution Was a Party: How Privatization Was Invented in the 1960s." *Boston Globe*. October 20, 1991.

Wellock, Thomas R. "Stick It in L.A.! Community Control and Nuclear Power in California's Central Valley." *Journal of American History* 84 (December 1997): 942–78.

West, Elliott. *The Way to the West: Essays on the Central Plains*. Albuquerque: University of New Mexico Press, 1995.

White, Richard. "The Current Weirdness in the West." *Western Historical Quarterly* 28 (Spring 1997): 5–16.

Whorton, James. *Before Silent Spring: Pesticides and Public Health in Pre-DDT America*. Princeton, New Jersey: Princeton University Press, 1974.

Wickenden, Leonard. *Our Daily Poison: The Effects of DDT, Fluorides, Hormones, and Other Chemicals on Modern Man.* New York: Devin-Adair, 1956.

Wiebe, Robert. *The Search for Order, 1870–1920.* New York: Harper and Row, 1967.

Willey, Zach. "Behind Schedule and Over Budget: The Case of Markets, Water, and Environment." *Harvard Journal of Law and Public Policy* 15 (Spring 1992): 391–425.

Worster, Donald. "Cowboy Ecology." In *Under Western Skies: Nature and History in the American West.* Pp. 34–52. New York: Oxford University Press, 1992.

———. *Dust Bowl: The Southern Plains in the 1930s.* New York: Oxford University Press, 1979.

———. *Nature's Economy: A History of Ecological Ideas.* 2nd edition. Cambridge: Cambridge University Press, 1994.

———. *Rivers of Empire: Water, Aridity, and the Growth of the American West.* New York: Oxford University Press, 1985.

———. *The Wealth of Nature: Environmental History and the Ecological Imagination.* New York: Oxford University Press, 1993.

———. "The Wilderness of History." *Wild Earth* 7 (Fall 1997): 9–13.

———. "Wild, Tame, and Free: Comparing Canadian and U.S. Views of Nature." In *Parallel Destinies: Canadian-American Relations West of the Rockies,* edited by John M. Findlay and Ken S. Coates. Pp. 246–73. Seattle: University of Washington Press, 2002.

Yandle, Bruce. "The Emerging Market for Air Pollution Rights." *Regulation* (July–August 1978): 21–29.

———. "Escaping Environmental Feudalism." *Harvard Journal of Law and Public Policy* 15 (Spring 1992): 517–39.

———. *The Political Limits of Environmental Regulation: Tracking the Unicorn.* Westport, Connecticut: Quorum Books, 1989.

———, ed. *Land Rights: The 1990's Property Rights Rebellion.* Lanham, Maryland: Rowan and Littlefield, 1995.

Yohn, Susan M. "Will the Real Conservative Please Stand Up? Or, The Pitfalls Involved in Examining Ideological Sympathies: A Comment on Alan Brinkley's 'Problem of American Conservatism.'" *American Historical Review* 99 (April 1994): 430–37.

Zakin, Susan. *Coyotes and Town Dogs: Earth First! and the Environmental Movement.* New York: Viking, 1996.

Index

Fernow, Bernhard, 10
The Fight for America (McCarthy), 60
Fire on the Mountain (Abbey), 152–54, 157–58
Fish and Wildlife Service, 11, 46
fisheries, commons problem, 124
Fleming, Arthur, 64
fluoridation programs. *See* antifluoridation movement
Food and Drug Administration (FDA), 61–62, 63
The Fool's Progress (Abbey), 145
Ford, Gerald, 93
Foreman, Dave, 175–76
Forest Service, 10–11, 46, 104, 109–10, 117–18, 128–29
"Forward" (Abbey), 175
Foundation for Research on Economics and Environment (FREE), 127, 128, 134
"Freedom and Wilderness, Wilderness and Freedom," 167, 169, 171
Freedom Center, 75
free enterprise argument: environmental-backlash movements, 102–3; as Goldwater philosophy, 49; hydropower generation, 38–41
FREE (Foundation for Research on Economics and Environment), 127, 128, 134
free-market environmentalism: commonalities with Progressive conservation, 136–37; critique themes, 130–34, 167–68; intellectual roots, 122–30; principles of, 16–17, 113, 115–16, 120–22, 134–35; private citizen role, 119; public land management failures, 116–19; regulatory agency limitations, 119–20; rise of, 114–15, 130
Free Market Environmentalism (Anderson and Leal), 129–30, 132
Freyfogle, Eric, 131
Friedman, Milton, 125
Friends of the Earth, 96, 106
Fulbright, William, 40
Fuller, R. Buckminster, 162–63

Fulton, Richard, 40

G

gay rights, Goldwater's support, 21, 111
George Washington Hayduke character, in *The Monkeywrench Gang,* 173–74
Germany, forest management, 136–37
Gila River, 43
Glacier Bay National Monument, 101
Glen Canyon Dam: in Abbey's fiction, 173–74; approval of, 36; Earth First! demonstration, 175–76; Goldwater's positions, 6, 43, 90–92; silt deposit changes, 81, 85, 199n8
Goldberg, Robert, 25, 32, 111–12
Goldman, M. C., 67, 69
Goldwater, Baron, 24, 27
Goldwater, Barry: Abbey comparison, 6–7; childhood/youth, 23–27; development of environmental concerns, 80–86; Grand Canyon raft trips, 29–32, 84–85, 199n8; ideological complexities, 5–6, 16–17, 19–23, 111–13; photography interests, 27–29; retirement, 110–11; between Senate terms, 49–50; Watt relationship, 106
Goldwater, Barry (political positions): overviews, 32–33, 106–8, 190n30; environmental regulation, 86–87, 98–103, 107–8; federal hydropower, 37–39; Grand Canyon National Park, 92–95, 107; reclamation projects, 37–46, 106–7, 192n52; renewable energy, 88–89; river protections, 89–92; supersonic aircraft, 96–98; wilderness designations, 47–49, 89, 103–5, 108–10
Goldwater, Bob, 24–26, 50
Goldwater, Carolyn, 24–26
Goldwater, Josephine (born Williams), 24–26, 27
Goldwater, Michel "Big Mike," 24, 32
Goldwater, Peggy, 27
Goldwater, Sarah, 24

P

WEYERHAEUSER ENVIRONMENTAL CLASSICS